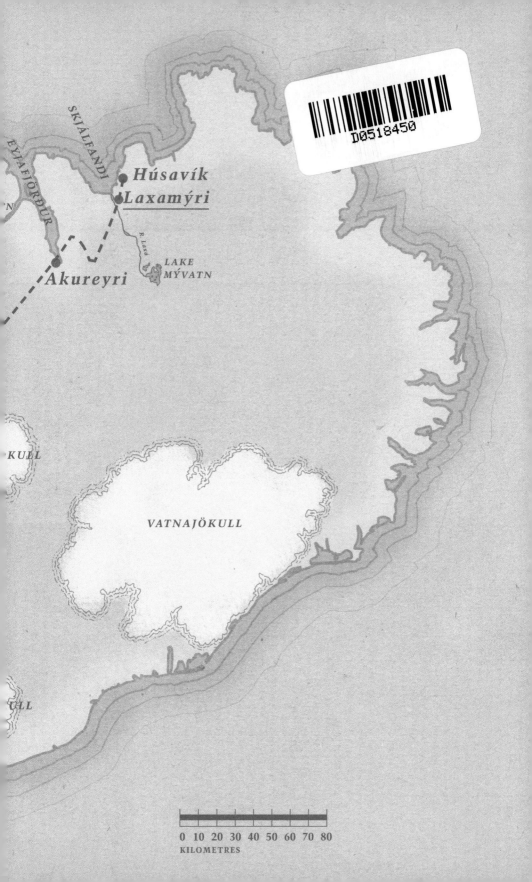

Dreaming of Iceland

Dreaming of Iceland

THE LURE OF A FAMILY LEGEND

SALLY MAGNUSSON

Hodder & Stoughton
LONDON SYDNEY AUCKLAND

Sally Magnusson is grateful to Bill Holm for permission
to quote from a revised version of his poem,
'The Icelandic Language', as printed in *Xenophobe's Guide
to the Icelanders* by Richard Sale, Oval Books, 2000.
The original version of the same poem can be found in
The Dead Get by with Everything by Bill Holm,
Milkweed Editions, Minneapolis, Minnesota, 1991.

British Library Cataloguing in Publication Data
A record for this book is available from the British Library

ISBN 0 340 86250 5

Typeset in TrumpMedieval by Avon DataSet Ltd,
Bidford-on-Avon, Warwickshire

Printed and bound in Great Britain by
Clays Ltd, St Ives plc

The paper used in this book is a natural recyclable product
made from wood grown in sustainable forests.
The hard coverboard is recycled.

Hodder & Stoughton
A Division of Hodder Headline Ltd
338 Euston Road
London NW1 3BH
www.madaboutbooks.com

For my mother

Contents

Acknowledgements

I am grateful to many people in Iceland for their help with this book, not least my kinsman Árni Sigurjónsson who, after supplying a stream of ideas, advice and tactful correction to aid the writing of the original, ended up translating it all into Icelandic as well. My warm thanks go also to Guðni Halldórsson and Björn Sigurðsson in Húsavík; Atli Vigfússon at Laxamýri; Jón Hjaltason and Hallgrímur Aðalsteinsson in Akureyri; Sigurjón Sigurðsson, Jóhannes Helgason, Jón Viðar Jónsson, Viktor Aðalsteinsson, Erlendur Sveinsson and the late Líney Jóhannesdóttir in Reykjavík; Unnar Ingvarsson in Sauðárkrókur; Örlygur Kristfinnsson in Siglufjörður; and translators Ingibjörg Águstsdóttir and Dröfn Guðmundsdóttir.

Marta Guðjónsdóttir, Kjartan Gunnar Kjartansson and Ragnhildur Guðjónsdóttir supplied me with food, wine, books and Icelandic lessons, and Vigdís Finnbogadóttir laid the foundations of my love for Iceland many years ago.

Nearer home, I am hugely grateful for the encouragement of my literary agent Giles Gordon, who died suddenly in November 2003, leaving all his authors bereft. His sunny belief in this book kept me, and it, going forward.

And not least there has been my father, translator, mentor and unstinting support from beginning to end, who by some miracle is still talking to me. I hope he will accept this book as a kind of thank-you, for everything.

Laxamýri Dynasty

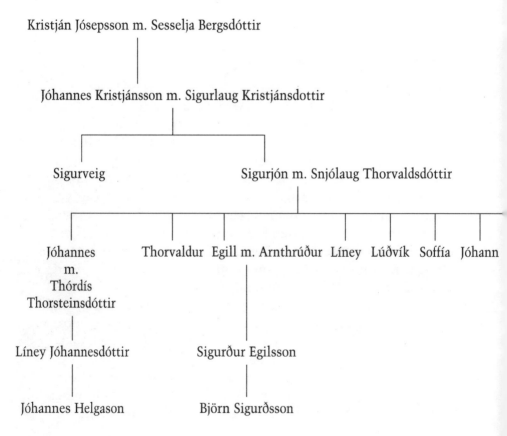

Kristján Jósepsson m. Sesselja Bergsdóttir

Jóhannes Kristjánsson m. Sigurlaug Kristjánsdottir

Sigurveig

Sigurjón m. Snjólaug Thorvaldsdóttir

Jóhannes
m.
Thórdís
Thorsteinsdóttir

Thorvaldur   Egill m. Arnthrúður   Líney   Lúðvík   Soffía   Jóhann

Líney Jóhannesdóttir

Sigurður Egilsson

Jóhannes Helgason

Björn Sigurðsson

C A S T

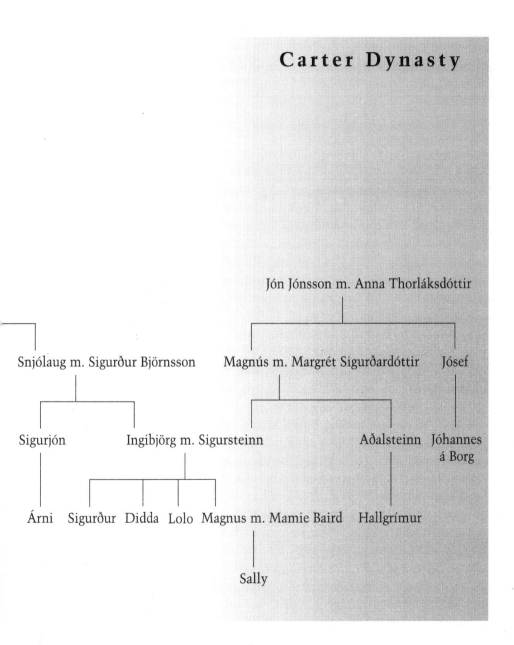

Carter Dynasty

Jón Jónsson m. Anna Thorláksdóttir

Snjólaug m. Sigurður Björnsson   Magnús m. Margrét Sigurðardóttir   Jósef

Sigurjón   Ingibjörg m. Sigursteinn   Aðalsteinn   Jóhannes á Borg

Árni   Sigurður   Didda   Lolo   Magnus m. Mamie Baird   Hallgrímur

Sally

A Note on Pronouncing the Unpronounceable

There is no getting round it: Icelandic names are confusing to non-Icelanders. To this day my inveterately English husband insists on calling my sister 'Snoogaloog', because he has never been able to master the name 'Snjólaug', which recurs in just about every branch and generation of our family. But with a few phonetic rules to hand, anyone ought to be able to make a better fist of it than he does. Here are some tips to help with the names of people and places which crop up in this book.

First of all, you can't go wrong by pronouncing everything in sight. Nothing is silent. The emphasis is always on the first syllable of a word.

The letter which looks like a crossed *d* is called 'eth' and is pronounced like the voiced *th* in *then*. Hence, *Sigurður* is pronounced *Sigurthur*. (The unvoiced *th*, as in *thin*, is a different letter, *þ*, which to avoid confusion I have transcribed everywhere as 'th'. But it is worth remembering that when you meet, for instance, the historic parliament plains of *Thingvellir* on an Icelandic map, the name will appear as *Þingvellir*.)

The letter *j* is always pronounced like the *y* in *yellow*, which means *Jóhann* is pronounced as *Yóhann*. And the double *ll* in *Egill* is pronounced *dl*, giving something like *Ay-yidl*.

The pronunciation of the vowels is strongly conditioned by their accents. Hence:

a as in *father*

á as in *owl*

e as in *get*

é as *ye* in *yet*

i as in *bid*

í as in *seen* (*Líney* is thus *Leenay*)

o as in *got*

ó as in *note* (*Jóhann, Jóhannes* and *Sigurjón* all have this long ó)

u as in French *peu*

ú as in *soon* (my father's name in Icelandic, *Magnús*, is pronounced *Magnoos*)

y and *ý* are exact equivalents of *i* and *í* (thus *Laxamýri* is pronounced *Laxa-meerie*)

æ as in *life*

ö as in French *fleur* (my grandmother *Ingibjörg*, for example)

au as in French *oeil*

ei and *ey* as in *tray*

As for *Snjólaug*, the best policy is to take the word in its two Icelandic parts and then a deep breath. Try *Snyoh-loeig*. Or you may prefer to stick with Snoogaloog.

Iceland is the sun colouring the mountains without being anywhere in sight, even sunk beyond the horizon.
W. H. Auden in an interview with *Morgunblaðið*,
14 April 1964

When the legend becomes fact, print the legend.
The Man Who Shot Liberty Valance, 1962,
directed by John Ford, screenplay by James Warner Bellah
and Willis Goldbeck

Prologue

My father hops out of the car with an alacrity which practically bellows his relief at having survived the mountain roads of north Iceland with his eldest daughter at the wheel. Through his open door, I can hear the wind whining over the moors of Laxamýri.

I follow him from the car to the memorial on the edge of the heath, struggling to adjust a hood of such Arctic efficiency that I can barely see out of it. He glances back and raises an eyebrow. His own tweedy jacket is flapping like a flag.

'Bit parky, isn't it?' I hazard from deep within this fleece-lined, wind-cheating, snow-repelling anorak – a little *de trop* for May, even in Iceland, but who's laughing this afternoon, I want to know. The sun has gone and the wind is blustering straight up from the sea.

'Nonsense,' he replies bracingly. My father, thin, checked shirt open at the neck, would rather sit for ten hours in a non-smoking aeroplane than admit he might be finding Laxamýri cold.

'Oh come off it. Feel that wind,' I mutter, still struggling with the hood. 'You must be freezing.'

He draws himself up straight. 'Men, as I think I've had occasion to mention to you before, dearest, do not limp while their legs are the same length.'

Oh, I see. That makes it perfectly clear. Yes, he's cold, but no, he has not the slightest intention of buttoning up his jacket. My father is a Viking.

The sculpture mounted on a plinth not far from the roadside is strikingly simple. The letters J and S have been sculpted into a sinuous embrace above a plaque which reads:

Jóhann Sigurjónsson
Skáld
19.6.1880–30.8.1919

Jóhann, the celebrated Icelandic playwright and poet (*skáld*) from the estate of Laxamýri in the north of Iceland, was my father's great-uncle. He was the family hero, adored by my grandmother Ingibjörg, who would have been flutteringly thrilled at the honour done to him with this monument erected in 1980. To her, Laxamýri was a kind of B-movie kingdom, in which Jóhann starred as the Crown Prince and dark deeds were done before violins sighed for the titles.

I glance at my father, who is looking suspiciously moist in the eye himself, although it could be the wind. His mother never stopped talking about this place; both he and I grew up believing it was the nearest thing on earth to heaven itself.

'Laxamýri,' Ingibjörg would sigh, taking a full second on that *mýr* and savouring it like a sweet on her tongue, as fondly as you might croon the *dear* of *dearie*. I always knew there was a story in the reverent way she breathed the word rather than spoke it, although I was never sure exactly what the story was. It was just another mysterious bond with Iceland.

I am related to this country, every last car-rattling stone of it, by blood and by story. My ancestors lived in it and my father was born in it, but my own relationship has been largely forged in the imagination, through stories – fittingly, perhaps, since Iceland owes its very identity to the collective memory of saga. Some nations are born of conquest, some by the schemes of others, some on the strength of an idea. This is a nation built on words.

But what do you do when the stories are so good you don't know what is true? When your view of your kin and their country is based on a type of story-telling wryly captured by the Icelandic novelist Halldór Laxness in *Christianity at Glacier*? 'It is pleasant to listen to the birds chirping,' observes Pastor

Jón. 'But it would be anything but pleasant if the birds were always chirping the truth.' It is a comfortable enough position to be in, until the time comes when you find yourself wanting some fact from the charming birdsong of your family legends and some substance to the lifelong consciousness of another country in your blood.

What do you do? You persuade your father, none too reliable conduit of stories ancient and modern, to travel it with you, share his own Iceland along the way and help track the stories to their source.

Say it quickly enough and it sounds simple.

A Modest Proposal

Even by my standards it had been an impulsive suggestion, one I knew my father would regard with the utmost suspicion. An expedition of which he would not be in charge? Dreamed up by an impetuous daughter whose reliability in matters of punctuality and organisation he had long ago decided could not be trusted? Dream on, daughter.

We were in the study of his home in the countryside north of Glasgow, a teeming lair of books and strewn papers through which some brave vacuum cleaner had attempted to mow a path between door and desk. I was half-sitting against the window-sill and he was a few feet away in his leather armchair, filling his pipe. I watched him packing it with fresh brown strands of tobacco and stabbing these thoughtfully with the blackened rump of a red pencil. I felt as if I had been watching this ritual, from exactly this perch beneath the window, for the whole of my life.

Today, though, I was nervous. The last time I had come darting into this room with a proposal to take him somewhere he might enjoy my father had laughed, thanked me profusely, and said that on the whole he rather thought he wouldn't bother. It was only an invitation to the theatre. How on earth was I going to winkle this man out of here and on to a plane for Iceland?

Iceland. So much a part of us both. So constant a backdrop to my childhood that the 3-D map on his study wall is as familiar to me as pipe-smoke. How often I used to run my finger over its moulded contours, feeling along the tiny areas of flat green which hugged the serrated coastline, surprised by how quickly I would bump into brown mountain and awed by how long it took to slide across the vast white glaciers. There seemed to be so few frail ribbons of coastal green, so staggeringly little that was not brown, or white, or desert black. Long before I came to know the country for myself, I understood that Iceland was a very singular place indeed.

It provided a vaguely exotic dimension to my Scottish childhood, which I milked for all it was worth. Decades before Icelandair dreamed up the wheeze of flying holidaymakers to Florida via Reykjavík, I basked in the smug glow of privileged knowledge. At school the geography class was disdainfully informed that Iceland was, of course, green and Greenland icy. I expressed weary indignation that anyone could believe there were igloos there (the thought of my well-bred grandmother in one, smoothing out her foxtail collar in the ice-wall mirror, made me giggle). I even took it upon myself to disabuse the history class of the notion that the Vikings had worn horned helmets. It was an arcane point, this, but I pursued it with fervour because my father was up in arms about it at the time.

Having an Icelandic father who came dashing out of his study yelling '*Ég er farinn*' at the top of his voice to indicate that he was off, and insisted that we say '*Takk fyrir matinn*' to offer thanks at the end of a meal, was an acceptably minor degree of foreignness, if only his name had not been so embarrassing. Donald Macdonald would have been infinitely preferable to Magnus Magnusson in a Glasgow playground. Of course, now that our playgrounds ring to the names of domestic footballers like Lopez Ufarte and Raphael Scheidt, my father's doesn't seem half so bad, but in those days Magnus Magnusson really did feel excruciatingly odd. There was no anonymity with a name like that, and anonymity was what I craved more than anything in the early boom years of the BBC's *Mastermind* quiz show (which he went on to present for twenty-five years), when every conversation with anyone I had just met would begin, 'Magnusson? Any relation?' followed, more often than I can bear to remember, by the hilarious witticism, 'I've started so I'll finish. Ha, ha, ha.'

But the name was worth it for the rest of the package which came with my Icelandic blood. The stories of saga-heroes and giants conjured through a fog of pipe-smoke in my father's study. The language with the strange lettering which transfixed me when I was allowed to trawl through his books. The beguiling Christmas Eves, celebrated amid the rustle of long gowns and the heady whiff of cigar-smoke around a tree flaming with candlelight, while the rest of the country had nothing better to do than put out milk and biscuits for Santa Claus. And the grandparents, they especially, my *amma* and *afi* in Edinburgh, whom I dimly understood to be offering a window on a civilisation which was somehow different and valuable.

Laxamýri was part of it, this word which my grandmother kept saying with a sigh, this place I could never quite get a handle on, which belonged to our family past and was beautiful, rich and irretrievably lost. It seemed to hover like some ghostly presence around all our family gatherings.

'Let me look at you, *Sallý mín*,' one of my grandmother's gustily affectionate sisters murmured fondly when I visited Iceland in the late 1960s with my parents and younger sister. 'Ah yes, there's no doubt about it, *elskan* [darling]. You have the look of Laxamýri.'

I hadn't the faintest idea what this meant. I took it to be a compliment, although my great-aunts said the word exactly as my grandmother did, making it ooze plangency and sound like an elegy.

My grandmother said something similar once. She was standing in the kitchen of the city centre apartment in Edinburgh to which she and my grandfather moved in later life, slicing slivers of the smoked lamb known as *hangikjöt* which we all loved. I must have asked something about this name I had heard on people's lips so often because I can see her now, patting back a wandering strand of dark hair and telling me that Laxamýri, ah, beautiful, beautiful Laxamýri, was far in the north of Iceland and that her family had once owned it for a long time. 'A very long time, *elskan*.'

She walked over to the Frigidaire, which was as big as a

wardrobe (the first in Edinburgh, my father always said) and stocked the Icelandic delicacies which were sent from home or arrived from time to time in the suitcases of visiting compatriots.

'And you, *elsku Sallý mín*,' she added, pulling the silver bar on this pungent Aladdin's larder, 'have Laxamýri eyes.'

I am still not sure if she meant the colour, blue like hers, or the shape. But I was as flattered as she surely intended me to be. To have Laxamýri-anything was to be blessed indeed.

I wonder now how much of her calm social confidence my grandmother owed to her lifelong consciousness of descent from the clan of Laxamýri. No matter that she lived almost the entire fifty-six years of her married life in Edinburgh, Ingibjörg Sigurðardóttir never forgot that she came from a family which had once owned one of the greatest farming estates in all Iceland and produced the nation's first sensationally successful playwright. In her sweet-natured and never less than charming way, my grandmother sailed through Edinburgh society with the serene aplomb of a princess in exile.

She was beautiful. I loved the contrast of those sapphire eyes against the dark brown hair which never, to the end of her life, attracted more than a few stray threads of silver. I loved her neat nose and generous bosom. I loved her habit of mixing up English and Icelandic words in uniquely fetching combinations, and her continued insistence, over more than half a century in the city, that she lived in 'Edinboro'.

My grandfather adored her. Even after the fractious disorientations of old age had begun to set in and he was barking at his grandchildren as if he had never met them in his life, he treated her with consummate tenderness, like an infinitely precious thing.

He came from humbler stock than she. Sigursteinn Magnússon was the academically high-flying son of a carter from the town of Akureyri in the north of Iceland, not so very far from Laxamýri but an ocean of social standing apart. His own background was quickly marginalised by the glittering Laxamýri aura which my grandmother wore like a crown. Their older daughter Margrét, known to everyone as Didda, grew up knowing so little about Sigursteinn's family that she was well into adulthood before she realised that she had been named after his mother. Sigursteinn, a proud man who bore himself like a stately warrior to the end, resigned himself to living in the shadow of Laxamýri. He called his younger son Magnús, after his father, and made sure his children did at least hear about the achievements of his cousin Jóhannes, the strongest man in Iceland and a world-renowned circus performer of whom his wife's family faintly disapproved. But he was up against it with Laxamýri. How could a roistering wrestler rival a romantic poet? How could Sigursteinn Magnússon's upbringing in the house of a poor carter compete with the kingdom of heaven?

He had brought his family to Scotland in the summer of 1930, sent by the Icelandic Co-operative Society to open a new office for fish exports at Leith, the port of Edinburgh. Young Magnús was then eight months old. In the Scottish capital, where Sigursteinn later became Iceland's consul, he and Ingibjörg established a well-to-do household which was in many respects a microcosm of the bourgeois Reykjavík the couple had left behind. An Icelandic maid saw to the housework. Ptarmigan sent across on the steamer *Gullfoss* hung whiffily in the larder. Delicate pastries, which Ingibjörg had learned to bake to feather-light perfection at a domestic college in Denmark, sat crowned with cream on the tea table. Coffee was strong, dark and sweet. When travelling Icelanders were disgorged at Leith, they headed straight for the consul's house and joined the family in boisterous Icelandic songs around the piano, gamely accompanied by Didda and her sister, Snjólaug (known as Lolo), until their fingers sagged. Late in the night, over vodka and snuff, Sigursteinn and his guests debated the vexed political question of how to persuade the Danes to relinquish the final remnants of sovereignty over Iceland. They could almost have been in their smart apartment on Laugavegur Street back home. In fact, possibly my grandparents' sole concession to non-Icelandic custom was carpets. No one needed them in Reykjavík once the boiling water under the ground had been harnessed for indoor heating; but east-windy Edinburgh was not so blessed.

Traditional Icelandic feast-days were observed with exquisite cuisine and considerable panache, and none more so than Christmas Eve. In a development which astonished the neighbours, a glittering fir tree appeared in their window the first

Christmas after the family arrived in Edinburgh. Presbyterian Scotland was not accustomed to pagan winter festivals, and the appearance of the tree, ablaze with candles in a window from which the curtains had been wantonly tied back so that everyone could see it from outside, caused a small sensation. Within a few years, Sigursteinn was happily boasting that people had started to copy him. I'm not sure he didn't come close to suggesting that he personally had introduced Christmas to the benighted Scots.

On Christmas Eve, at 6 p.m. exactly, the family gathered in their finest clothes in the small lounge they called the *bláa stofa*, or blue room, where Sigursteinn played his cherished gramophone record of an Icelandic choir singing the carol which defined their Icelandic Christmas, *Heims um ból*, the hymn we know as 'Still the Night'. Then they would sit down to a dinner of thick rice soup mixed with cinnamon and sugar, dark ptarmigan with red cabbage, and a frothy Danish pineapple mousse for dessert called *fromasse*, which melted in the mouth like foam. After the meal, Sigursteinn disappeared into the lounge, lit the candles, and revealed with a dramatic flourish the sight the children had been artfully denied since it arrived in the house the day before: the tree, candles flickering against the dark window, with presents heaped below. The family sidled around it, hand in hand, first one way and then another, singing carols until the last flame had died. It was an evening, replicated to a degree in my own childhood, which still reduces my father to wordless sighs of remembered bliss.

Icelandic remained their language at home. Magnús spoke little else until he went to school and his English has retained to this day the precise modulations of the learned second tongue. By the time he set up his own home with a Scottish wife, the newspaper reporter Mamie Baird, the *u* in his name had lost its accent and his Icelandic was confined to extended family gatherings and a few catchphrases. Teaching his Scots-born children to say '*Takk fyrir matinn*' before leaving the table was the extent of my father's efforts to pass on the mother-tongue to the next generation.

But my grandparents were a different matter. Ingibjörg would chatter to us in Icelandic all day if we let her, blissfully forgetful that her grandchildren could rarely grasp more than the gist of what she was saying. She frequently spoke it when she thought she was speaking English, sliding happily from one language to the other and back again, often within a sentence. Even when she alighted steadfastly on English, her grasp was never completely secure, although no one was much inclined to correct her. Who would not prefer to bring their school *chumps* home for tea? Or thrill at the prospect of the soldiers in Edinburgh Castle going on *gooard*? Or have the heart to explain why the grocer was baffled by her polite request for two *libs* of flour?

Heim was one of the first Icelandic words I grew to recognise, perhaps because it is also the old Scots word for 'home'. Neither of my grandparents ever called Iceland anything but home.

'This summer, *elskan*,' Amma would say in her eclectic way, 'we're planning to *fara heim*.'

And from an early age it seemed to me entirely natural that her home should be both there in Lygon Road, Edinburgh, and also far across the sea where she and those mellifluous Icelandic cadences of hers belonged and where, in a way I could not even have begun to articulate, I felt I did too.

Their home was steeped in the culture of the Icelandic sagas, medieval narratives about life in Iceland in the generations after it was first settled. Sigursteinn's study was lined with beautiful leather-bound volumes of *Njáls Saga* and *Laxdæla Saga*, *Egils Saga* and the rest, which he ensured were read, recited and discussed in Edinburgh as avidly as they were in homes around Iceland. Sigursteinn believed passionately that the sagas were word-for-word historical fact. He was hotly opposed to the theories starting to gain ground in 1940s academic circles that the sagas were actually inspired works of historical fiction, merely based to varying degrees on the lives of real people. My father, studying English and Old Icelandic at Oxford, was on a hiding to nothing when he argued the new line that they were none the less brilliant for being literary creations rather than holy writ. It was like living in a Strict and Particular Baptist household and trying to suggest there was an element of poetry in the Creation story.

My grandfather's irascible fundamentalism mellowed in the end, as the heresy gradually became orthodoxy, but the sagas remained as personally inspirational to him as any religion. The stories of heroism in a once-free Iceland fed the patriotic struggle for independence to which he and his generation of Icelanders were passionately committed. They drank in the sagas until their speech and very thought-patterns echoed them.

Sigursteinn's cousin Jóhannes, a brawny youngster who became the strongest man in Iceland and competed as a wrestler in the 1908 Olympics in London, was a case in point. He modelled himself on the fêted saga outlaw, Grettir the Strong. Family lore has it that at the age of about eight Jóhannes started hauling on to his shoulders each day a foal born on his father's croft in the north, until by the time the foal was grown and Jóhannes was eleven, he could lift a full-sized Icelandic horse. The story has suspiciously Herculean overtones, but Jóhannes recounted it in later life with such gusto that my teenage father, soaking up every word the old man told him on their fishing days together in the west of Iceland, never for a moment thought of questioning it.

Jóhannes lived his whole life like a saga character. He went on to become a champion wrestler and, if not horses, he certainly flung men around with merry abandon. He then travelled the world, inviting all comers to take him on (no weapons barred except pistols) and living to tell the tale at colourful length. I was delighted to discover an internet website for martial arts enthusiasts dedicated to the great Jóhannes Jósefsson, exponent of the ancient art of Icelandic *glíma* wrestling. He would have revelled in the description of himself as 'this martial arts sensation'.

After a flamboyant career, Jóhannes prepared for a hero's death. When my father, still a very young man, went to see the old boy in Iceland after he had suffered a heart attack, Jóhannes was lying prostrate in bed. They talked for a while and then Magnus made to go. Jóhannes at once waved him towards a sword and scabbard which he wanted him to have as a gift. I'm sure my father would have preferred his fishing rod, but he was touched. Then he saw that his uncle was struggling to sit up in bed.

'No, no, please don't sit up,' he said, terrified the old man was going to expire on the spot. 'Just say goodbye. I'll see you again.'

Purple in the face, Jóhannes pulled himself up so that he was half-leaning on the pillow and his back was straight.

'I do not take leave of my kinsmen lying down,' he gasped. 'We shall not meet again.'

Nor did they. Their final parting was straight out of the sagas, and I suspect my father would be only too glad to contrive something of the sort for his own demise.

Suspect? I know it.

My father's brand of patriotism is literary with a vengeance – an apt enough phrase for a saga-lover, if you remember the plots. It is rooted in the most revered period of Iceland's history, when the land was free, men were men, and (this bit is true) Icelanders were writing some of the most glorious literature in the world. Over the years those characters from a thousand years ago have welded themselves to his personality. His family can only be thankful that he has shown a clear preference for honour and valour over murderous pique.

This is a man who nearly burned the tip of his finger off once to prove that he could hold it longer over a flame than anyone else, who in his heyday would rather have had his arm broken than concede another man's superiority in arm-wrestling. He is a man whose word is his bond in an absolute fashion which, like his literary idealism in general, sometimes sets him apart from the more pragmatic style of modern Icelanders.

These Viking proclivities of my father's have fairly infested his language. (I find 'Viking' useful shorthand, by the way, but I doubt if he would use it himself, since the vikings – probably taking their name from *vík*, or bay – were actually multi-national Nordic seafarers who never existed as a single people and don't even strictly merit a capital letter.) His conversation is full of aphorisms, tossed in with no intention of displaying erudition, but never entirely tongue in cheek either. As a child it took me a long time to realise that these were ancient books he was quoting and literary heroes he was emulating, and that the very rhythms and idioms of my father's speech, even in perfectly honed English, were as Icelandic as his prickly pride and cavalier generosity.

The unanswerable 'Men do not limp while their legs are the same length', employed to rebuff any warranted or unwarranted fussing over his health, is his act of homage to Gunnlaugur Adder-Tongue, a saga-hero with a stoical bent who earned the reverence of many a manly Icelander for his reply when challenged about a boil on his instep which was leaking pus all over the Earl of Norway's best floor.

'Why are you not limping, Icelander?' demanded the earl.

'Men do not limp while their legs are the same length, Sire,' retorted young Gunnlaugur, successfully silencing his earlship. It is a reply which manages, in the way of the sagas, to be both so preposterous and so admirable that it suits my father in stoical Viking mode down to the ground.

For his epitaph, though, I suspect he might prefer a line or two from Óðin. He likes the code of honour attributed to the chief of the Norse gods in a poem called *Hávamál* from the body of mythological Norse poetry called the Edda, composed around AD 800. He especially treasures Óðin's concept of immortality as 'word-fame'.

'Wealth dies, kinsmen die, a man himself must likewise die,' he will observe solemnly when a philosophy of life is called for, sounding like Gandalf preparing for the off in his grey ship. 'But one thing I know which never dies – word-fame, if justly earned.'

Anywhere outside Middle Earth this is, of course, a conversation-stopper, of the kind you hope doesn't have to be followed up by an inquiry about whether he would like an egg for his tea. But although my father can be easily teased into laughing at himself, the maxim is deeply felt. Word-fame is important to a man who wore his television celebrity lightly and has long scorned what passes nowadays for fame.

The first time I placed a tape-recorder under my father's reluctant nose with a request to tell me all he knew about Laxamýri, we got nowhere. It is a sad axiom that we start to become curious about our family history at exactly the point when it is too late to ask anyone who has a chance of remembering. My grandparents were gone. The last of my breathlessly loquacious Icelandic great-aunts had also died. My father roundly declared himself an inadequate replacement.

He hummed and shuffled and prevaricated, protesting (truth-fully enough as it turned out) an appalling memory and such a compulsive instinct for embroidery that he could never be sure how much he had heard and how much invented. But one day, after much nagging, he settled down in the armchair in the study, ready for business. I perched on the window-ledge, the way I used to when he was outlining a hundred ways to fell your enemy in saga-times, and listened.

As far as he knew, he said, Laxamýri had been one of the greatest and richest estates in the whole of Iceland. His voice went all dreamy, just the way his mother's used to. It was a place with tremendous natural resources of river, land and sea. Its period of real greatness had been in the second half of the nineteenth century, when his great-grandfather, Sigurjón Jóhannesson, was in charge.

'He was a brilliant farmer, driven and far-sighted, but cursed' – my father paused theatrically – 'with a potentially fatal flaw.'

'Which was?'

'An over-fondness for the drink.' He grinned. 'Not unknown in the Laxamýri family.'

Then, one especially inclement winter's night, Sigurjón's wife went into a difficult labour while he was too drunk to help, or even to fetch the midwife. By some miracle both wife and baby daughter survived, and in his gratitude and shame Sigurjón swore never to touch another drop again. He never did, but hurled his formidable energies instead into building a farming empire which became a legend even in its own time.

'Such a wonderful place it was,' my father said, so wistfully you would have thought he had spent half his life there; you would certainly have wagered a generous slice of your salary that he had at least seen the place. 'Ah yes,' he sighed, and I could hear my great-aunts in that sigh, 'it was rich beyond the dreams of Icelanders, and very beautiful.'

Then, he said more briskly, everything had turned sour. He wasn't sure what had gone wrong exactly, but the story went that it had been gambled and drunk away by a generation of feckless sons, with all sorts of unspecified rumours of villainy afoot, until it ended up being sold to strangers in 1928, the year before he himself was born. The family's irreplaceable treasure had been thrown away and everyone had been terribly upset about it for a long time.

'Here, listen to this,' he said suddenly, leaping up to select a book from the shelves. 'This is what sums up for me all the wasted promise of the House of Laxamýri.'

The book fell open at the page he wanted – he must have been there often – and he began to recite a poem. He knew it so well that he hardly glanced again at the page. Then he read me a translation he had laboured over years ago.

Alone I sit with a wine-glass,
the long afternoon of winter;
from golden goblet arises
the aroma of ancient flowers.

Einn sit ég yfir drykkju
aftaninn vetrarlangan,
ilmar af gullnu glasi
gamalla blóma angan.

Joys which long are departed
spark to life in my spirit;
sorrows long dead and
    forgotten
yet once more are weeping.

Gleði, sem löngu er liðin
lifnar í sálu minni,
sorg, sem var gleymd og
    grafin,
grætur í annað sinni.

Death waits behind me;
his mighty hand is bearing
the fathomless night heavens,
poured to the brim with darkness.

Bak við mig bíður dauðinn,
ber hann í hendi styrkri
hyldjúpan næturhimin
helltan fullan af myrkri.

The poem was written by Jóhann Sigurjónsson, the Laxamýri poet who wrote like an angel, enjoyed a few years of stardom, drank prolifically and died in his thirties, like Robert Burns, at the height of his fame. My father believed it was his generation of brothers who had squandered the inheritance. For him, Jóhann's lethally golden glass had long evoked the lost paradise that was Laxamýri.

Later I sought out his elder sister, Didda, to ask if she was any the wiser about what had gone on up there on the family estate. I rang the bell of her detached Edinburgh villa and waited, eyeing the name of the house painted in flowing letters above the front door: *Laxamýri*. There ought to be a tale or two here.

Didda did have one juicy story to add to my collection that

afternoon. In a conspiratorial whisper, she confided that Ingibjörg's mother, my great-grandmother, Snjólaug, had been 'cast off' from her Laxamýri home for marrying beneath her, banished for ever by the implacable Sigurjón.

'She got nothing from the estate, nothing at all,' murmured my aunt into her teacup, 'except a handful of gold coins from her mother.'

These coins had been smuggled out to the banished one in conditions of deadly secrecy. Ingibjörg had inherited some of them, and Didda herself now had one in her possession, a small, shiny, golden piece bearing the head of the Danish king.

Didda's recollections should have come stamped with an even bolder health warning than my father's, as I might have realised sooner if I had not been as seduced as she by the romance of my family history outdoing Dickens for plot. But I was only too eager to file this one alongside his as stories too good to forget. Drunken epiphany, smuggled gold, doorsteps which must never be darkened again, stern father, ne'er-do-well sons and paradise unjustly lost: this saga had the works.

So there I was on a grey Scottish winter's afternoon, watching the flame of my father's lighter dart into the tobacco, breathing in my fix of heady aroma and wondering how I should frame the proposal that we make a journey to Laxamýri together. So carried away was I with the idea of spending time with him in Iceland, just the two of us, that I felt ridiculously apprehensive. We had not been away alone together anywhere, ever, since the evening he took me out to a posh Glasgow restaurant to celebrate my sixth birthday. I was afraid he would pat me on the knee, thank me graciously for a most invigorating idea, and change the subject.

'Er, Da-ad,' I ventured.

He was alerted at once. In the old days, 'Dad' with two syllables would have prefaced a pranged car confession or, at the very least, some wheedling request for a holiday sub. The pipe hovered in mid-air and he looked at me warily.

'I just wondered,' I said, 'how you'd fancy coming with me to Iceland.'

Discovery

I had forgotten how brown the south coast looks in late spring. You burst through the clouds and see nothing whatsoever which might have prompted Ravens-Flóki to name this country Iceland. Amid every nuance of hessian, the only legacy of winter is a few modest rivulets of snow stuck in mountain crevasses. There are no glaciers to be seen, no floating slabs of ice, none of the things which made the disgruntled Norwegian explorer Flóki Vilgerðarson turn his tongue, and his back, on the land he discovered more than eleven centuries ago.

Ice or no, it is a thrilling sight for a returning Icelander and his daughter, especially when they have spent the previous few minutes of the flight over the Atlantic arguing.

We had started out that late May morning in fine spirits. Even when I tested my father's patience by rolling up at his house to collect him half an hour late, so that we made it to Glasgow airport with what I cheerfully suggested was a comfortable margin and he denounced as cutting things criminally fine, all was well. In fact, my father trying to be tetchy and not carrying it off felt exactly as it should be. Even when he typically offered the wrong answers to the luggage questions at the check-in desk (a private protest at the illogicality of security procedures which once earned him a strip-search at Tel Aviv airport), he did it with such a jovial smile

19

that the girl smiled uncertainly and handed him his boarding card. Any minute now he would be quoting Óðin. He must be happy.

I certainly was. Four days lay ahead without work or children, and with nothing more to worry about than trying to be early for planes and not tipping my father into genuine irritation. It was so long since the pair of us had gone anywhere together that I had forgotten how comfortable, in a sparring sort of way, we could be in one another's company. I had also forgotten how we shared the journalistic zest for a story. It was this which had tempted him in the end, the idea of going on a quest, the chance to dig and ask questions and form theories about the past. I noticed that his briefcase was bulging with books, a sure sign that he also regarded this excursion as the nearest he ever allows himself to a holiday.

When we reached the plane, he greeted the stewardess on board with such a sunny '*Góðan daginn*' – even as she confirmed that he was indeed to be parted from his pipe for a whole two hours – that I knew he was seriously preparing to enjoy himself. Thank goodness for that. I knew there had been times over the past few months when he could happily have dropped both me and every last ancestor of ours deep into the North Sea.

On one of my illicit raids on his bookshelves I had unearthed a slim, densely printed book containing a memoir written by Sigurjón Jóhannesson shortly before his death in 1918. My father, if he had ever read it, had forgotten what the book was about. It also contained funeral orations in honour of Sigurjón (and before that, his father), poems, photographs and an extremely long introductory genealogy. It was just what I needed to understand the first two generations of the Laxamýri clan. Unfortunately, it was in Icelandic.

I had smiled at my father in what I hoped was a winsome manner. He ran his fingers through his hair with the air of a man who sees no escape.

'Not the whole thing? You don't really want it *all* translated, do you? Good heavens, dearest, must you?'

But I did want it all translated. This was gold-dust and my feeble conversational Icelandic was not up to it. He put the task off for weeks (some pathetic excuse about having work of his own to do), but when he did finally give in, he tackled it in the way he does everything: with a fastidious zeal for perfection which far exceeded what I needed and nearly drove me up the wall. He sat in his armchair in the study with the book in one hand and a dictionary on his knee, while I tapped the translation into a computer on his desk.

'Could we maybe just say "etc, etc" with a few dots here?' I implored, as we waded through page after page of genealogy stretching right back to the settlement of Iceland.

'Certainly not,' came the bark from across the room. 'It's important to get it right.'

'Yes, but these are only notes. I know I said I wanted it all but . . .'

'IT'S IMPORTANT TO GET IT RIGHT.'

Oh, well, in that case . . . I'm now delighted to be in a position to report that Guttormur Ormsson of Thykkvaskógur's father was Ormur Snorrason of Skarð, the son of Snorri Narfason of Skarð, the son of Reverend Narfi Snorrason of Kolbeinsstaðir, the son of Reverend Snorri Narfason of Skarð, the son of Reverend Narfi Snorrason of Skarð, the son of Snorri Húnbogason of Skarð [*that's enough Snorris – Ed.*], the son of Húnbogi Thorgilsson, the brother of Ari (the Learned) Thorgilsson whose father, Thorgils Gellison of Helgafell, was the son of Gellir Thorkelsson, whose mother – this particular paragraph ended with a flourish – was Guðrún Ósvífrsdóttir, heroine of *Laxdæla Saga*. Actually, that bit was quite interesting.

It was at this point that my father got up from his chair and strode across the room towards the desk.

'Let's see if you've got all those accents right,' he said, peering suspiciously over my shoulder. I shifted guiltily. 'And what do you think this is? You haven't put in any at all!'

The accents do all sorts of important things to Icelandic vowels and I fully intended to put them in later. But I thought the task in hand would go quicker if I sort of ignored them for the time being. He snorted. If he was going to put his own work aside for who knows how long to help me, we would do it properly. No short-cuts, no messing around, and no putting accents in later.

This is going to take weeks, I thought, searching the keyboard for the combination which produces á, ö, ý, æ and the rest of the distinctively Icelandic alphabet. Sure enough, it did.

My father saw me off the premises on the final day with a weary pat on the shoulder. When I whooped in a few weeks later to show him my next find, a lyrical memoir by a relative who had spent her childhood at Laxamýri, he looked so hunted that I didn't even ask. I hired a translator. If I didn't give him a break from long-dead relatives, I would never get this man to Iceland.

The plane is surging out over the empty seas north of Shetland and my father's eyes are gleaming with enjoyment.

'See that sea?' he says, looking past me out of the window. I stare down at the black expanse of water, scarily empty. 'Imagine Ravens-Flóki navigating that in an open boat without a compass.'

Of all the Norse explorers who braved this ocean to reach virgin Iceland in the second half of the ninth century, Flóki Vilgerðarson is my father's favourite – probably because he had the sense to be a fan of Óðin. Flóki set out from Shetland with a few companions around the year 860 to check out reports of land to the north-west. His fellow Vikings were busy plundering up and down the coasts of the British Isles, but Flóki thought he would try heading in the opposite direction. The land up there had not been settled, by all accounts, and was worth a look. After several days at sea, he decided to try the Noah trick of releasing birds to guide him towards land. As a devotee of Óðin, he had three ravens with him. The first winged its way with all speed back to Shetland and the second flopped straight back down to the boat again, but the last one saved the day. It headed straight for the horizon and disappeared. Ravens-Flóki, as they called him after this, set course in the same direction.

I have always felt rather sorry for Ravens-Flóki, the plucky but hapless Neil Kinnock of early Iceland. He braved these seas without navigational tools and with only one sail, had the brainwave of following his raven, made it to the new island, settled down with his companions to enjoy its fruits – and then blew it. He spent a wonderful first summer hunting, gathering eggs and fishing in the teeming north-west fjord where he had made his final landing, but there was nobody around to warn him about the Icelandic winter. He omitted to gather in hay for the animals and they all died. The spring was also desperately cold. Thoroughly disgruntled, he climbed a mountain one day and, looking north towards the coast, spotted a fjord choked with drift-ice. You can just hear him muttering 'Huh, Ice Land' to himself on the way down.

All he wanted now was to get back home to Norway, but the sailing weather remained so bad that he had to spend a second winter where he was. The story goes that when he made it home at last, there was no holding back his disgust. 'That place is Iceland,' he grumbled to anyone who would listen, and the name *Ísland* stuck, Flóki's lasting and no mean contribution to the country's heritage. Sadly, though, Flóki has gone down in history as the man who missed his chance. A new leader coming up behind would earn instead the title of official First Settler of the new land.

But ice has only ever been half the story of Iceland and my father never lets me forget that there was another would-be settler in Flóki's party, a man called Thórólfur, who remembered the same expedition very differently. Not for him the chill, snow-blasted memories of winter. He waxed lyrical about summer-time when butter, he claimed, 'dripped from every blade of grass'. Perhaps if Thórólfur had had his say first, the Tourist Board in Reykjavík would be welcoming visitors today to Butterland and I could be happily introducing myself as a half-Butterlander.

I mention this to my father, and then wish I hadn't.

'Yes, quite,' he says thinly, in that subject-closing way of his which I take to be a sign that I should lay off any disrespectful line of speculation about the country's name.

His defences have leapt into action now that we are nearing Iceland. This is a country he has made it his life's work to promote. He has become an unofficial ambassador to the rest of the planet, translating Iceland's literature, singing its praises and picking away at the world's ignorance in books, articles and television documentaries since before I was born. He has done everything, in fact, except go and live there. If more people than ever now know that Iceland is a large volcanic island just south of the Arctic Circle with a population of only 284,000, an extraordinary literature, no igloos and a history which would make anyone want to wave the tiny flag he keeps on a ledge in his study until their arm ached, then my father can take at least some of the credit. But the responsibility does make him chippy at times.

He comes over all prickly again a few moments later in an extended altercation about the exact shade of Icelandic moss. I can't remember how we got started on this, but there is all at once a distinct chill in our section of the cabin. My father is deeply afraid that I might say – or, worse, write – something which would hurt his compatriots' sensibilities; and the list of things which might cause offence to somebody somewhere turns out to be longer than I thought.

I am taken aback to discover that using the phrase 'sickly green' to describe the shade of the vegetation covering a lava-field I once walked across might be construed as a gross personal insult to one of Iceland's greatest heroes, the moss. It seems I had underestimated the affection for this tenacious plant. Its work over the centuries in colonising Iceland's stone-hard deserts of lava, and breaking that lava down into soil, has won it god-like status in a land which never forgets a hero.

'The moss matters to Icelanders,' my father is saying huffily. 'Go and offend people if you like, but I'm sure you could find a better way of describing it.'

Icelanders are famously touchy, and my father is no exception. Sensitive to affronts himself – a very Viking flip-side to the scrupulous sense of honour – my father is pre-emptively offended on his countrymen's behalf, personally offended by my failure to see why it matters and, well, just offended.

I snap my notebook sulkily shut, offended myself now, and we sit there glaring into the backs of the seats in front. If my mother were here, she would blame it on the Icelander in us both, tell us we were too alike for our own good and defuse the situation with a joke. But we're on our own now. The mood of merry optimism which had swept over me at the airport is fast dissipating. It is my fault for underestimating his protectiveness, being too flippant about an environment he loves and too careless of a public he respects, but on the other hand this is my father being tetchy without even trying, and carrying it off very well indeed.

I feel mutinously adrift here. How much better to be an uncomplicated native crusader like him, with no shades of grey (or green) in his appreciation of the country, or else a detached outsider like the rest of the Iceland travel pack, who never need to waste a second worrying about whether they might be insulting anybody or anything at all. But what kind of hybrid creature am I? I start to wonder gloomily whether the whole exercise will end, as it is in danger of beginning, in tears.

Fortunately, there are other matters to engage us. The last wisp of cloud has cleared and below us, in clear, jagged outline, is the coastline of Iceland. My father cranes past my shoulder to take in the view as the plane glides along the south-western extremity and prepares to swoop inland towards Keflavík. These gaunt cliffs and infertile lava-plains in their muted colours may not be as spectacular as some of Iceland's natural wonders, but they thrill us all the same. It is good to see the place again.

My father has been travelling here on his resolutely Icelandic passport all his life. Every summer after they moved to Scotland, his homesick parents would steam across from Leith on the doughty *Gullfoss*, bringing their four children to visit the Laxamýri clan in the capital. Only the closing of the seas after the outbreak of the Second World War put paid to the annual visit for a few years. (In fact, my father's older brother Sigurður was stranded in Iceland after war was declared in 1939 and carried on his schooling in Reykjavík, eventually settling there as a doctor.) Later Magnus spent long university vacations in the country, working on farms, fishing boats and once, memorably, in a Reykjavík shipyard where he managed to break his arm and render himself useless in the first week.

As a newspaperman, he returned often to report on the many so-called 'cod wars' which Britain and Iceland pursued for several years with intermittent vigour and a few casualty-free clashes between Icelandic gun-boats and British warships. His mission was to expand the British public's understanding of the situation by stating Iceland's case for limits to protect her precious fish stocks as eloquently as the equally partisan newsdesk of the *Scottish Daily Express* would tolerate. In later years he came back as a broadcaster and made programmes about sagas, about ice and fire, about Vikings, about anything which gave him a chance to tell the world what they were missing in this extra-ordinary country.

I have been here less often, but the visits have also spanned a lifetime. My first approach as a two-year-old was, like this one, by plane. 'Come soonest. Bring Tootle' was my father's instruction on the telegram home. He was already in Iceland reporting on the first cod war, and he wanted my mother to join him. Without a passport for me, she was obliged to present the telegram nervously to the British authorities as evidence that the said Tootle's father really did want her to leave the country.

There followed more childhood holidays, a few months as a student behind the reception desk at the State Tourist Office, my own journalistic assignments for newspapers, television and radio, one unrepeatable family excursion to introduce my children to their *afi*'s homeland (unrepeatable because we would have to take out a mortgage to afford it again) and now this whimsical trip with my father. This time, perhaps for the first time, I want to see as well as look. I want to understand our relationship with Iceland.

My father has a huge grin on his face as he leans over to watch the sea foaming at the hem of the cliffs. Differences forgotten, we both smile stupidly out of the window, taking in the view, saying nothing.

I am thinking about Ingólfur Arnarson – as one does. What if his pillars had ended up stuck among these bared teeth of rock instead of in the tranquil bay he was to dub Reykjavík? I mean, think of it. This second Norwegian explorer sails all the way to the island which Flóki and Thórolfur have been gossiping about back home, heaves his household pillars into the sea, and pledges to settle wherever they fetch up. He lands and then spends three years looking for them. What if he had spotted them down there, wedged into the cliffs, with nowhere you could so much as light a fire on for miles around?

But Ingólfur was the Tony Blair of Icelandic settlement (to continue what my father will undoubtedly tell me is a very silly and tasteless analogy) and he was lucky. Or, as he saw it, the pillars carved with images of the Norse gods, which he had brought on the voyage from the high-seat of his Norwegian home, did what he had trusted them to do. They parleyed on his behalf with the guardian spirits of the new land and then led him many miles away from this barren stretch of coastline to the most perfect spot any settler could have dreamed of.

The date, according to the sources, was 874, which later became formally accepted as Iceland's official year of settlement. Thus did Ingólfur Arnarson win the accolade which Ravens-Flóki had missed out on ten years or so previously. Flóki returned to live in Iceland some time after, but it was too late. The title of First Settler, with capital letters, had gone to his successor.

As the plane banks to the right, my father is leaning across again to look out of the window. Below us, the brown of the cliffs has given way to dimply plains of hardened lava, blanketed in moss. Green moss, Dad, plain and simple. The ground is cracked and cratered like an ancient face.

'Miles and miles of bugger all,' my father observes cheerfully. 'You can see why it was an ideal place to put the Americans.'

It is strange, and not a little painful for some Icelanders, that the first thing you see on Icelandic soil when the air hostess trills *'Velkomin heim'* should be a NATO military base built by the Americans. The sudden display of primary colour as you glide in to land is not the native airport, but the red, green and blue roofs of the NATO staff houses. The presence of foreign troops in a touchily independent country with no armed forces of its own has long been a source of unease and quietly simmering controversy in Iceland. But as a founding member of NATO, the nation has by and large accepted it as the price of the island's strategic importance in the north Atlantic. And the poor American servicemen and women, stuck out here in the big toe of the Reykjanes peninsula in the middle of – to paraphrase my father – nothing much, have proved to be much less intrusive than was once feared.

This toe of land was part of a huge swathe of south-west Iceland which Ingólfur staked out after he had found his pillars and settled at Reykjavík. When friends and family followed him to Iceland in the late ninth century, he secured their allegiance by parcelling out key districts as gifts. He gave this chunk to a widowed kinswoman called Steinunn the Old, who cannily insisted on sealing her ownership by making a payment for the land. She paid with an embroidered, hooded cloak, which we are told came from Britain, probably snaffled from some unsuspecting Hebridean on a raiding trip.

'It was the first recorded real-estate deal in Iceland,' my father tells me gleefully after we land. 'Now how many international airports can claim to be built on land acquired over a thousand years ago for the price of a tartan cloak, eh?'

'You've got me there,' I say. But he is just getting into his stride.

'This really is the most beautiful air terminal in the world,' he enthuses as we walk towards the hub, our shoes sinking soundlessly into the beige carpet which is lining both corridor and walls. A large scenic poster on the wall is advertising Iceland Moss Extract Throat Lozenges. 'Natural Cool', it ripples, neatly encapsulating the country's two current selling points. The moss on the poster, I notice, is very, very green.

I should mention that not long after our visit, this arrivals area was extended. The luxury of plane to carpet is now no more; you are off-loaded into a tastefully austere cavern which could be anywhere. But the centre, when you reach it, is as entrancing as ever.

'All this stained glass,' my father is raving, 'and the first aeroplane ever built in Iceland hanging from the ceiling. You must admit it's quite, quite lovely.'

I do. I remember as well as he does the modest shed in the middle of the NATO airfield which used to welcome visitors to Iceland. The more I have trudged around the tacky airports of the world, the more this one has retained its capacity to ravish. So it is really very childish of me to cast furtively around the gleaming terminal for an architectural horror to undermine my father's enthusiasm. Still feeling adversarial after our spat on the plane, I draw his attention to the exposed ventilation pipes across the ceiling of the lounge. They were all the rage in the eighties, but now look as if the architect had forgotten something.

My father merely grunts. He knows that I know that this place is a gem. There are glossy duty-free shops where you can spend money on the way in as well as out, walls faced with local lava, basalt floors and the classiest airport cafeteria you will find anywhere. At the back, brilliant light floods through three giant stained-glass panels on the theme of flight, a stunning work of art at which newly arrived passengers have been known to gape so long that they lose their place in the currency queue.

But the best of all is above our heads. There, suspended from the ceiling like an Airfix model, is a little plane, so frail that it looks as if it is made of cardboard. Hard to believe it is real, but this is Iceland's first (and last) home-designed and home-built aircraft, a single-seater bi-plane, constructed in a Reykjavík bakery in 1931 and assembled in the (then empty) National Theatre by two young Icelandic mechanics. It took the pair until November 1940 to launch the plane into the sky, but it managed only three or four flights before it was brought to earth with at least a metaphorical bump by the British defence forces occupying Iceland during the war. They put an end to the adventure by banning any further flights in case the tiny plane was mistaken for an enemy German aircraft. The Ravens-Flóki of Icelandic aviation had flown for precisely one hour and thirty minutes. Now restored, repainted and hung in its fragile glory, the plucky pioneer is off the ground again.

We walk out into bright, chilly May sunshine, taking a moment to adjust to the incomparably sharp Icelandic light. There is a Windowlene clearness about it which catches my breath. My father has changed some British currency into *krónur* and issued me, disconcertingly, with pocket-money. As I have organised the trip, he wants to take over the remaining expenses which, since he is striding towards the taxi rank rather than the airport bus for the 50-kilometre drive to Reykjavík, I can see may be considerable. Feeling lightheadedly free of all responsibility and approximately twelve years old, I follow him to the car.

As the taxi pulls away from the terminal, we pass the airport's last two extravagant flights of imagination: a huge steel bird with elongated beak emerging from a giant egg, and then the final curve of a rainbow in glass and steel, images of travel, flight, Iceland, home. My father settles back in the front seat, lights up an illegal pipe under the benign dispensation of the taxi driver, and smiles contentedly. He is back where he belongs, and he's ready to roll. I roll meekly along behind.

The Blue Lagoon

There is absolutely no point in trying to persuade my father to take a dip in the Blue Lagoon. I last saw him in a pair of trunks in the 1970s, and even then I don't recall them coming into contact with water. But he is the one who tells the taxi driver to turn off the main road between the airport and Reykjavík to have a look, just a look, mind, at the new facilities there. He also, for reasons which now escape me, wants a word with the chef at Iceland's trendiest resort.

'Do you know his name?'

'Oh, it's probably Siggi,' he breezes. 'All chefs in Iceland are called Siggi, or Hilmar.'

The road to the Blue Lagoon takes us across miles of grotesquely formed lava where heroism beyond the call of duty has long been demanded of the moss. Volcanoes have been spewing lava over this peninsula for so long that it looks in places like some wacky moon-desert for a *Star Trek* shoot. In fact, there are places in Iceland where American astronauts really did practise for their moon-landing. The country has never stopped seething with the volcanic activity which brought it into being twenty million or so years ago, and this is the result.

I can remember – just – how excited my father was when an eruption under the sea off Iceland's south coast gave birth to a brand new island in 1963. It came to be called Surtsey, after the fire-giant Surtur. We all sat clustered around the television that night, awestruck by this immense fire exploding out of the sea. Even in black and white, the sight of creation bursting into action in front of our eyes was staggering. Iceland still bubbles with that kind of energy today. It still feels like a country in creation, so young geologically, so busy boiling and exploding and moving, that there is an overwhelming sense here of being close to the beginning of things.

Iceland has always been on the move, ever since it came into being at the point where two submarine plates began pulling away from one another on the earth's crust. The American continental plate separating from the Afro-European one created volcanic action on the ocean floor which produced what is known as the Mid-Atlantic Ridge, which runs right through the country. The awesome thing is that these plates are still separating. The country is literally pulling apart under our feet. Not at a cracking pace, to be sure – somewhere between one and two centimetres a year is the best estimate – but enough to make you feel wobbly just thinking about it.

You can see the effects of the subterranean pull quite starkly here and there. Over the millennia it has created a giant rip in the landscape, running always in the same direction from south-west to north-east and flamboyantly visible in different parts of the country. You can see it most dramatically some miles from here in the great gorge above the plains of Thingvellir, my father's favourite place in the world. You can also catch a glimpse of the rift much nearer to where we are now, at a spot I had visited the last time I was in Iceland. The road bumps over a ragged chasm in the lava at that point and the tourist guides stop their buses to announce gravely that you have just crossed from Europe to America. Or is it America to Europe? Whatever the direction, it is an odd experience to hop continents by strolling from one end of a bus to the other.

My father looks suspicious when I tell him about this. 'Where *was* that cleft in the lava?'

'Can't remember exactly. Somewhere near the tip of the peninsula. Middle of nowhere.'

He snorts. I'm not sure if this is at my vagueness, matched only by his when it comes to place names, or because a site which is not mentioned in the sagas belongs in his view to a lesser category of sightseeing spots. I am secretly pleased to have been somewhere he has not.

But he does enjoy the joke which the guide on that trip had recounted with some relish as my fellow tourists and I rattled through the lava. It goes like this. An Icelandic bus driver and a bishop both died and found themselves together at the gates of heaven. 'In you come, my good man,' said St Peter to the bus driver, beckoning him forward. The bishop was disconcerted that a mere bus driver should be ushered into heaven ahead of such an eminent churchman as himself, and demanded an explanation.

'Ah,' said the gatekeeper, 'we're merely showing our appreciation. When you, bishop, were delivering your sermons, everyone was fast asleep. But when the bus driver was carrying people along the Icelandic roads, they were praying hard.'

Travelling off the highways can certainly be a bone-shaking experience, but St Peter was hardly doing justice to the Icelanders' recent successes in road-building. You only need to look at the lava to wonder at the feat of making any impact at all on this rearing and bucking nightmare of a surface. The moss, clinging for dear life to every wild contour, is of course doing its best.

'Greatest bulldozer in the world,' my father says, throwing me a baleful look. 'Just look at it. Thanks to the moss, this lava will be good soil one day. Five or six thousand years at the most. It's wonderful stuff.'

In the meantime the Icelanders have been doing some bull-dozing of their own. It is a considerable feat to have forged as many roads as they have through lava-fields like this, given how few of them there are to do it and to pay for it.

There were 284,000 of them at the last count, a population smaller than Cardiff scattered across a country bigger than Ireland. There were even fewer of them in 1974 when they managed to complete a 1,406-kilometre ring-road around the perimeter, spurred on by a determination to have it done by the eleven-hundredth anniversary of Ingólfur's settlement. They have been assiduously laying tarmac on the most extensively travelled thoroughfares ever since. Adventurers looking forward to roughing it in four-wheeled drives may be perversely disappointed to find themselves cruising from the airport towards Reykjavík along the Icelandic version of the M1.

Indeed, the roads in this part of the peninsula are so good that it is easy to forget how few of them exist further in towards the interior and, for that matter, how bad they used to be, even in these parts. But it only takes the sight of a car on a track off to our right, showering stones and trailing clouds of dust as it speeds towards the horizon, to remind us.

'The Beetle,' my father murmurs. 'Remember that awful Beetle?'

In the summer of 1967, he drove my mother, younger sister Margaret and me around some of the historic sites to which he was planning to lead a coach-load of saga enthusiasts from Britain in his forthcoming holiday job as a tourist guide. It was the only time the pair of us travelled Iceland together before now. We jolted along rutted tracks and across glacial streams in an ancient hired Volkswagen so dusty that we never discovered its original colour. The Beetle had been handed over without a jack, which meant that each one of our many punctures involved collecting stones and piling them high under the teetering car before we could change a wheel. Not, of course, that finding stones was difficult; the roads, if you could call them that, were bracingly bad. At one point we crossed the cratered desert where the American astronauts had indeed been practising for their forthcoming excursion to the moon. Nowadays it's a visitor attraction. 'We will take you to the moon,' proclaims a robust poster in the Reykjavík Tourist Office, with a picture of a large jeep whizzing across flying rocks.

The Beetle bumped us over a wide swathe of south-west Iceland, from farm to farm and holy hill to historic mound, while my father practised on us the stories of romance and revenge which he was preparing to inflict on his unsuspecting tourists. The sagas (from the Old Norse word for stories) are prose narratives written in the Middle Ages about the men and women who lived in Iceland in the years after settlement. Nobody now believes, as my grandfather once did so fiercely, that events necessarily happened exactly as the writers describe. But the stories are based in the main on real people who fought and loved in recognisably the same Icelandic landscape as we are driving through now. And some of the events they describe turn out to have been spine-tinglingly closer to historical fact than the sceptics might allow.

'Just there,' my father said when we clanked up to Bergthórshvoll, where the climactic scene of *Njáls Saga* is set. 'That's where the Burning happened. Imagine it.'

I remember him striding around that day in his tweed jacket, the breeze ruffling his hair. The hair was reddish-blond in those days, and his jacket such a close relative of the one he is wearing today that it could have been the same one. It probably was. He pointed to the knoll where Njáll's house is thought to have stood, seeing it all in his head. My sister and I sat on the grass and imagined.

'See where their enemies would have ridden in at nightfall. Think of old Njáll and his wife lying down on the bed with their young grandson between them as they waited for the flames to come. Imagine their son Skarphéðinn trapped by a falling rafter and yet holding himself upright, biting his lip hard to stifle a cry as the fire licked around his legs.' He paused for effect and his voice dropped. 'When they found him later, his legs were nearly burnt off at the knee.'

This was powerful stuff. Skarphéðinn's burnt stumps are up there in my memory with the giant bottle of cod liver oil which lay in wait for us every morning on the breakfast buffet of the travel lodge. But the drama of it was enhanced when my father revealed that archaeological investigations had proved con-clusively that there *had* been a fire at Bergthórshvoll during the Saga Age, more or less around the time *Njáls Saga* was supposed to have been set. It was definitely worth shivering on the grass even longer than usual to hear that.

Njáls Saga was, and remains, my father's passion. When I came to read it later for myself, I was surprised at how familiar it felt. I felt him in it, and not just because he had done the Penguin Classics translation. Naturally I couldn't wait to reach the bit about Skarphéðinn's legs, and I wasn't disappointed:

He had held himself upright against the wall. His legs were almost burnt off below the knee, but the rest of him was unburnt. He had bitten hard on his lip. His eyes were open but not swollen. He had driven his axe into the gable with such violence that half the full depth of the blade was buried in the wall, and the metal had not softened.

My father's ultimate act of homage to the brave but brutish Skarphéðinn was to call the next family spaniel Skarpi. Fortunately, he proved to be an inoffensive hound who never lived up to the alarming expectations of his name.

We covered many a saga other than Njáll's that summer, and I doubt if anyone could people an anonymous mound or a bare rock with murderous life better than my father. Even after the fifth boulder and the tenth slaying of the day, it was a talent which held his audience more or less upright. The doughty Beetle kept us going to the end, too, limping back to Reykjavík at the end of the fortnight several pounds of dust heavier.

We are speeding now along the smoothly surfaced approach to the Blue Lagoon, and I notice that my father is beginning to look apprehensive. Precisely because he is so inordinately proud of Iceland and all its works, he worries in a paternal way about whether things have been done properly. The Blue Lagoon is now a tourist mecca, a magnet for every visiting journalist on a magazine freebie, and he badly wants to be reassured that the expensive upgrading work has been successful. But as the complex appears up ahead amid various effusions of steam, he is perceptibly overcome by foreboding. No fewer than seven international flags are fluttering on a battalion of flagpoles outside the resort, and this he takes to be a bad sign.

'The number of flags is usually in inverse proportion to the quality of the establishment,' he growls.

The Blue Lagoon is a huge natural bath created by the run-off from a nearby geothermal plant. The Icelanders have become so adept at exploiting the heat under their feet that they have even found uses for left-over water. The plant at Svartsengi makes hot water by pumping up steam from 2,000 metres below the earth, pumping up desalinated water from the sea, and then mixing these together. The burning hot water is then carried along a pipeline to wash the dishes and supply the showers of the people of the Reykjanes peninsula. A lagoon has formed from the overflow, rich in minerals, silicon and algae, which have bestowed on the place both its reputation as a spa and its allegedly blue hue. The water has always looked more white than blue to me, but photographs taken from above in the right light do catch an azure tint.

A sign on the pathway announces that the new visitor centre, begun in 1998, was built from lava formed during a volcanic eruption in 1296. This is young as lava goes, and explains why the moss in these parts is still struggling. Rounding a corner we receive our first eyeful of the refurbishment, and my father mouths a small whistle of relief. The primitive bathing huts and old sheds which I remember from my first dip here have been replaced by a chalet-style hotel, constructed of wood and gleaming glass. The lava has been banked up on either side to enclose the lagoon, which is now straddled by wooden walkways and dinky bridges.

It has been stylishly done, with lava boulders and sulphurous steam perpetuating the feeling of a wild outpost, while casual touches of elegance add the classiness for which my father was hoping. Here are art and light; earthy colours to blend with the black sand and grey stone; sapphire-coloured glass jugs glinting on the tables; marigolds swimming around a candle in a blue vase. This, it strikes me suddenly, is modern Iceland in miniature: stylish, expensive, tastefully simple and right on the edge of chaos.

It is interesting to see how post-war prosperity has enabled the Icelanders, a nation once so poor that for centuries they could barely afford the visual arts at all, to make art of their chaos. They put lava on their walls, flaming volcanic colours in their paintings, limpid light in their stained glass, the sinuous movement of a river in their sculptures, rough earthiness in their wool. The wilderness is given form, but that very form, constantly drawing its inspiration from land, sea and sky, means that even in the most elegant city home you are reminded of the other Iceland shifting beneath your feet.

My father relaxes. Prepared now to smile at the flags as a harmless ostentation, he wanders off happily in search of the chef, who is indeed reported to be called Siggi. I linger at the edge of the lagoon and wonder if I dare kick off a shoe and trail a toe in the milky water, maybe even a leg. Hey, perhaps no one would notice if I just stripped off and popped in here and now. The bracing eggy aroma rising from the sulphur-laden pool, authentic smell of the Icelandic bathing experience, is calling me. The steam playing wispily over the surface is seducing me with the promise of water which is truly hot; none of your tepid British nonsense, but water which still has the heat of the earth's crust in it, water you can wallow in for hours while your face tingles in the cold.

Chance would be a fine thing. Illegal entry without submitting to the full martial discipline of the changing rooms would land me in hotter water than even a lifetime's paternal intimacy with the chef could divert. The Icelanders find the rest of us disgustingly casual about hygiene. They are a laid-back race as a rule, but they do come over all authoritarian at their swimming pools. Try to sneak out without a shower, or without due attention to what the gimlet-eyed gauleiters on patrol refer to delicately as your 'parts', and you will be despatched humilia-tingly back to strip off and scrub harder. In more prudish times the experience proved a challenge to the iron modesty of British matrons on holiday, who used to lurk in the communal ladies' shower-room, clinging to the last vestige of swimming costume, while a bulky attendant in white uniform waited menacingly outside to enforce full disclosure.

Since chlorine is not in the Blue Lagoon's cocktail of ingredi-ents, the zeal is understandable. The main ingredient is silica clay, which is said to be good for skin conditions like eczema and psoriasis. Today I can see a few enthusiasts slapping handfuls of squelchy grey mud on to limbs and faces, but the ones I envy are floating about in the warmth, closing their eyes and going nowhere, merely bumping majestically from time to time into other serenely floating bodies hidden from view by the steam.

The steam is as thick as an Isle of Skye mist in places, drifting across in the breeze from the big geothermal plant behind the lagoon and up from the water itself. It reminds me of the plight of a Scottish television presenter who was sent to Iceland more than thirty years ago to interview the Prime Minister. According to the account which circulated in taverns the length and breadth of Glasgow on his return, he was invited to a preliminary chat in a Reykjavík hot-pool. Nothing unusual in that. 'Politicians in hot water' has an entirely innocent connotation in Iceland, where there is a long tradition of discussing manly affairs in the bath. To this day, government ministers think nothing of pondering affairs of state from the inner ledge of a hot-pot, up to their shoulders in water.

So at the appointed time the visitor emerged shyly from the changing rooms and edged over to the pool. Noticing that he appeared to be the only one who had bothered to put bathing trunks on, he lowered himself self-consciously into the water. Clouds of steam were billowing across the surface, through which he could dimly make out several men chatting on a bench inside the rim. On being directed to one of them, he lurched across and reached underwater for what he took to be the Prime Minister's hand; only, as he realised with horror, it wasn't his hand at all.

It was the most embarrassing moment of his life, he claimed, and by all accounts the gleeful talk of journalistic circles back home for weeks.

My father has now wandered back, having learned that Siggi the chef is not yet on duty. Since a meal here would probably clean him out for the week, bosom buddy of the chef or not, I reckon this is a lucky escape. On the way out, he insists on buying me a supply of geothermal creams, a silicon mud-pack and an ice-cream.

'No need to use up your pocket-money,' he says expansively, and I'm not sure if he is joking or not.

The taxi driver is waiting for us with a contented eye on the meter and we drive back to the main highway linking Keflavík with the capital. My father, delighted with the Blue Lagoon, banters heartily in Icelandic with the driver, who tells him in tones of deep gloom that property prices in Reykjavík are still shooting up, and no wonder, what with 160,000 people living in and around it now, more than half the population of Iceland.

There is no sign of any of them here, though. The lava is undulating into the distance on every side as far as we can see, a grey misshapen desert relieved only by the cone-shaped mountain Keilir off to our right. My father tells the driver that we'll be staying in Reykjavík tonight and then pushing on up north tomorrow to Akureyri, Húsavík and then Laxamýri, where his mother's people came from. He says he is glad of this opportunity to experience a slice of Iceland with his daughter. I am touched. Struggling to follow the conversation from the back seat and belatedly penitent about not practising a few declensions before we arrived, I am glad of the opportunity, too.

My father is already slipping into the tour-guide role I remember so well, his elbow resting on the sill of the open window, pipe in hand. All in all, it is a pleasure to be twelve again.

He points out the small cairns scattered here and there by the roadside – road markers, laid at intervals, stone upon stone, to mark the route for early travellers as they picked their way across the lava on foot or horseback. The cairns are a quiet reminder, as we speed past on the motorway, of how difficult travel used to be in these parts in centuries past.

'Let's look in on the Chapel in the Lava,' he says suddenly, still thinking of the travellers of old. This is a small ruined shrine on the edge of a lava-quarry, which we'll be driving by any minute. It was uncovered by archaeologists in the 1950s, along with a fifteenth-century figurine of St Barbara, patron saint of dynamiters, who in Iceland was rather inventively called into service against eruptions and lava-flows. Although there is not much to see, my father adores it. He never needs to see much.

'I find it every bit as romantic as the discovery of Troy,' he declares roundly on the way along.

I take this to be patriotic hyperbole and prepare to argue the toss. Just because Iceland doesn't have many archaeological remains, it is surely nonsense to argue that one tiny figurine dropped on the floor of a roadside shrine measures up in the romance stakes to the discovery of an ancient civilisation.

But, then again, he does have a point. In a country which

really can't boast anything in the way of relics, except words and landscape, it is precisely the power of the imagination which evokes the past, and you actually need very little to do it. I suspect the rise of Atlantis itself would struggle to compete with the pleasure my father takes in imagining those wayfarers in distant times, fearful and cold as they journeyed over the dark lava amid who knows what rumblings and shakings of the earth, to find rest and reassurance in the sanctuary of St Barbara.

As it happens, we forget to look in on the Chapel in the Lava. There is nothing to mark the turn-off in the road which leads behind the quarry and up to the little shrine, and by the time we reach it we are too busy talking about elves to notice.

The taxi sails on, skimming the long aluminium factory opposite. I had been asking whether any diversions were made for the Hidden People when they built this motorway. My father says he doesn't know about this one, but other roads have definitely been realigned out of respect to an elf-mound or a dwarf-rock.

'It's a fact,' he says, ignoring my look. 'Experience has proved it's pointless to try and build where the Hidden People are said to live because bulldozers just break down, equipment fails and in a country with as much space to choose from as Iceland, you might as well build elsewhere.'

The taxi driver nods sagely. There are countries in which the two of them might be quietly sectioned, but this is Iceland. Ever since Ingólfur Arnarson sent out his pillars to negotiate with the guardian spirits of the land, the Icelanders have been pragmatically respectful of the supernatural. A law in 930 required visiting Vikings to remove the gaping dragon heads on their ships before landing in Iceland, so as not to affront these guardian spirits. When the country converted to Christianity in the year 1000, a canny decision based on parliamentary decree rather than spiritual conviction, pagan beliefs and superstitions remained close to the surface. Living in a landscape of eerily formed lava on ground which boiled beneath their feet, and with an oral tradition haunted by ogresses, trolls and capricious gods, it is perhaps not surprising that Icelanders continued to hedge their bets on the Hidden People.

'But do people honestly believe in elves still, or is it just the . . . you know . . . ?' I trail off, not wanting to offend the taxi driver.

My fearlessly rational parent, once the target of some of the most vicious green-ink attacks known to TV man for questioning the authority of the Bible in a BBC documentary, shifts in his seat. 'Ah well,' he equivocates, 'it's all very tongue-in-cheek, of course, but it's basically about having respect for the spirits of the land. Just like Ingólfur did.'

He tells me a folk story I had never heard before, about the elves being created by God when He visited Adam and Eve unannounced one Saturday, which was traditionally bath night in Iceland. Eve, having only managed to bathe half her children before the visitor arrived, was in a flap. Ashamed to place dirty children before Him, she panicked and hid them away. When God asked if the well-scrubbed line-up represented her only children, she said yes. The lie was instantly detected and punishment pronounced: since Eve had not let God see these children, they were to be kept from the sight of men as well, for the rest of time. The 'hidden people' became the elves – life-sized beings living parallel lives to ours, but never seen.

My father adds defensively that the revered Icelandic scholar Sigurður Nordal used to believe in elves and he was as wise an old bird as they come, which ought to settle the matter.

Why should I be surprised? After all, his mother was as fey a creature as ever graced the douce bridge tables of Edinburgh. I never heard Ingibjörg on the subject of elves, but she was a firm believer in signs, omens and dreams. She claimed to have had a dream before Magnus was born in which her own mother appeared, telling her the child she was expecting would be a fine writer one day. My father dismisses this demurely as 'a load of crap', but he acknowledges that his mother was a pure Icelandic distillation of centuries of spiritual eclecticism. Icelanders weathered the country's overnight conversion to Christianity by simply adding the new faith to whichever remnants of the old one remained helpful. In my grandmother this produced a whimsical attachment to omens and fate overlaid by genuine Christian piety. In my father it has allowed a formidable rationalism to be infiltrated by a soft spot for the Norse gods and a weakness, yes, a definite weakness here, for elves.

In this he merely reveals himself, as in so many other ways, to be extremely Icelandic. In a survey conducted for the psychology department at the University of Iceland some twenty-five years ago, but probably not hugely out of date in its findings, 64 per cent of the polled Icelanders claimed some experience involving the supernatural; a 55 per cent majority believed that the existence of elves, and also ghosts, was either possible, likely or certain; and a full 97 per cent considered themselves rather religious – a finding which the official Lutheran Church must have found challenging, since 92 per cent admitted to never reading the Bible.

This may be the Celt in them. Genetic research has shown that the Icelandic settlers must have had a healthy mix of Celtic blood in their veins, picked up (as were the girls) on Viking forays up and down the coasts of Scotland and Ireland before they arrived in Iceland. Maybe it is that which has tipped the Icelanders towards the feyness so prominent in my grandmother, not to mention a marked preference for poetry over philosophy, epic narrative over abstract discourse, and verbal fencing over the analysis of ideas.

The writer Sigurður A. Magnússon, one of the most entertaining interpreters of the Icelandic psyche as well as the fastest talker I have come across in any language, has even argued that it may be the Celtic blood in the Icelanders which explains why they, of all the Nordic nations, produced great and enduring literature in the Middle Ages. If so, it also explains why the story-telling tradition which has brought me to Iceland is as colourful, compelling and unreliable as it is.

But back to the elves. By this time we are driving into Hafnarfjörður, a harbour town on the outskirts of Reykjavík where elf-respect is so engrained that I was once told that 20,000 people live here – 'the ones you can see, anyway'. The rest are said to live among the rampaging lava on which the town is built. I also heard that one lady here had made a map showing precisely where the Hidden People live: in houses with curtains and flowers in the windows exactly like ours, she said, except that you couldn't see them.

The Hafnarfjörður tourist industry has now swooped in on the act, offering to take visitors on a 'Seeing is Believing' tour to explore the hidden worlds of Icelandic folklore. 'Hafnarfjörður,' the publicity informs us gravely, 'is home to Iceland's largest community of elves, dwarfs and Hidden People.' No doubt about that, then.

Actually you only need to consider the landscape to understand where all the folklore comes from. The person who first showed me how to look was Vigdís Finnbogadóttir, a blonde bombshell of a theatre director who became the country's president in 1980, thereby entering the record books (as Icelanders were quick to work out) as the world's first elected female constitutional head of state. In the days when she was still an ordinary citizen and I was spending a summer vacation working in *Ferðaskrífstófa Ríkisins*, the State Tourist Office in Reykjavík, we spent every weekend driving around the country in her big Volvo.

Every now and then she would stop the car and point. That clump of bulbous-headed boulders was an ogress with her children, frozen to stone when dawn broke on their way home from visiting her lover. Those lava rocks were the homes of the elves. The mountains hid the lairs of trolls who could smash the land and everyone in it. The lakes were full of wishing-stones which floated to the water's edge on hallowed nights and gave you everything your heart could wish for, if only you could find one.

Over yonder was Helgafell, the holy mountain, which was said in *Eyrbyggja Saga* to have opened up before a wide-eyed shepherd, revealing great fires burning within and the noise of feasting and revelry. There, on another day, was the circular hot-pool at Reykholt which the thirteenth-century saga-historian and statesman Snorri Sturluson had built for gossiping in with his cronies; he was murdered later in his cellar only a few yards away. That was the site of Njáll's farm, or Egill the warrior-poet's home, or Gunnar Hámundarson's High Noon stand against his enemies after his wife refused to give him a strand of her lustrous hair to mend his broken bow-string. Weekend after weekend my head was reeling with stories, every one rooted in the landscape.

Vigdís tried to explain why they mattered so much. She said that in a huge island with no cities, towns or even villages until quite modern times, each isolated farmstead formed a kind of intellectual unity. With no materials to create art with, except words, they made poetry and told stories about the supernatural creatures they imagined into the curious shapes of their land-scape, and recited sagas about the deeds their ancestors had done in olden times. During centuries of calamitous conditions, record-beating poverty and oppressive colonial rule from Denmark, the Icelanders had kept themselves alive as a nation by remembering. Their whole identity was wrapped up in the memories of how they had begun, how the first people came there, what they had done and what they were like, memories told and written in the language Icelanders still spoke today. That was why they protected their language more fiercely than the Académie Française.

'If we forget the language,' Vigdís was always saying, 'then we forget the memories.'

On our way through Hafnarfjörður my father asks the taxi driver to pull up, so that we can slip out and look at the volcanic gift which gave Harbour-Fjord its name. The harbour is impress-ively benign, formed by a broad tongue of rolling lava which stopped conveniently in 5000 BC just before it blocked the head of the fjord. For centuries it was a key Icelandic port. Idling along the waterfront, we recall that this was where the nation's precious memories, collected into a body of literature by a tenacious Icelandic antiquarian, were sent off across the sea to Denmark in the spring of 1720.

Árni Magnússon, one of the most genuinely revered heroes in the country's pantheon, had travelled the length and breadth of Iceland, buying, borrowing or accepting as gifts as many of the original saga and history writings as he could lay his hands on. People said he could sniff out old saga-manuscripts like a bloodhound. He found one piece of vellum that had been cut to make an insole for a shoe, another page which had been trimmed by a tailor to make a pattern for the back of a waistcoat.

Árni's priceless collection was carried on thirty laden pack-horses to Hafnarfjörður and loaded on to a ship bound for the Danish capital. The expedition had been commissioned by the monarch of the day, anxious for evidence of his own country's great past as preserved in the sagas of Norse kings. Eight years later, much of the collection was lost in the Great Fire of Copenhagen, and it must have near broken Árni's heart: he died only fifteen months later. But the rest of Iceland's treasure, the surviving documents of the oldest living literature in Europe, enshrining the origins of Icelandic society and the memories which had sustained it as a nation, remained safely in Denmark for the next 250 years. In the 1970s, amid scenes of jubilation in Iceland, the Danes returned them.

'That's why I've always supported the case for Britain voluntarily returning the Elgin marbles to Greece,' my father murmurs, gazing out to sea. 'There was no compulsion on the Danes to return the manuscripts. The scholars hated the idea, but two consecutive Danish parliaments voted for them to go back. And with that one simple gesture of friendship and understanding, they wiped clean the slate of centuries of colonial grievance.'

He starts to head back to the car. 'They gave us back our identity, you know. That's how much it mattered.'

1874 and All That

Let me tell you about 1874, the year the king visited Iceland and my great-great grandfather, Sigurjón Jóhannesson, put the finishing touches to his new house on a farm called Laxamýri.

Iceland, this country where a tourist spa has marigolds in crystal glasses and the airport boasts better art than many a gallery, was an almost unimaginably different society then. Six centuries reeling from one natural disaster to the next – volcano, flood, earthquake, disease and famine – had left the population no more numerous than it was when the state was founded in 930. Reykjavík could muster a mere 2,000 souls and there was barely a village anywhere else on the island. Most trade was in the fists of Danish merchants.

The country had no roads, few harbours and a mere handful of small bridges over the glacial rivers which surged down from the mountains to the sea. Farming remained primitive, and fishing was still done largely from open rowing boats in conditions barely less hazardous than back in 1700 when a total of 165 men – 0.33 per cent of Iceland's entire population – had died on the same day.

There would not be a lighthouse in the country for another four years. Even that first one collapsed in an earthquake and it was 1908 before a new one went up, guarding the point of the Reykjanes peninsula to this day amid the noisy fussing of thousands of birds in the crevices of the great cliff.

In the north, life was so precarious and the poverty so hopeless that people had started to leave. Travelling in the area only the previous year, the English writer William Morris had stopped to drink coffee with a family who lived in a turf-house in a long, green-sided valley. He found the people to be 'depressed and poor'. The previous tenant, he was told, had emigrated to America on a ship which 200 people had rushed to board, but was only able to take 100. 'It seems the people here have had many bad years together and it has sickened them of it,' Morris wrote sadly.

But not everyone had it so bad in the far north of Iceland. By the astute purchase of land and wily manipulation of the trading system, Sigurjón of Laxamýri was accumulating untold wealth. While agents for the Canadian government were roaming the countryside, offering desperate farmers a home in Manitoba, Sigurjón was supervising the construction of a fine new house for himself with wood imported at considerable expense from Norway. The timber had been brought across the snow on horse-drawn sledges during the previous winter and was being assembled on the estate by as many as twelve workers. It was one-storey high, with a sunken cellar beneath and lava slabs partitioning the rooms.

Compared to the draughty, smoke-filled turf and stone houses in which most people lived, it must have seemed a fabulous place, a fairy-tale house. And Sigurjón was lord of it all, not only of the manor, but of a wide swathe of some of the best land in Iceland, with numerous tenant farms beneath him. He was like a duke running a small dukedom. I am tempted to say he was like a king in his kingdom, which is certainly how future generations thought of him, but I would hate to insult the man touring in the south that same summer of 1874, who really was the king.

Christian IX was the first Danish monarch ever to set foot on Icelandic soil. He was there to deliver a constitution to his restless Icelandic subjects, who were starting to agitate for home rule after nearly five centuries under Copenhagen's rule. This constitution, placing legislative and financial power in the hands of the renascent Icelandic parliament, was less than the Icelanders were by then demanding, but it was symbolically important all the same. The plan was for the king to deliver it with due ceremony on the one-thousandth anniversary of Ingólfur Arnarson's settlement of Iceland in 874.

My father has started to tell me all this as we are climbing into the taxi to leave Hafnarfjörður. He says that Christian sailed into this very harbour to launch his historic tour. Indeed, the king's visit that summer was so momentous that the very first road for wheeled transport was constructed to accommodate the royal party.

'They had to build a road to get the king from the harbour at Hafnarfjörður to Reykjavík because his bottom was too big for the small Icelandic horses,' he assures me with the breezy authority of someone well up – if you'll pardon the expression – on the posteriors of Danish monarchs. 'He was a fat old boy who was used to being carried around in a carriage in Copenhagen.'

I imagined this pampered old king being prised out of his ship at the harbour and carried to a specially primped Icelandic cart, where he settled his gigantic rump into the plump purple cushions and was then hauled by the strongest horse in the country along the smooth new road to Reykjavík. Such a good story. And such a pity it didn't happen.

My first inkling that all was not well with the vignette came after we were home. I spotted a contemporary drawing of Christian in Iceland that August, being welcomed to the festivities by a grave-faced poet in a frock-coat. Good grief, was this tall, slim, straight-backed, dark-haired fellow in his snug-fitting naval uniform really the king? The man was positively sexy. Then I discovered that he had been widely admired at the time in Iceland for, of all things, his horsemanship. A little more digging produced the revelation that the bearded Adonis had not landed at Hafnarfjörður at all, but at Reykjavík, where he arrived with a fleet of three Danish warships at noon on 31 July and stepped ashore (sprang ashore, more like) through an archway decorated in red cloth with a golden crown above it, to be warmly received by the great and good of the town.

You perceive the problem. It is hard to see why the king's

ceremonial arrival at Reykjavík, with cannons fired and the quayside kitted out in flags and bunting, would have precipitated the building of a road from the nearby fishing station at Hafnarfjörður. It had a good harbour for sure, but so, obviously, did Reykjavík by this time. Sure enough, the story was news to the Icelandic roads department. Road-building did begin in the 1870s, but they reckoned the first was somewhere else altogether. The curator of the Hafnarfjörður museum also sent a polite e-mail regretting that he was 'unable to confirm' my father's story.

Back in his study, his story unravelling like a yoyo, the great spinner of yarns was duly contrite. He said he was sure he had heard the story somewhere, probably from his blood-brother, the late Icelandic playwright and unapologetic teller of tales, Jökull Jakobsson, and even more probably when the pair were in their cups.

I should explain here that if 'blood-brother' sounds like something out of the sagas, that is because it is. In devoted imitation of an ancient ceremony described in *Fóstbræðra Saga*, the pair slashed their wrists on the front lawn of Iceland's ambassador to Denmark in the summer of 1951. They were students in Copenhagen. My father was studying for a post-graduate doctorate in Old Norse, and the ambassador, Sigurður Nordal, was his tutor (a man of such inerring judgement that by the end of the summer he was advising Magnus, who had regaled him with exaggerated accounts of his extra-curricular exploits every morning over breakfast, that he would be better suited for the story-telling realms of journalism than the academic life).

Nordal looked on with unruffled amusement when his students took it upon themselves one balmy night to cut up not only their own wrists but the ambassadorial garden as well, with the aid of a carving knife stolen from a Copenhagen restaurant.

('Stolen?'

'Well, borrowed. We were drunk, dearest.')

Judging from the position of the scar my father still bears, he for one narrowly missed an artery. Crouching on the grass, he and Jökull held the wounds together under a sod of turf hewn from the manicured lawn, and dreamily watched their blood mingle. The next day, everlastingly bonded and much hung over, they took their butchered wrists to the nearest hospital for stitching.

I can still remember, far back in childhood, my father and the flame-haired Jökull doubled up with laughter together at our house in Glasgow. 'Did he just make that sort of stuff up, then?' I asked. 'First road in Iceland? Fat royal bottoms?'

'Well, he made plenty of other things up.' My father smiled indulgently; he had loved Jökull. 'That man was perfectly capable of inventing anything. He also claimed that Ingólfur Arnarson brought golf to Iceland – In*GÓLF*ur, get it? – and that Lake Mývatn in the north was so called because a giant used to piss in it.'

'I thought Mývatn meant Midge Lake.'

'Yes, but Jökull argued that it could have come from *míga*, meaning to pee. He ... oh, God, why am I telling you this? You'll just go and put it in that bloody book.'

'Of course not,' I said soothingly.

And so an excellent story bit the dust. Thank goodness I had never tried boasting that the Icelanders discovered golf as well as North America, but I was sorry to lose the tale of Iceland's first road being built to accommodate a king's bottom. It was only the first of many charming legends which would have to be reassembled as the result of our journey to Iceland. Stories are both a glorious strength and an occupational hazard of this country. Sifting them for fact can be as hard as combing through centuries-old ash at Bergthórshvoll for signs of the Burning of Njáll.

If I forget every other lecture my father has given me about Iceland, all the other places which have made his imagination blaze and his eyes shine, I will go to my grave remembering a grassy plain called Thingvellir.

'Such a magic, incomparable place,' he sighs as soon as I mention King Christian's journey there in 1874. 'I don't suppose we could squeeze a visit in, could we? Couple of hours tomorrow?'

Oh dear. Terrible is the temptation to do Thingvellir, as Bertolt Brecht almost said. This, you see, is the big one.

As I seem to have been hearing all my life, Thingvellir is where the country's settlers began gathering once a year, within a generation of Ingólfur's arrival, to formulate laws and settle disputes. It was an ideal social arena for the world's first parliament, with space, shelter, water and pasture for horses, along with a mighty rock from which the Speaker proclaimed the laws. The family chieftains rode there every summer from the furthest reaches of the land, setting up camp on the plains at the foot of the unsettling Almannagjá gorge for two weeks of law-making and revelry, later boisterously immortalised by the saga-writers. Icelanders still revere the site. Ever since the anniversary celebrations held there the year the king visited Iceland, they have been flocking back in their thousands to commemorate the momentous occasions in the nation's history.

Yes, I could give lectures about Thingvellir. I dare say I could even pen a learned essay on whether this *Althingi* really was the first parliament in the world, as Icelanders like to claim, or merely a form of oligarchy. (I would doubtless conclude, as my father has, that it was at the very least an astonishing medieval experiment in republicanism and a kind of democracy.) All in all, I can tell you more about Thingvellir than I have ever known about Hampton Court, Westminster, Dunfermline, Culloden or any of the other landmarks of British history, and that is because Thingvellir has an emotional resonance for Icelanders which none of the British symbols can match for either the Scots or the English. If a nation can have a soul – and in this country you find yourself just about believing it – then the Icelandic soul reposes at Thingvellir.

When the crowds pour down through the gorge for the big occasions, to listen to speeches and wave their flags, it can be extremely moving. The republic of Iceland was established there at 2 p.m. on 17 June 1944, when a fifth of the entire population turned out in heavy rain to hear the bells of the little Thingvellir church ring out in celebration, followed by a minute's silence. The rest of the country listened on the radio. The wartime military forces had forbidden the broadcasting of any allusion to the weather, but the announcer is said to have been so carried away by the occasion that he could not help describing the Thingvellir flags being 'soaked by the tears of heaven'.

Fifty years later, in June 1994, the nation returned to Thingvellir to celebrate the first half-century of independence – again in a way which, as my sister Anna reported, managed to be neither jingoistic nor toe-curlingly sentimental. It has to be said that, quarrelsomely individualistic though they may be, the Icelanders make a rather dignified sight *en masse*. Whatever the mysterious glue which unites this nation and keeps bringing its many wanderers home, it is something to do with landscape, kin and history, and it is expressed most poignantly in these gatherings at Thingvellir.

I can't for one moment imagine my father waving a flag, although he does it metaphorically all the time, but he is wholly Icelandic in his emotional attachment to Thingvellir. Bowling towards the suburbs of Reykjavík, we debate whether we should delay tomorrow's crack-of-dawn flight to Akureyri and nip 51 kilometres up the road for a quick obeisance. Surprising us both with my ruthless time management skills, however, I suggest that if we keep diverting to our favourite places, we will never make it to Laxamýri.

'Anyway,' I say, 'we've been there together once already.'

Which is true. It was the summer he was planning his saga tour, as he remembers all too well.

'I was trying to work out how I would present the place to those ruddy tourists, wasn't I? I remember wondering what on earth those stone ruins were all over the place. Of course they were the foundations of the booths where people sheltered, but I couldn't believe the booths had been that small. The sagas seemed to suggest they were bloody great marquees. You were dragging along behind, as I recall, looking fed up.'

Really? I recall showing a bright and intelligent interest beyond my years, but there you are. I certainly remember being impressed by the awful chasm of the Almannagjá, which we had to walk through to reach the parliament plains below. I am sure I didn't know at the time that this searing gash in the landscape was caused by the shifting dinner service on the earth's crust; my father would have been too busy working out where Njáll's booth was to bother about continental plates. But the gorge was an unforgettably arresting sight, which made me feel very small and transient. It must be at least thirty centimetres wider by now, maybe sixty. I tell you, this country is moving.

I also didn't know then that the grassy nooks and crannies along the chasm, sprinkled with tiny white and blue flowers in summer, had long been a popular weekend haunt for couples. I learned much later that my grandparents had done much of their courting there. Ingibjörg was coaxed into an unguarded admission that her eldest child, Sigurður, had been conceived in just such a sheltered hollow during their betrothal. When her children teased her about not being married at the time, she went only slightly pink. The Icelanders have long been rather relaxed about sex.

As far as I am aware, King Christian had no such diverting prospects awaiting him at Thingvellir. Arriving in time for the final day of anniversary celebrations, there was kingly work to be done. It was the first national festival the country had ever held and the organisers from the Icelandic Patriotic Society, formed three years previously, had gone to town.

By 1874 the old Althing was long defunct, but for the newly politicised Icelanders the parliament plains were the natural place to remember the glory days. The Law Rock and the ruined booths which would one day puzzle my father immortalised a precocious experiment in democracy which had lasted longer than it plausibly should: government with legislative and judicial authority, but no executive power to enforce its laws, is ultimately on a hiding to nothing. The Icelanders had made a decent fist of preserving law and order without a ruler for 300 years but, in the end, overcome by bloody family rivalries, they sealed the country's colonial fate in 1262 by swearing allegiance to a unifying outside agency, the King of Norway.

When the Norwegian throne was united with Denmark's in 1380, Iceland went too, as part of the package. The country would remain tied to Denmark until 1944. It was only towards the middle of the nineteenth century that Icelandic scholars and poets began the long political struggle to win back autonomy. Christian's visit, bearing a constitution enshrining some measure of home rule, was an important landmark on the way to independence.

Not everyone on the welcoming committee at Thingvellir that August thought they had much to be grateful for, though. Even as the king was nearing the great cleft overlooking the plains, frantic consultations were still going on behind the scenes as to whether the Icelanders should go so far as to thank him for the gift he was bearing. Some felt it had too many flaws to deserve thanks; others argued the even more haughty point that they had fought Danish interests so hard to achieve this that it could hardly be considered a gift anyway. The meeting hastily broke up when someone rushed over to report that the royal party was approaching.

In the event, no one thanked the king. If he noticed, he did not say so, which shows what a fine fellow he was. He received a pointed welcome instead to 'this former seat of freedom and heroism' and submitted manfully to a stultifying round of speeches. He also had to listen to the first performance of the new Icelandic national anthem, a flowery hymn composed for the occasion by the poet Matthías Jochumsson to a tune which soars and plunges so demandingly that it still needs a full choir to do it justice. (Icelanders joke that the rest of the world lives in fear of their ever winning an Olympic gold medal because the anthem would empty the stadium.)

Christian also listened in some bemusement to several long poems composed in his honour in the old skaldic tradition and watched a display of native Icelandic wrestling, the *glíma* of which my grandfather's cousin Jóhannes would one day become national champion. He rounded off the festivities with just the sort of gesture I would have expected of him. He told his prickly subjects (in Danish) that he would personally ensure that the Crown Prince and his other children were taught Icelandic forthwith.

See? An officer, a gentleman and a very smooth operator.

As a matter of fact, the symbolism of Christian's 'gift' was misleading, because until recently the Icelanders did not have the original document enshrining the 1874 constitution in their possession at all. It was only in April 2003 that it arrived at last, borne across the skies by a Prime Minister rather than by a king in a battleship. In a formal ceremony in Reykjavík the Danish premier Anders Fogh Rasmussen presented it to Iceland, along with other documents, on permanent loan.

The gesture, which was not on the scale of the return of the saga manuscripts, nor intended as such, left many Icelanders cold. But my father, who loves to see things coming home, was enchanted. He for one is prepared to say thank you this time.

We are nearly at Reykjavík now, driving through Garðabær, a suburb which has been plonked unceremoniously in the middle of the lava. I am struck again by how precariously Iceland's civilisation teeters on the wildest of foundations. My father feels it too. He twists round to me in the car, waving his pipe at the lava and saying he feels as if all that energy is just waiting underneath to burst through. We both sense something untameable here, on which man is barely keeping a lid.

And yet, improbably, it *has* been tamed. Town life proceeds equably in neat chalet-style homes on top of the volcanic debris of the centuries, enjoying the comforts of twenty-four-hour hot water and central heating straight from the boiling earth. They even grow trees in the contorted gardens, something you don't see much of in Iceland. The country has long been short of trees, which is why Sigurjón of Laxamýri had to import his timber from Norway. The sagas say the country was 'wooded from mountain to sea' when it was first settled, so we know it was forested once, mainly with birch trees and shrub willow. But most of the native woodland was squandered by settlers for fuel, while volcanic eruptions destroyed more. Once sheep were introduced, it was the beginning of the end.

'Sheep can be very destructive,' my father is musing. 'After they had eaten the shrubs, the wind took the topsoil and the vegetation couldn't regenerate. Remember the joke?'

Cue for the oldest joke in Iceland. The taxi driver grins. This one is almost as antique as my father's Christmas turkey joke (don't ask) and one of the few in his repertoire to which he can attach a punchline.

'What,' he asks portentously, 'do you do if you get lost in an Icelandic forest?'

This is also one of the few punchlines I can remember. 'Stand up,' I reply smugly.

It is almost as good as the one about the American troops at Keflavík, who were encouraged to accept a NATO posting to Iceland with the ambiguous promise of a beautiful blonde virgin under every tree.

Tree-planting is now a national duty in Iceland. Every summer a couple of planes fly over the country dispersing fertiliser and seeds, and teenagers are employed to help make footpaths so that nobody walks in the areas where seeds have been planted. They may be lucky to get two to three centimetres growth in a year, but in places like Garðabær they have certainly made a start. Rowans, dwarf willow and birch have struggled up in wiry clumps.

'Another thousand years,' says my father comfortably, ever one for the long view, 'and we'll be nice and well wooded again.'

Ahead of us Reykjavík is sprawling haphazardly in the late afternoon sunshine, its exuberantly coloured roofs flaunting their usual red, green and blue defiance of whatever the climate may hurl at them. There is nothing too challenging today. The sea, glinting here and there beyond the houses, is rippling so peaceably in the protective embrace of Mount Esja that the English journalist A. A. Gill, who forced his frozen fingers to record that the ocean around Reykjavík 'smashes and grabs at the impertinence of human habitation with corpse-white fists', would be astonished. Instead of the huddled, head-down, white-knuckle town of his tormented winter memory, he would find a small city dreaming placidly beneath the rays of a sun which will not set until late tonight.

It is Flóki and Thórólfur all over again. On a day like this you forget the long, dark, wind-blasted, ice-laden days of winter. You start raving about butter dripping from every blade of shining grass. It is just as well that Ingólfur Arnarson had been in Iceland long enough to see both by the time he discovered where the gods had deposited his household pillars. And in Reykjavík they had chosen well.

Reykjavík

My father is so fastidious about grammar that it is like hanging out with Dr Johnson. An unwary ellipsis, a lazy colloquialism, and he is on to you like a wolf.

We have dumped our bags at Hótel Esja and are considering how far we dare wander in Reykjavík before we are due for dinner at the home of my grandmother's youngest brother.

'What's the time now?' he asks on our way to the old city square.

'Half five.'

He stops in his tracks and glares at me. 'Surely you mean half-*past* five?'

This is when I realise that our expedition is going to be my longest period of remaining verbally at attention since I left the parental home for university long ago. In Icelandic, 'half five' (*hálf fimm*) means half-past four. My father has always found the English ellipsis annoying, and in my case downright ignorant. On Norse turf it is clearly too much to bear.

I know how much he cares about words. He likes precision. He prizes elegance. A split infinitive can spoil his morning, and the surest way of irritating him in a piece of writing is to use 'that' as a relative pronoun, a crime which (note that *which*) he considers downright heinous and is on a rampant crusade to banish. On a battlefield overrun by wandering apostrophes and mindless syntax, my father stands waving aloft an uncompromising standard for semi-colons and thoughtful English. But, oh, his company can be linguistically taxing.

To deflect his wrath, I suggest that we try talking Icelandic together. This is a smart move because although my grammar there is a mangled mess, he is delighted I can manage anything at all. Truth to tell, he is a mite rusty himself. I horrified him by asking on the way across on the plane if he could remind me how to decline *bók*, a word I knew would prove useful. The nominative for 'book' was no trouble, but we were nowhere near the eight case variations, including all the plurals, before he gave up. And this is the man who is supposed to be fluent.

But then, Icelandic is a seriously tricky tongue. We are talking about a language which has twelve different forms for every number from one to four. *Twelve*, I tell you. Everything which moves is conjugated, declined and mystifyingly altered. They would modify your grandmother if you let them. As a matter of fact, they do modify your grandmother: *amma* becomes *ömmu* when she is the object of a sentence.

That is the price you pay, or at least non-native speakers pay, for a language which has hardly changed since its written form took shape during the twelfth and thirteenth centuries. It is as though there were some isolated island in the Mediterranean where Latin were still the native tongue. For that we can thank nigh-on 600 years of almost total isolation and the Icelanders' habit of reading and copying their old literature. At least there are no dialects to contend with (curiously, considering how scattered the communities always were), but the antiquity of the grammatical forms does make learning the language hard work.

It is bad enough for my father, who absorbed it at his mother's knee and spoke nothing else at home in Edinburgh until he went to school. But I had to learn it the hard way. I remember once listening to a curly-haired girl, who looked about three, chattering to her father in a Reykjavík café. He was smiling and nodding as she talked, interrupting fleetingly now and then to pop in the correct form of a word she had used. Lightly, unconsciously almost, she repeated it and carried on. I thought then of how I used to spend my lunch-breaks from my summer job at the tourist bureau poring over a battered brown grammar book I had found in a second-hand bookshop at home. I had sat day after day in a café just like this one, muttering declensions and trying to remember that you follow the Icelandic word for 'am able' with a past participle, not an infinitive. Yet I was still stuck for an answer longer than one word when the waitress asked how I was enjoying myself in Iceland. Suddenly I was wildly, hotly jealous of that little girl.

Bill Holm, an American writer descended from Icelandic immigrants to the New World, has caught something of the longing respect we second- or third-generation Icelanders feel for the language, in a poem which goes in part:

> You must sit down to speak this language,
> It is so heavy you can't be polite or chatter in it.
> For once you have begun a sentence, the whole course of
>   your life is laid out before you,
> Every foolish mistake is clear, every failure, every grief,
> Moving around the inflections from case to case and gender
>   to gender,
> The vowels changing and darkening, the consonants soften-
>   ing on the tongue
> Till they are the sound of a gull's wings fluttering
> As he flies out of the wake of a small boat drifting out to
>   open water.

The line about not being able to chatter in Icelandic must be poetic licence, or he never heard my great-aunts. But I know all about the foolish mistakes. My father and I do try a desultory conversation in Icelandic for a few minutes, but I am wildly out of practice and we are both self-conscious. We lapse quickly into silence.

By now we have reached the grass-sown square which the old histories record as the site of Ingólfur Arnarson's home field, just a short walk from the seashore where he found his house-hold pillars more than eleven hundred years ago. Ingólfur had been hunting for three years, pushing west, until one day he spotted puffs of white steam rising to the sky in the distance. Following the steam, he came to an area of hot-pools, seething and bubbling a few kilometres above a great basin of a bay. Down in the bay, washed up on the shore, were the pillars.

It was an ideal spot to settle. Some of Ingólfur's companions worried about the lack of a natural harbour, but the place was rich with grassland and woods; the sea, warmed by the Gulf Stream, was full of a variety of fish and a nearby river teemed with salmon. Above all, there was an abundance of natural hot water in those open pools which smoked under the summer skies, producing the steam which had guided him here and was to give the settlement its name: *Reykjavík*, Bay of Smokes.

Ingólfur promptly laid claim to a huge area of land around his homestead and right across the peninsula. As word spread, kinsfolk began joining him from Norway, and Ingólfur parcelled out land to them. Steinunn the Old received her share at Keflavík and paid with her embroidered cloak. Subsequent settlers sailed further north and east, claiming more land around the habitable rim of the island.

Slowly the landscape began to accumulate names, every one of them a story. The headland where Ingólfur first came ashore became Ingólfur's Head. The braided rivers on Reykjavík's doorstep took their name from the settler Ketilbjörn the Old's ship, *Elliði*. The water cascading over the lava cliffs at Thingvellir was called Axe River, because Ketilbjörn lost his axe trying to break the ice there one winter. There was White River and Hawks' Dale, Holy Hill and Harbour Fjord, Thrush Wood, Swans' Ness, Salmon River. (This last is *Laxá*, of which there are several in Iceland, including the greatest of them all which thunders through Laxamýri.)

Of course, we all have our Bearsdens and Gleneagles, our Grafty Greens and Oathlaws. The difference in Iceland is the number of people who remember the stories behind the names, a phenomenon which, like so much else in this country, is down to the sagas. It is extraordinary to hear farmers and fishermen still talking as if Ingólfur had just moved into Reykjavík the other day and the people who came after were personal buddies of theirs: Njáll, Gunnar, Gunnlaugur of the pus-filled foot, Grettir the outlaw and the rest of the immortal band who lived in Iceland in the years when the country was young enough still to need names. They were the men who fought and bargained at the Althing each year, who refused to limp while their legs were the same length, and bit their lips when fire seared their flesh, who lifted impossibly large boulders, and mingled their blood in foster-brother ceremonies, who loved feisty women, courted word-fame and only rarely died in their beds.

On our family trip here thirty years ago, we jolted and clattered one day to Hlíðarendi, where Gunnar Hámundarson, the most attractive character in *Njáls Saga*, lived and farmed in the tenth century. The farmer greeted us as if it were the most normal thing in the world to be interrupted in the middle of shearing your sheep by four strangers asking for the story of a man who lived on your land a thousand years ago. In Iceland, it probably is. He nodded happily when my father asked him about Gunnar, who had died, as recounted in one of the most poignant scenes in *Njáls Saga*, because he could not bear to leave this hillside for exile. The farmer pushed back his hat and recounted the story with verve, gesticulating towards the landmarks as he talked.

Gunnar had been sentenced to outlawry and was about to escape his enemies by sailing abroad and leaving Iceland for ever. With the whole household standing outside to see him off, he vaulted into his saddle and rode away. But as he rode down towards the river, his horse stumbled and he had to leap off. In that moment, he glanced back towards his home and the slopes of Hlíðarendi. ('Over there,' grunted the farmer, gesturing behind.)

'How lovely the hillside is,' Gunnar murmured to his brother, and when you read this amid the spare prose of the saga, the burst of lyricism is surprisingly moving. 'More lovely than it has ever seemed to me before. Golden cornfields and new-mown hay. I'm going back home. I will not go anywhere.'

That autumn, when his men had gone off to finish the haymaking, Gunnar was alone at home with his wife and mother, asleep. He awoke to the sound of a bloodcurdling howl of warning from his dog as an axe was driven deep into its head. He knew then that his enemies had come for him at last. In the siege that followed, Gunnar held the attackers off with a shower of arrows, until one of his assailants leaped up on to the wall and managed to slash through his bow-string. Gunnar threw him off the wall and turned to his imperious wife Hallgerður with a request.

'Let me have two locks of your hair, and help my mother plait them into a bow-string for me,' he asked.

'Does anything depend on it?' asked Hallgerður (a seriously scary woman).

'My life depends on it,' replied Gunnar, 'for they will never get at me as long as I can use my bow.'

'In that case,' said Hallgerður, 'I shall remind you of the slap you once gave me. I don't care in the least whether you hold out for long or not.'

'To each his own way of earning fame,' said Gunnar. 'You will not be asked again.'

He kept fighting until he was exhausted and his enemies felled him at last. Afterwards his mother said to Hallgerður, 'You are an evil woman, and your shame will long be remembered.'

Gunnar's leading attacker stood over his body and predicted that the last defence of this great champion would be remembered for as long as this land was lived in.

And so it has proved thus far.

Along with the nearby bird-haunted lake, the old square where Ingólfur built his farm is the most attractive part of the Icelandic capital. As my father and I walk across the grass in the early evening sunshine, I remember why I like it so much here. Farther out, Reykjavík has the flat-roofed, East European feel of a city cobbled together in haste. In the last fifty years, it has had to accommodate a dizzily expanding population (who have to pay, as our taxi driver pointed out, dizzily expanding prices for a home of their own). But here and among the gaily painted buildings by the lake, where in my tourist office days I used to share my lunch with a clamouring gaggle of ducks and swans, the city feels gracious and thoughtfully proportioned.

Along one side of the square, across from the cathedral and the parliament house, is what I consider to be the most elegant building in town, although I may be biased, of course. This is Hótel Borg, a white, five-storey mansion stretching almost the length of the square, which was built by our kinsman Jóhannes Jósefsson, the strongest man in Iceland.

My father and I step tentatively into the lobby with a flicker of the same apprehensiveness which had overcome him at the Blue Lagoon. Hótel Borg went to seed after Jóhannes died and neither of us has been inside since it was renovated. But this, too, seems to have been done well. The glittering art deco which must have had jaws dropping when the hotel opened in 1930 has been replicated with a panache of which the founder would surely have approved. My father is gazing around with a look of satisfaction.

'It's just as I remember it,' he grins. 'Just as I remember it when I was brought here as a child. It felt like a palace.'

The lobby area alone is a revelation. It has been turned into a compact, theatrically lit shrine to the founder, with display cases packed with his fishing rod and rifles, and a large bust of the man himself on a plinth, looking like Boris Yeltsin. The walls are hung with photographs of Jóhannes in his heyday, posing with the wrestling troupe he took around the London vaudeville houses in 1908, and smiling rakishly in a John Wayne cowboy hat.

Jóhannes *á Borg*, as they called him after he built his hotel (Jóhannes of the Town Hotel has nothing like the same saga-esque ring in English), earned the money to build Iceland's first proper hotel with a staggeringly exotic career as a professional strongman. His troupe started by demonstrating the art of *glíma*-wrestling against boxers, knife fighters and multiple assailants invited up from the London audiences. He later refined the act to include dramatic stage routines for which they dressed up as cowboys and Indians. Jóhannes would be tied to the stake and the audience brought to a frenzy of excitement until he escaped, tossed the Indians around the stage, and saved the girl. As Buffalo Bill had also discovered, the Wild West theme was popular everywhere. 'Johannes's Icelandic Stranglers', as the posters hyped them, were top billing in London, all over North America and later across Europe.

For a time he toured with Barnum and Bailey's circus, where

his troupe shared the billing with some Japanese Jiu-Jitsu fighters. Their wrestling contest on the roof of Madison Square Garden in New York turned into one of Jóhannes's most newsworthy exhibitions, when his two-year-old daughter Hekla started to cry in the middle of the contest, prompting him to abandon his opponent and pick her up. The moist-eyed ringside reporters reported admiringly that Josephsson, as they called him, nevertheless went on to win the bout.

Towards the end of his touring career, Jóhannes became so blasé about his invincibility on stage that he was inviting onlookers to challenge him with any weapon they liked, except a gun. He told my father that when he was playing Lisbon once, the local knife champion stepped forward to oppose him. In a moment of carelessness, he allowed the man to skewer him through the hand. Getting kebabbed was bad enough, but when he felt the knife being twisted, Jóhannes became, as he said, 'irritated' – doubtless a euphemism for a rage of berserk proportions. He forced the Portuguese challenger on to the floor and was methodically killing him when the audience erupted and surged on to the stage. Jóhannes promptly upturned his half-comatose opponent and manoeuvred himself underneath, so that the blows of the enraged audience rained on the hapless knife champion's back. The Icelandic Strangler then crawled out between their legs, fled off the stage and escaped through a toilet window. He tore through the streets of Lisbon in his wrestling trunks and vest.

As he toured the capitals of the world, revelling in the luxury of their grand hotels, Jóhannes began to form an idea. His homeland was beginning to taste the prosperity which would transform it beyond recognition in the course of the twentieth century; it was developing a fishing industry, raising cultural institutions, governing itself and aspiring to full independence. The capital of such a country needed a hotel of international standards, and Jóhannes vowed he would not go back to Iceland until he had enough money to build one.

In 1927, nearly twenty years after leaving Iceland to try his luck at the Olympic Games, Jóhannes finally went home. He returned, as saga-heroes do, replete with fame and fortune, and immediately used both to fulfil his vow. The cash dollars he had amassed abroad enabled him to ride the Depression and erect his glittering monument on the edge of Ingólfur Arnarson's home field. In a typically astute publicity coup, he opened it in January 1930 to coincide with the one-thousandth anniversary of the Althing, which attracted scores of visitors to the capital and hordes of admirers to Iceland's first real hotel.

One photograph in the lobby shows him as an elderly man with uncombed hair standing high off his forehead. He really does look like Boris Yeltsin.

'That's how I remember the old boy,' says my father fondly as we inch along the portrait gallery. 'He would have loved all this. He was such a showman.'

I am peering at the giant candelabras next door and wondering if even my father's seemingly bottomless wallet on this trip could afford us a night here.

'Go on, ask!' I hiss, shaking his sleeve like the importunate teenager I have metamorphosed into in the space of an afternoon.

He does, but the hotel is full. We have a coffee instead, in an extravagantly furnished room gleaming with mirrors and polished black surfaces, and discuss what to do next. There is still a little time before we are expected at my great-uncle's house, and I know, even before he tells me, where my father would really like to go.

'It would be fun to see it together, wouldn't it?' he says.

Yes, it would. We step back out into the sunshine and head for the long shopping street called Laugavegur.

My father was born at number 42 Laugavegur in October 1929. He was christened Magnús Sigursteinsson, but it was a name he lost before he even knew he had it. It lasted him only the eight months of his residency in Iceland.

Icelandic names are a mouthful for foreigners, especially if they are not familiar with the custom of creating a surname by adding *son* or *dóttir* to the father's name. When the family moved to Britain in the summer of 1930, Sigursteinn took pity on their host nation by giving everyone the common surname Magnússon, his own patronymic. He reckoned that 1930s

Scotland was not ready for the bewildering and faintly scandalous overtones of a household in which the father was Magnússon, the mother (retaining Ingibjörg's own father's name) Sigurðardóttir, the two sons Sigursteinsson, and the two daughters Sigursteinsdóttir. Even the one name with which they left themselves caused confusion enough among the worthy citizens of Edinburgh. The family eventually found itself absorbed into that obscure Scottish clan, the MagNoossons.

In October 1929 Sigursteinn was working at the headquarters of the Icelandic Co-operative Society in Reykjavík, managing imports and exports. He was a rising star of the Co-op, a clever young man who had been head-hunted from his school in Akureyri and trained at a business college in Hamburg. He and Ingibjörg were part of a growing class of educated, well-off Icelanders in a city which was enjoying a pre-Depression boom in prosperity. New buildings were starting to be constructed out of reinforced concrete because of the danger of earthquakes, and they lived in one of the smartest. Their first-floor apartment was above one of the clothing stores which were opening up and down Reykjavík's main thoroughfare – if 'thoroughfare' is the word for a street in which the only traffic was an occasional small lorry, a car or two belonging to the doctor or some of the wealthier Danish merchants, a few horses riding out on a Sunday, and *in extremis* a model-T Ford doing service as a fire-truck.

Magnús, the couple's third child after Sigurður and Didda (the youngest, Lolo, was born in Scotland), was delivered by a tiny lady with tight grey ringlets and a face so ancient it seemed to be made of parchment. *Tanta* Thórdís, as they called her, had delivered Ingibjörg herself once, as well as her sisters and brothers, and all their children. She was the adopted daughter of Sigurjón of Laxamýri, one of a clutch of waifs and strays he had taken under his wing at the teeming northern farmstead. Nearing the end of a busy life as the family midwife, she was a frail, almost ethereally old link to a place which none of the babies she delivered would ever know.

My father and I walk up Laugavegur, scanning the shops and apartments for number 42. This is one of the main roads out of town. Keep going here and you reach the smoking hot-springs which drew Ingólfur towards his pillars all those centuries ago; nowadays these supply the city with a central heating system so wonderful that you rarely need to wear a sweater inside or wait for hot water in the bath. Cars crawl along the road, bumper to bumper. The shops are stylish and expensive, the pavements crowded with the young and fashionable. The aroma of good coffee wafts out from small, studenty cafés and navels clank with gold. This is modern Reykjavík, a city 'as hip and happening as it is possible to be', according to one of the more excitable internet sites.

It is an image which mesmerises the younger end of the tourist market. The rest of the world has been alerted at last to young Icelanders' formidable capacity for partying non-stop from Friday until Sunday, with Saturday night spent wrapped fondly around one of Reykjavík's elegant lamp-posts. Laugavegur and the surrounding streets are now a clubbing magnet for the planet's youth. In the absence of any teenagers of my own to mortify, I did wonder fleetingly if I should suggest checking out this scene in the interests of journalistic research. But the last club I visited in Reykjavík has barely opened its doors by the time my father and I are due on the plane tomorrow morning. He would never have come anyway. Inebriated youths littering the streets are not the Iceland he likes to see.

What he likes are washer-women, preferably the sort who lived a thousand years ago. Laugavegur (Hot-Springs Way) started out in the mists of saga-times as a path trodden by women on their way up to the hot-springs to wash their laundry, and he loves the romance of his moment in history beginning where families as far back as Ingólfur's (who knows?) were sending their smalls up his road.

The story of the washer-women, wearing down a path as they hauled their loads up to the hot-pools every week, burning their hands in the boiling water before plodding back with even heavier damp bundles, has always bothered me.

'No chance of the men ever lending a hand with the laundry, I suppose?' I suggest half-way up the road. 'Or were they too busy poncing around on their horses, looking for someone to kill?'

My father stops in his tracks. 'Dearest!'

He is caught, I can tell, between the impulse to defend his heroes and an opposite tendency to be irreverent about them. At home he would laugh, but here he will be weighing up how much latitude he can allow me, in case it leads to the casting of moss-like aspersions on Iceland's manly heritage. He starts to walk again, opting for a safe, professorial reply.

'Well, the men did do some work, you know. They worked as farmers. Somebody once called the saga-heroes "brawling farmers", which irritated the hell out of devotees like my father. But that's exactly what they were. It's interesting how often the sagas do describe men being attacked while they're at work in the fields, which I suppose proves your point in a way, although I'm not sure *poncing* is quite the right word. The women certainly did all the back-breakingly heavy work, as they did in most medieval societies.'

The exchange deposits us neatly at number 42, which is on a corner where one of the smaller streets crosses the main road. It is a handsome apartment block, still housing a clothing shop beneath. My father has not been here for a while and is amused, in a resigned sort of way, to find that his birthplace now houses a fashionable boutique with a brash poster displayed prominently through the glass. He stands in front of it and harries me across the road to take a photograph from the other side.

I nip between the shuffling traffic and click the camera from so far away that I can barely see him. He is hopping about between window-shoppers trying to give me a clear view: a man with his head full of blood-feuds and washer-women, posing gravely in front of three scantily clad mannequins and a banner saying FCUK. The collision of two Icelands has rarely seemed so stark.

There is another birthplace in Laugavegur. Twenty-seven years before my father, Iceland's most renowned novelist, Halldór Laxness, was born at number 32. He won the Nobel prize for literature in 1955 for a series of monumental novels which, as well as drawing universal truths from the wryly observed experiences of Icelanders through the centuries, also encouraged the modern nation to see itself in an entirely fresh way. It was an achievement – no mean feat in a country of only a quarter of a million people – which happily confirmed the Icelanders' self-image as a literary nation.

None is more proud of it than my father, who translated five of the novels into English and always cherished his friendship with Iceland's greatest man of letters. I remember them strolling in the sunshine outside the Laxness home at Gljúfrasteinn in Mosfellssveit during the summer we toured the saga sites. I lay in the grass gazing up at a flawlessly azure sky and listening to the murmur of their voices as they discussed their next project. My father was smoking his pipe; Halldór waited for evening to bring out the cigars.

Number 32 houses another fashion shop now. My father pauses respectfully. I pass as reverently as is possible for someone with only half a mind on literature. In keeping with my new juvenile status today, I am actually looking out for an exhibition of penises.

Laugavegur's supremely daft Icelandic Phallological Museum is set, appropriately enough, down a back passage off the main street. I study goggle-eyed a notice declaring that inside you will find exhibited the phallus of every mammal in Iceland, eighty in total, including twenty-seven from whales, one polar bear, and eighteen seals and walruses. Beside me my father is still manfully pretending to calculate how old Halldór Laxness was when he died in 1998.

The museum appears to be closed, which means, to my parent's inordinate relief, that we are unable to ascertain whether the old farmer who had agreed to donate his wedding tackle after his death has yet had the opportunity to do so. My father turns gratefully on his heel and strides off. It is time for dinner.

The Patriarchs

The man gazing out equably from the cover of my Laxamýri book is plump-faced and burly. His hair is white, parted at one side and tapering into two artful curls above his left ear. The snowy side-burns, like stuck-on Santa Claus fluff, meet his beard in such a seamless loop under the jaw that it looks as if his face is tied up in a bandage.

When I first found the book languishing forgotten on a shelf in my father's study, I thought this must be the face of Sigurjón Jóhannesson of Laxamýri, the man who finished his new house in the year the king visited Iceland. But this hardly looked like the visage of someone famed for his ferocious energy and implacable will. There was a hint of humour at the corners of this mouth. The hairstyle suggested at least a passing acquaintance with curling tongs, and the bulky physique was surely that of a man who had discovered how to relax.

Indeed it was not a portrait of Sigurjón at all. This was his father, Jóhannes Kristjánsson, the man who first put Laxamýri on the map.

And why does it matter who put Laxamýri on the map? Who cares what happened in a small corner of northern Iceland 200 years ago? Have I been seduced by the siren strains of the legends into believing that my family history is important? After all, making us feel that our own legacy is special is exactly the function of this kind of lore. The stories cherished by a people or a family may be truly improbable or probably true, but they all feed someone's self-image somewhere. That is why they thrive.

Look at the way Muriel Spark's redoubtable heroine in *The Prime of Miss Jean Brodie* relishes her ancestral link to Willie Brodie, Edinburgh cabinet-maker and designer of gibbets, 'who died cheerfully on a gibbet of his own devising in seventeen-eighty-eight', as she reports regally to her girls. Miss Brodie glories in her descent from a man who kept two mistresses, played dice and fighting cocks, and became a night burglar for the sheer danger of it. 'It is the stuff I am made of,' she declares. Just as surely was Laxamýri the stuff of which my grandmother was made.

Spotting the unconscious revelation of values and priorities is part of the fun of other people's stories. But the deeper pleasure comes from opening a more intimate window on to different times and cultures. What excited me in trying to penetrate my own legends and reconstruct the epic saga which began with Jóhannes Kristjánsson was that in following him and his descendants through four generations (five, if you count my father), I was uncovering the history of modern Iceland itself. Suddenly light was being flung into all sorts of areas which had refused to come to life before as anything more than dry chapter headings in the history books: poverty, economic recovery, entrepreneurial disaster, cultural revival.

It was always going to be difficult to find the truth behind some of the stories, but the prize would be to understand better a heritage which had long been there for me, but only fitfully grasped. It didn't matter that what I discovered might undermine the best efforts of the myth-makers to portray our family as uniquely exotic and the fate of Laxamýri as the product of tantalisingly dark secrets. Wearing away at myth is bound to dilute the bolder colours and expose the banalities behind mystery. It is a sort of reverse tabloid effect, which I relish because it brings unremarked lives and humble side-shows to the fore in the process.

Ultimately, though, a single family's story is important because it illuminates a larger one. The big story here is Iceland.

Jóhannes Kristjánsson was born in the area of Reykjadalur in the north of Iceland on 11 March 1795 and lived with his parents,

Kristján Jósepsson and Sesselja Bergsdóttir, on their farm at a place called Halldórsstaðir. Everyone lived on farms then, except the tiny number in the embryonic southern village of Reykjavík, which had been no more than a big manor-farm itself until the middle of the century. But the farms on which most Icelanders lived are better described as smallholdings, on which the lucky ones managed to sustain a precarious living in extraordinarily harsh conditions. Iceland was a peasant subsistence society, which had barely developed in the five centuries it had spent as a colony of Norway and then Denmark.

By the eighteenth century the country was so destitute that even the Danish crown, casually oppressive in its time, was becoming alarmed. A census in 1703 had recorded a population of just over 50,000, in which one person in every ten was a pauper. Later in the century, King Frederic V commissioned an Icelander by the name of Skúli Magnússon to see what he could do to develop native commerce, and Skúli obliged with some bold ideas for transforming the royal manor-farm of Reykjavík into a modern industrial centre. In 1752 he began building a row of timber houses along Ingólfur's old bridle path to the sea, which he turned into workshops for wool-processing and cloth-weaving, with a forge, a tannery and a cooperage. He tried to encourage Icelandic farmers to grow grain again and pioneered an experimental sheep farm. But none of these ideas came to anything. The fledgling wool and skin industry was thrashed in the competitive European export market and Danish traders successfully undermined any native efforts which threatened their own monopoly. Even the sheep farm was a catastrophe: the imported rams from England turned out to be infected with scab, which ran riot through Icelandic flocks, forcing the slaughter of every sheep in the diseased areas.

Up north, Skúli formed a small brimstone factory in Húsavík, the fishing station near the farm-lands of Laxamýri, which processed brimstone from local geothermal sources into useful elements for making explosives. This enterprise fared better than his projects in the south; it was sold to the royal Danish arsenal in Copenhagen and lasted nearly a hundred years until 1850, by which time Jóhannes Kristjánsson, on whose doorstep it flourished, was in his fifties. Meanwhile the failures in the south had at least the encouraging side-effect of promoting the development of Reykjavík. In 1786 the estate where Skúli had set up his factories received its royal charter as a market town. Iceland's future capital, boasting a grand population of 167, was on its way at last.

But there was nothing remotely comparable in the north to the budding Reykjavík. There the harbours continued to be little more than trading stations, controlled by Danish merchants. Farms like Kristján's and Sesselja's, scattered among the mountains and around the coast, were isolated outposts in which survival remained a chancy business.

The century which was ending when Jóhannes was born in 1795 had crippled Iceland. Reykjavík's modest progress flickers like a lone beacon in an ocean of disasters. Decade after decade, the Icelanders had been battered by catastrophe. An epidemic of smallpox (or 'big-pox', *stórabóla*, as they call it) killed a third of the entire population between 1707 and 1709, reducing numbers to about 35,000, the lowest point since the country was first settled. Volcanic eruptions repeatedly devastated the land, including one in the Öræfajökull glacier which lasted almost a year and wiped out farms and livestock. Earthquakes finished off more. An eruption of the volcano Katla in 1757 led to widespread famine. And in 1783, in an event never before recorded in the history of the planet, the earth literally split apart. A 25-kilometre-long fissure opened in the Laki mountain range in the south, revealing more than a hundred separate craters, from which lava flowed for ten months over 565 square kilometres of land.

Like the rest of the country, Kristján and Sesselja would have been enveloped in the nightmare effects of the Laki eruptions. The ash-clouds poisoned the atmosphere as far away as northern Europe and the whole of Iceland was shrouded in a bluish haze. Pastures became so toxic that little grew and three-quarters of the country's livestock died. In the famine which followed, at least 10,000 people, a fifth of the population, died. The tragedy was so immense that the Danish crown again felt impelled to take action. Money was collected to help ease conditions in the colony and there was serious talk of relocating the surviving population to the moors of Jutland. If that had happened, Iceland would have joined St Kilda as the haunting relic of an extinct people and my great-great-great-grandfather Jóhannes Kristjánsson would have been born a Dane.

Thankfully, Iceland didn't. And Jóhannes wasn't. For which (notwithstanding my admiration for that paragon of Danish manhood, Christian IX) I am also very grateful. Instead he grew up in Iceland, on his parents' farm, in conditions described with saga-like understatement in the sources as 'great poverty'. So straitened were his circumstances that he never learned to write his own name as a child, which was unusual for the time, since Lutheran ministers were supposed to be ensuring by then that children could read and write before they were confirmed at fourteen.

But Jóhannes had several personal traits in his favour. He knew how to work hard. He was ambitious and planned ahead. He eschewed alcohol (which was a big advantage, much commented on at a time when meagre profits were often drunk away). Crucially, he was also in possession of something which no Icelandic man of destiny should be without: a defining experience in his youth which in later years he liked to think had set him on course for success.

One day Jóhannes was visiting a farm in the area, when he overheard a sickly old vagrant asking for assistance. The tramp wanted help in fording a river called Calves' Stream, which was in spate. When Jóhannes heard the people at the farm saying they were too busy, he offered to take the old man across himself. He was a brawny lad and in no time was wading through the rushing waters with the emaciated figure slung over his back. When they reached the other side, the tramp was so grateful that he said a blessing over the boy and prayed that his life would be happy and prosperous. Jóhannes took the words as a prophecy.

After working on his parents' smallholding, Jóhannes began to be hired out to others. Labouring hard, he earned enough to buy himself seven ewes and a horse, and by the spring of 1819 had accumulated enough to rent his first piece of land. After he had been farming for a year, he married a young girl, Sigurlaug Kristjánsdóttir, from the farm at Breiðumýri (Broad Moor). This proved to be a wise business move as well as a happy personal match. She not only brought him a dowry of one cow, six ewes, a bed and some small household articles, but within a few years he was able to take over the whole of her parents' farm.

All the while the family was expanding. Sigurlaug had sixteen children in all, of whom eight survived, including their indomitable eighth child Sigurjón, born at Breiðumýri in June 1833. Two foster-children, probably orphans, also shared their turf-roofed cottage.

There was another farm in the area, a neglected place now, although it enjoyed a reputation for having produced community leaders in the previous two centuries. It was not one of the very oldest Icelandic farms, but the name was well enough known thereabouts: Laxamýri, the farm on the salmon moor next to the sea.

Jóhannes had never given it a thought. Laxamýri was not a particularly desirable piece of real estate: its buildings were in ruins and the land itself was in multi-ownership. But during his eleventh year of farming at Breiðumýri, his friend Thorsteinn Daníelsson, who owned an eighth part of Laxamýri, got wind that another eighth was available and asked Jóhannes to buy it on his behalf. For some reason, Thorsteinn did not specify how much he was willing to pay for this extra portion, which seems an oddly substantial oversight. Nevertheless, Jóhannes waded in and bought it for 300 *spesía* in the old coinage and fifty old ewes, which his friend promptly said was much too high a price and refused to pay. That left Jóhannes high and dry with an eighth of a farm he never wanted in the first place.

But this was not a man to panic when destiny beckoned. He took a closer look at Laxamýri, made his calculations, sorted out some loans, and set about relieving Thorsteinn of his original portion as well. Then, flying in the face of local doubters who thought he was taking too big a risk on a property with so little going for it, he proceeded to buy a third eighth of the land. His credit-rating is said to have been high, and it must have been.

In 1838, Jóhannes moved his household into the ramshackle turf and stone farmhouse, and gradually took over the remaining Laxamýri land by purchase or exchange. Thus began the ninety years of occupation celebrated in our family annals.

By the time Sigurlaug died in 1859, to be buried in a new

family plot in the churchyard at Húsavík, Jóhannes had done well enough to confound the local doubters and add several smaller farms to the original land. He had even bought the whole of the small island of Hrísey, way over in the next fjord. They called him *Jóhannes ríki* now – Jóhannes the Rich – and he had an estate to match. Laxamýri's reputation was growing. The son who would turn it into a legend was waiting in the wings, biding his time.

'Have you noticed how many Jóhanneses there are in our story?' I ask my father. We are in a second taxi, driving along the coast road which hugs Reykjavík's bay, and mulling over what we hope to find out from our kinsman this evening. 'At least four.'

'Good heavens, are there really?' My father looks alarmed. His punctilious attention to the spelling of his forebears' names rarely stretches to remembering who they are.

'And you know what?' I say, wondering vaguely if I've missed one. No, he was a Jóhann. 'I like them all.'

Actually I'm not sure what I do like so much about Jóhannes Kristjánsson. The admiring funeral orations I had read at home make the Laxamýri patriarch sound as wise and noble as the great Njáll himself, but that hardly takes us far; Icelanders are always the most improbably fine of fellows at their funerals. We are told Jóhannes served as chief of the district for ten years, granting legal advice to all who sought it in a manner as magnanimous as his hospitality to all who passed his door. According to the minister who conducted the service, he was 'composed, courteous, prudent and foresighted, courageous and reliable, loyal to his friends, polite and tactful, of noble bearing, well-built, manly and handsome'. Whew.

All the same, there was definitely something attractive about Jóhannes. He had a quick intelligence, unrefined by book-learning, and a humane approach to life which his burgeoning prosperity enhanced rather than pinched. There is a quality in that immaculately coiffed portrait of his which strikes me as good-natured and restfully wise.

Then again, perhaps I like him because I fancy a similarity

about the mouth (just humour me here) to my father and my son Siggy. I also find the trace of all too human vanity in the carefully primped hair endearing, likewise his cuddly physique, which ran so much to fat in later life that he had to be helped on and off his horse. But what I most admire in Jóhannes is that he never forgot how difficult it was for a young man who had never learned to write to make his way in life. He reached the top himself, and in time managed to pen his own name on official documents in a movingly awkward signature; but in one eloquent action towards the end of his life there is an indication of the struggle he had found it to be. He donated a large sum of money to provide a teacher to circulate among poor and promising farmers' children in each of the districts in which he had lived, so that no one else would have it quite so hard again.

Sunshine is still glancing off the sea as my father rings the doorbell on a house directly across the road from the shore. Great-uncle Sigurjón is something of a patriarch himself now, the last of my grandmother's siblings and one of the few people left in the clan with a direct connection to the old estate. His mother was Sigurjón of Laxamýri's youngest daughter, Snjólaug, granddaughter of Jóhannes.

He greets us as graciously and gallantly as ever. In his younger days, Uncle Sigurjón used to remind me of a debonair matinee idol, something I found difficult to reconcile with his job as Reykjavík's chief of police; it's hard to imagine Cary Grant wearing down suspects. Even in his frail eighties he is still darkly handsome. His memory, which he had claimed was deeply faulty, turns out to be as sharp as an icicle. But his charm does not preclude fixing me with a mild but penetrating eye over dinner and informing me that one or two of the stories I have brought with me are, not to put too fine a point on it, nonsense. Of which more later.

We sit around the table in a long room facing the sea, joined by his wife Sigríður and some of their grown-up children with husbands and wives. I listen, riveted, to what he can tell us of his mother's life at Laxamýri and his views on its demise. Then we turn to Jóhannes Kristjánsson. My great-uncle can add little to what I know already, but he is very knowledgeable about the family tree backwards and forwards from the patriarch.

At once the level of conversation round the table rises to a babble. The Icelanders do like to talk ancestry. It is a more common topic of conversation than the weather – and, believe me, in a country where you can be served up a light dusting of snowflakes, followed by sunshine, rain and then a feet-lifting blizzard all in the course of a day, that is saying something.

You can hardly last two minutes among strangers without someone asking '*Af hvaða ætt ertu?*' ('What line are you from?') and there is at least a page a week devoted to genealogy in one national newspaper. An internet database opened by Decode, an Icelandic company devoted to researching the country's small and compact gene pool, proved an instant hit. Merely by logging on to *Íslendingabók*, as it is called, every Icelander can immediately follow his or her ancestors from both parents several generations back. Within weeks of its being set up, a third of the nation had registered for a password and Decode was claiming smugly that genealogy had become even more popular than handball, the sport which currently empties the streets when Iceland is playing. Even more than with the weather, that really is saying a lot.

The genealogy game is gloriously, bewilderingly, wackily complicated, and the more labyrinthine it gets, the more everyone loves it. My father is in his element. Jóhannes's ancestors can wait for the moment. He has decided that this is the moment to record on tape, once and for all, who is doing what and related to whom across the entire family, right down to Uncle Sigurjón's smallest great-grandchild. My father's relish for recording, typing up, annotating and organising this sort of minutely detailed information is matched only by his complete inability to remember it afterwards. My mother is well practised at steering him round family gatherings with a whispered commentary running in his left ear: 'Your mother's sister's husband's sister's son, married to the lady you've just been talking to. Remember?'

The womenfolk around the table throw themselves into the exercise with gusto. Icelandic women have perfected a system of speaking on the in-breath which is a wonder to behold. It means they never need to pause for breath at all, ever. My father leans across with his tape-recorder and I sit there hypnotised by the wave of names and relationships streaming unstoppably from my great-aunt, Sigríður. My old grammar book was no match for this. The recurrence of the same names in every generation makes the stream even murkier. Just when I have latched on to one Snjólaug (Ingibjörg and Uncle Sigurjón's mother), I realise they have slipped away to another one, Snjólaug's own mother. Or was it her daughter? There have been seven generations of Snjólaugs in several different branches of the Laxamýri clan. The name is virtually unique to the family, a lovely one in Icelandic although tortuous for anyone else to pronounce. Its literal translation is Snow-Hotsprings (from the same root as *Lauga*vegur), which I somehow can't see catching on over here, although in America my cousin Árni's daughter was inventively dubbed Snowlake, which just might.

However many Snjólaugs there have been in the family, I think we had covered every single one of them by the end of the roast lamb and potatoes. But then again, I can't be sure.

You do begin to see why the Icelanders have historically been so meticulous about writing down their family genealogies. After Ingólfur's followers had claimed farm-lands the size of Liechtenstein, it was a nightmare trying to keep track of successors when there were no family surnames and just about everyone was called Sig-something, Jó-something, Ing-something or maybe Hilmar if you were a chef. The solution they came up with was simply to write down the names, generation by generation. Every saga is prefaced by a genealogy of biblical proportions. This means Icelanders have always known where they come from, and it still makes them excited.

Me, too. Or else why am I here in Iceland now, chasing the ghosts of grandfathers with so many 'greats' in front of them that I am developing a stutter? It is undoubtedly why my father, for all his initial reluctance, is now throwing himself into the exercise like some mad amanuensis. We love it because we like to know who we are. It means that when we talk (all at once and without pausing for breath) about Jóhannes Kristjánsson, the-man-who-helped-a-tramp-over-the-river-who-became-the-father-of-Sigurjón-the-father-of-Snjólaug-the-mother-of-Sigurjón-the-brother-of-Ingibjörg-the-mother-of-Magnús-the-father-of-me, we all know exactly about whom we

are talking and how he relates to each one of us. Er . . . more
or less.

We also enjoy it because all Icelanders – and I include myself
– are genealogical snobs of the highest order and take pride in
proving our descent from the men and women of the sagas,
preferably taking in a bishop or two along the way and ending, if
we can possibly swing it (and nearly everyone can), with one of
the kings of Norway. Nobody, as one Icelander told me smoothly,
wants nobodies as forefathers.

In fact, this was precisely the reason Ari the Learned gave for
writing his history of Iceland all of 900 years ago. Ari, I am
delighted to say, appears on the Laxamýri family tree. He wrote
two histories in the 1120s – the original *Íslendingabók* (Book of
Icelanders) and *Landnámabók* (Book of Settlements), scrupu-
lously sourced from people whose inherited memories bridged
the couple of centuries between him and the time of Ingólfur
Arnarson. This was a country young enough to be able to
remember its origins with considerable clarity. What Ari did
was to transfer these remarkably fresh oral traditions into
literary form. It was his histories which the writers of the sagas
drew on in the thirteenth and fourteenth centuries for their own
imaginative accounts of the lives of the settlers. Ari said he
wrote the histories so that Icelanders could 'all the better meet
the criticisms of foreigners when they accuse us of being
descended from slaves or scoundrels, if we know for certain the
truth about our ancestry'. It seems as good a reason as any.

By the time dessert is over and the most recent generations
have been exhaustively inspected, we are ready for the kings
and bishops. We move to a small lounge at the end of the dining
room for coffee. My father peers at his tape-recorder, shakes it,
and mutters 'Testing, testing, one, two, three' in an incipiently
fed-up voice. His passion for examining every leaf on the family
tree is waning and I'm sure he is starting to wonder if volun-
teering to be sound-recordist on this trip was a good idea.

I, meanwhile, am coming into my own. All that tedious
transcribing of genealogy back home has given me something to
add to the conversation at last. Illustrious names from the
Laxamýri line pour from my lips with unwonted fluency. There
was Ari the Learned himself of course. Nice to have a historian

in the family. Before him was Guðrún Ósvífrsdóttir, heroine of the romantic *Laxdæla Saga*, who was considered the most beautiful and intelligent woman in Iceland, although men did tend to get themselves murdered around her.

Jón Arason was one of ours, too, as of just about everyone else in Iceland. 'The last Catholic bishop of Hólar in the north, executed in 1550 for his heroic resistance to Danish imposition of the Reformation,' my father pops in, by way of an aside. As if we didn't know. Jón is a hero of his, not least because he managed to sire about fifteen children between masses. Only in Iceland could a bishop be revered as the nation's favourite ancestor.

More recently in the line came Jónas Hallgrímsson, best loved of Iceland's lyrical poets, and Hannes Hafstein, Iceland's First Minister when the Danish parliament granted Home Rule in 1904.

Saga-heroine, historian, bishop, poet and the Donald Dewar of Icelandic politics – not bad to be going on with. I am bound to admit there is no king immediately in sight, but, really, nothing could be easier to remedy. My father points out that the line begins with Ingólfur Arnarson, who was such an aristocratic cove that he must have been related to one ruler of Norway or another. That will do us royally for now.

We are sitting, I need hardly remind you, in the most ardently republican republic in the world.

Our host refills the coffee cups and sits back. It is growing late, but light is still flooding through the window, bathing the room in a mellow glow which suits our mood. We have had fun with the family tree, but the evening has been a reflective one. The mission which has brought my father and me to his home is one my great-uncle takes seriously. He has ransacked his memory, and as many old letters as he could find, for everything he knows about Laxamýri. Now, as we look forward to our journey north tomorrow and start considering how Jóhannes's son Sigurjón took up the inheritance, there is something he wants to impress on me. He does it so lightly that I barely realise, until thinking about it later, the significance of what he is trying to say.

'These things you are asking about – they didn't happen so very far in the past, you know. When *afi* Sigurjón died, I was two or three years old.'

There is something immensely tender about this word *afi*, the Icelandic for grandfather. It is the word children use for their grandpa. I used to call Sigursteinn *afi*; my own children call my father *afi*. My great-uncle was gently reminding me that the man who took over from Jóhannes at Laxamýri, his own namesake, was not a character from the distant past, but his granddad. He was asking me to remember, as I sift the truth of stories and try to probe the motivations of people in an era which seems long ago to me, that for others these times are not yet history.

'Yes,' I say. 'I'll remember.'

Uncle Sigurjón has one more story for us to ponder. In the spring of 1928, he was spending a holiday with his aunt and her husband in Hafnarfjörður, the elf-haven into which the king assuredly did not sail in 1874. He was twelve years old. Riding back to his aunt's and uncle's smallholding one afternoon, he heard the clatter of hooves behind him. Someone was riding hard from the direction of Reykjavík. The rider slowed down beside him and asked who the boy might be.

'Sigurjón Sigurðsson,' said the lad. 'I'm staying with my Uncle Árni, the minister at Garðar.'

A quick mental flip through the genealogical file in every Icelander's head enabled the stranger to place him immediately.

'Then your aunt is Líney Sigurjónsdóttir. That means you are named after your grandfather, Sigurjón of Laxamýri.'

The man slapped his thigh. 'What a strange coincidence. I have just signed the contract for the purchase of Laxamýri. I'm on my way home from Reykjavík now. I am the new owner.'

Jón H. Thorbergsson, farmer at nearby Bessastaðir, had bought the family estate that very day. My great-uncle was the first to hear the news.

'It was a very sad blow,' he tells us, putting down his coffee cup and shaking his head. 'A very sad blow.'

Sigurjón of Laxamýri

We are quite astoundingly early for our early morning flight to Akureyri. I was going to call it our crack-of-dawn flight to Akureyri, but night gets such a paltry look-in at this time of year that I'm not sure there actually is a dawn. If one did happen to crack this morning, believe me, I would have noticed, because my father and I were undoubtedly up earlier than anyone else in the entire country.

Iceland's summer weather is as chancy as Britain's, and I had drawn back the curtain of my giant picture window high up in Hótel Esja not knowing whether to expect sheets of rain, pea-soup fog or perhaps a gusty smattering of unseasonal snow. You just never know. It took a while to find out, because it was a long walk across the room, hauling back the heavy curtain designed to fool guests into thinking it gets dark. But once the window was exposed, sunshine blasted me full in the face, deliciously fresh and golden.

Out in the bay the early morning sea lay still as glass, while directly across from my window a few puffy white clouds were trifling with the flat table-top of Esja, the mountain which benignly superintends the city from the north. People say it never looks the same from one day to the next, continually altering in shape and hue according to the play of cloud, mist, sunlight or snow. As such it provides an informal weather forecasting service which enables the citizens of Reykjavík to

87

judge what to wear on the basis of how much of the mountain's comforting bulk is actually visible. Light jackets today, I would say. Esja gave the hotel its name, although since our visit, in keeping with Iceland's galloping pace of change, the place has been extended, spruced up and prosaically renamed Hótel Nordica.

If Reykjavík's nightlife has bestowed on Iceland, heaven help it, an improbable reputation as the new Ibiza, then on a morning like this you can just about believe it. There will be a chill in that pellucid air for sure, but from my centrally heated cocoon up here, the city looks as if it is dozing in Mediterranean warmth. Only the insouciant collage of red and green roofs gives the game away. Reminding me less of Spain than of the jaunty face which the Hebridean town of Tobermory turns to the blustery Sound of Mull, these are colours for taunting the elements.

Full of the joys, I bounce down to what I know will be a gargantuan hotel breakfast. Iceland has been doing these groaning spreads of cold meats, herring, eggs, fruit, bread and incomparable coffee for decades, long before Britain caught on to the breakfast buffet. Keeping a wary eye out for cod liver oil, I carry a plate piled high as Esja to join my father, who is smoking his pipe and toying with a coffee cup in the corner. Aghast, I realise he is ready to go. No breakfast for him when there is a plane to be early for. He kindly concedes three minutes for me to eat, and we are off.

In keeping with a country which bypassed the Industrial Revolution, sidestepped the train, and vaulted from horse to aeroplane, Iceland's domestic airports operate like brisk bus stations, with elegance reserved for their international cousin at Keflavík. My father and I sit down at a table in Reykjavík's spartan terminal and I immediately wish I had held out for an egg. I could have worked my way through three breakfasts in the time we now have to wait for the flight north.

Never mind. My father is in high spirits this morning. Last night's dinner has whetted his appetite for the quest. He mulls joviously over what we have discovered so far and what we are beginning to learn about Sigurjón Jóhannesson, who bestrides the history of Laxamýri like a fidgety colossus.

I tell my father how his name had beguiled me from the

first, how it had seemed as redolent of adventure and romance as Lawrence of Arabia or Scott of the Antarctic. Jóhannes Kristjánsson might have created that estate, I say, becoming carried away (light head, not enough breakfast), but it was the son who took the name with him into history. Cleopatra of Egypt, Gordon of Khartoum, Jesus of Nazareth, Sigurjón of Laxamýri . . .

'Er . . . quite,' says my father, pushing back his chair and muttering something about the departure board. His own reaction on seeing the first photograph of Sigurjón had been to suggest that he looked like a grumpy old sod.

The people who boarded small boats from the makeshift wooden pier on the beach at Húsavík in the latter part of the nineteenth century, waiting to be rowed out to one of the great steamships which anchored periodically in Skjálfandi bay, must have looked towards the lands of Laxamýri and wondered at life's disparity of fortune. They were leaving for the other side of the world and a future they hoped would offer more than bare subsistence from a meagre croft or perilous sea. The Laxamýri estate, by comparison, encompassing much of the best land on the Tjörnes peninsula as well as the jewel of the Laxá itself, was almost indecently flourishing. It was as if all the miracles of nature had cascaded down at once upon one sea-girt pocket of plenty.

The salmon caught in traps at the point where the Laxá rushes over its last falls to the sea were the biggest and fattest in Iceland. The trout were so heavy they almost tore the nets, and so abundant that the men sometimes had to take their trousers off to carry them, tying the legs together to turn their breeches into reeking bags. Seals in the bay, tempting prey for large nets or shotguns wielded from a boat, provided fresh meat in winter. In the early spring lump-fish glided in to spawn in the hospitable waters. Ptarmigan came to lay their eggs on the moor, those tenacious, doting birds which would never leave their nests, not even at the threat of fire or the approach of a horse.

Even driftwood, a precious building material in a land without trees, turned up in careless abundance along the black shore, tossed up by the sea like an extra gift which God had scarcely bothered to wrap. There was quality hay, good grazing for sheep and thick, heathery cover for the ducks nesting in the grassy islets in the river. And of course there were the eider themselves, vulnerable and valuable, feathering their nests with precious down which filled duvets all over the north. Their eggs were so delicious that when you boiled big pots of them in the summer and then dipped them in whey, they tasted like soft cheese.

So much for one family to possess. So little for so many others. It is an unhappy irony that the period when Laxamýri was at the height of its farming glory was precisely the time when as many as 15 per cent of Iceland's population were leaving. With the encouragement of the immigrant-hungry governments of Canada and the United States, more and more families were turning their backs on unproductive soil, an unfair trading system and a particularly savage battering from the elements in the last quarter of the century. Successive ferociously cold winters, combined with a destructive volcanic eruption in the Dyngjufjöll mountains in 1875 and a wave of earthquakes in 1896, finally persuaded up to twenty thousand people to leave between 1870 and 1914.

Sigurjón, however, weathered it all. Fate and an assiduous father had handed him opportunities beyond the dreams of his countrymen, but he worked like a fiend to harvest the bounty and make the place pay. From a young age it was clear that Jóhannes's eighth child had the personality for the challenge. He took life at a run, always alert for danger, always darting ahead to the next plan, always, always on the move. No one ever recalled seeing him walking anywhere. Walking was a waste of time. Sigurjón ran.

He had the lean, wiry frame you would expect of a man who rarely paused, and even in portraits his face looks restless. From the photograph in my Laxamýri book, this was a man whom P.G. Wodehouse would have had no difficulty in distinguishing from a ray of sunshine. It is a long, thin face, with a blunt beard which lengthens it further and cheeks sucked so far into the bone that he looks gaunt to the point of being haggard and disapproving to the point of misery. A figure more unlike the stout Jóhannes of the Santa Claus whiskers and benignly twitching mouth would be hard to find. But there is a wily intelligence behind those close-set eyes and a stubborn set to the hirsute mouth, which are the key to everything.

It is possible to detect the strength of Sigurjón's will as early as the age of eleven, when he began keeping vigil over the precious eider-duck nesting sites on his father's new farm, wrestling with a shotgun nearly as big as he was to blast any gull, raven, falcon or sea-eagle which dared to threaten them. You can see it in the cool way he set about taking over the entire estate in the 1860s when Jóhannes decided it was time to retire. His father sold him half the land and gave him a quarter of what was left as his inheritance, but his three brothers had the rest. So Sigurjón bargained, cajoled and persuaded until he had bought them out. You see it again in the determination with which he then set about draining marshland, constructing dykes and an irrigation system, introducing a new-fangled technique called ploughing, rebuilding livestock sheds, buying ever more land, and wrangling indefatigably over fishing rights with his neighbours further up the river.

Sigurjón was unstoppable, and no one who worked for him was allowed to stop either. He was as likely to turn his big telescope on his own labourers as on the ducks he was supposed to be minding. The workers found it irksome to be spied on – it was not unknown for them to turn their backs, drop their breeches and offer him an eyeful he was not expecting – but his vigilance ensured the work was done.

That same determination was in evidence, too, in the way he recovered after over-reaching himself in the early years of his custodianship of Laxamýri, when he had to sell off everything except the land to pay his debts. Faced with having to build up his entire stock again from nothing, Sigurjón coolly called in a few debts of his own and asked for payment in ewes. Then he offered to look after the flock he had already sold to the store-manager at Húsavík, shear them, brand them and put them on the hill, in return for being allowed to lease back ten of the ewes who were expecting late deliveries and keep their lambs. In the autumn he rode far and wide buying more lambs, the best he could find, for which he paid with driftwood, sealskins and eiderdown. He had a celebrated talent for judging the quality of a sheep or a horse without laying a hand on it, and was said to be always right. For three years he bred and sold indefatigably until the debts on the estate were paid.

Laxamýri remained in the family, but this was a brush with commercial reality which taught Sigurjón to take nothing for granted. He never forgot how close he came to losing the farm altogether. For anyone disposed to romanticise Laxamýri, it is an early lesson in how easily things could go wrong in paradise.

Airborne at last, I suggest to my father that if Sigurjón had lost Laxamýri at that time, future generations would have been saved a good deal of sighing and head-shaking. What on earth would his mother have found to talk about?

'Don't you believe it,' he grunts. 'It would probably have extended the whole thing by about sixty years. Doesn't bear thinking about.'

The plane is flying north-east over one of the great ice-fields of Iceland's interior towards Akureyri, for a long time the country's second largest town, although the continuing expansion of the conurbations around Reykjavík has now pushed it into fourth place. From there we plan to drive on to Húsavík, just eight kilometres beyond Laxamýri, and then tomorrow we'll go to the old family estate and see for ourselves what all the fuss was about.

Right now my attention has been dragged away from nesting ducks and mooning labourers to the expanse of white below us. It goes on for so long that we reckon this must be Langjökull, or Long Glacier, Iceland's second largest ice cap. From this vantage-point, Ravens-Flóki was spot-on with the name Iceland. There is nothing for miles but dazzling virgin whiteness, pierced here and there by grey shafts of mountain. It looks like marble.

In fact, I can assure you with some authority that it is not marble. I have been on a glacier and I know. Admittedly it was one of the smaller ones near the south coast, but one glacier is much like another when you are flat on your back, listening to the roar of your riderless 'skidoo' careering off towards the grey horizon like the Lone Ranger. What you discover then is that glaciers are made of snow, and that the snow is deep and soft and very wet. Skidoos are the motorbikes on skis which have become as obligatory a part of the Icelandic tourist experience these days as jet-skiing in Malaga. They have opened up Iceland's terrifying ice-mountains in ways of which even the novelist Jules Verne never conceived when he had his hero descend into the depths of the majestic Snæfellsjökull on his way to the centre of the earth.

I nearly descended into the depths myself more than once. Far from being the gleaming ice-plain of my imagination, Mýrdalsjökull proved to be a foggy snowfield full of ridges and deceptive gullies. The guide took the keenest pleasure in assembling our party at the edge of the most innocent-looking of these to offer the cheerful information that anyone who wandered too close would hurtle down hundreds of feet to join an underground river from which he or she would be unlikely to emerge for some years. I had four children under eight on that excursion and must have aged several months in the next hour. It still makes my stomach lurch to look at a glacier, even from high in an aeroplane.

Thankfully the ice below us is beginning to recede at last, to be replaced by more conventionally snow-blanketed mountain ranges. This flight across the middle of the island is making it stunningly clear why habitation is confined to the rim of Iceland. There is nothing here for people at all. Nothing. It reminds me of the map on my father's study wall, the ribbons of green I used to trail my finger along. They looked so inconsequential in relation to the mountainous slabs of white and brown, and from here we can see why.

It is to the fertile swathes around the seaports of the north that we are heading now. Forebears from both sides of the family originated up here. Although my grandparents met in Reykjavík and seemed the essence of bourgeois metropolitanism by the time I knew them, this is where they hailed from, the feisty north with its tradition of political radicalism and proud disdain for the preoccupations of the south. My grandfather's people lived in Akureyri itself, and my father has high hopes of tracking some of them down today; Ingibjörg's people, as she never tired of telling us, were at Laxamýri, across the next bulbous finger of land to the east.

It was there, in 1874, that Sigurjón Jóhannesson completed his new house.

Travellers were always calling in at Laxamýri. At times there was barely room in the old stone and turf farmhouse for everyone to sit down. It lay on the main bridleway to Húsavík, directly in the path of all human traffic in a land bereft of inns or hostels. Passers-by came to shelter from the weather, paupers shuffled up to ask for alms, wayfarers called in for a bed, friends stopped by for a glass or two as they rode past. Everyone brought news, and in that summer of 1874 there was plenty of it to share.

King Christian of Denmark was due to visit the country soon, and the new constitution was the subject of animated debate far beyond the smoky pools of Reykjavík. The works of a new breed of politically aware poets, lyrically devoted to the independence struggle, were being widely read and discussed. Right on Sigurjón's doorstep, farmers were agitating for a bigger share of the trade which had been under Danish control for centuries. They were developing far-reaching economic ideas which would lead in 1882 to the formation, here in Húsavík, of the country's first farmers' co-operative, enabling members to market their own produce and buy in goods from abroad without crippling mark-ups from the middlemen.

Sigurjón made his own views clear enough. He had little time for politics and certainly no sympathy for any anti-Danish carry-on. His own success in buying and selling goods depended on a carefully fostered friendship with the Danish owner of the Örum and Wulff trading depot at Húsavík harbour, and he had no interest in rocking that boat. Besides, he had a lot on his mind at the moment. He had a house to build.

By early summer he had everything ready. The Norwegian timber was already there, brought from the harbour by sledge the previous winter when thick snow provided the easiest means of overland transportation. The workers had been hired, the plans prepared, and Sigurjón was itching to start. The old house inherited from Jóhannes, with its dark interior and grass roof sloping almost to the ground, was dilapidated and cramped; he wanted something modern, something big and light and airy, like the sleek villas which Danish merchants had started to build around Akureyri harbour.

Today Sigurjón's one-storey, twin-gabled house with foundations of lava and walls of wood sounds extremely modest. Then, to people still living in houses like his old one, it must have seemed like a palace.

Below the ground floor he built a sunken cellar in which he stored pickled food in enormous casks, along with a barrel with leftover fish parts for the dogs, and sieves for making the thick white Icelandic yoghurt known as *skyr*. Next door he erected another timber building, almost as big as the house itself, built from driftwood he had been collecting for the purpose. He used this storehouse for cleaning the eiderdown after it had dried in the sun, and as a smithy for his metalwork. There were racks there for hanging up washing, and sometimes fish. Salt-meat and smoked trout were stored at one end. He also built a small smoke-house with wood salvaged from some of the old buildings he had knocked down.

When the building was done, a local craftsman etched the Laxamýri symbols on a decorative door-frame in the west gable: a salmon, an eider duck and a drake. Later, the date 1874 was carved on the front wall. There were bigger and fancier dwellings by then in both Reykjavík and Akureyri, but a visiting Englishman who had travelled extensively around the island declared the Laxamýri house to be unique in the Icelandic countryside.

And where did all the building momentum come from? It is said to have arisen out of a great watershed in Sigurjón's life, an event so important to him that he devotes pages to it in his memoir. It is the first story I ever heard about Sigurjón of Laxamýri.

The previous year, on the night his wife went into labour, Sigurjón had decided to stop drinking. You won't be surprised to learn that one or two salient details about that fateful night in October 1873 are disputed, but my father was clear enough when he first explained the story some years ago.

'Sigurjón of Laxamýri, a very fine landowner, married a most beautiful young woman,' he had told me, in a version replete with fairytale superlatives which I recognised as having come straight from his aunts in Iceland. 'And when this beautiful young wife went into labour in childbirth, it proved to be a very difficult one and the midwife was miles and miles away, and my kinsman was unfortunately lying there too drunk to go out and fetch her.'

What he actually said was 'pissed out of his mind', but I doubt if that came from the aunts. Unfortunately it is not what Sigurjón says in his book either. Sitting on the plane with ears popping and the stewardess singing about seat-belts, I scrabble in my bag for the dog-eared *Laxamýraræættin* book and our laborious translation. We really must sort this one out before we reach Akureyri and plunge into a different set of ancestors.

'Now see here,' I say. My father raises his head from his own book and offers the long-suffering expression he reserves for challenges to stories he has no intention of defending. 'Sigurjón says in his memoir that he was lying in bed himself the night his wife went into labour, suffering from some strange disease that made his face swell and his eyelids balloon so much that he couldn't see a thing for three weeks. Sounds like mumps. He says he was so ill and blind that he couldn't do anything to help Snjólaug, who was writhing about the bed opposite in agony. You, if I remember correctly, said he was blind *drunk*, not blind.'

'That's what the aunts said,' he retorts. 'How the hell am I supposed to know what was wrong with him?'

'Might you have made up the drunk bit?'

'Quite possibly.'

He is about to return to his reading with an air of having settled the matter, when he looks up again. 'On the other hand, Sigurjón might have suppressed it – you know, done a bit of a PR job on his own story when he was writing it up later.'

Now this is an interesting proposition: that the oral legend might have captured a truth which the subject chose to edit out of his own account. Staggeringly, it would put one of my father's stories in danger of being right.

It certainly makes more sense of the rest of the tale, which no one has disputed. Whatever the exact nature of his condition on the fateful night of 6 October 1873, Sigurjón admits he had been over-indulging for the past six years. Two near-fatal falls into the salmon river had upset him so much that he began sitting up late at night over a bottle and eating too little. When his wife Snjólaug went into a complicated labour on a night of weather so vicious there was no chance of fetching the area's far-flung midwife, he was terrified he was going to lose both her and the child. Fortuitously a drinking buddy by the name of Pétur dropped in at the height of the crisis, several sheets to the wind but shocked into at least the appearance of sobriety when he looked around and summed up the situation. Pétur had helped scores of women in childbirth and none had died yet, so he rolled up his sleeves and got on with it. Young Líney Sigurjónsdóttir entered the world safely some time later. Her father, relieved and grateful, resolved there and then never to touch another drop of alcohol again.

By all accounts, including his own, Sigurjón kept his pledge, although he always had a bottle handy for others. Then, perhaps to hold temptation at bay, he hurled himself into the work of the estate with a renewed zeal so focused and so tireless that others found it remarkable.

My father declares himself inordinately cheered by our conclusion that the aunts had this story spot-on. Of course our kinsman had been drinking that night, or else why give it up in remorse? A more suspicious mind than mine might detect relief.

Stories about Sigurjón of Laxamýri abound. By having the foresight to write up a few selected memories only months before his death, Sigurjón managed to take control of his own myth-making, as of everything else. But the story I find most revealing was not one he cared to rake over in his memoirs, although he was happy enough to relate it anecdotally. This tale was about his obsessive concern for his hay.

Sigurjón, I ought to make clear, was not ungenerous by nature, as his occasionally reckless hospitality shows. In Húsavík he once saw a man who was waiting with his family to board a ship for America drop dead on the beach. Sigurjón's response was to sweep the homeless wife and nine children into his cart and take them home with him; some of those children were subsequently raised in his own household. But as a farmer he was careful, and Snjólaug's habit of giving things away without inhibition or thought for the future used to drive him wild with irritation – especially when it involved his precious hay.

Snjólaug Thorvaldsdóttir, whom he wed in 1862, was a quiet and steadfast foil to her husband's driven personality. She was the only person who ever managed to tell Sigurjón of Laxamýri what to do. Her own generosity was legendary: it was well known that she would give away her last bowl of *skyr* to anyone who asked for it. So Sigurjón should probably have realised that his hay was not in the safest hands when he set off to Copenhagen one autumn, leaving her in charge of huge quantities while he was away for the winter. It was his misfortune that the winter proved to be an appallingly severe one, which both delayed his return and placed the livelihood of the smaller crofters at home in a peril which the open-handed Snjólaug could not ignore.

He told the story long afterwards to a young farmer by the name of Jón Haraldsson, who found himself snow-bound at Laxamýri in January 1918. Sigurjón, by then in his eighties, invited Jón and a friend to sit down at a small table in his private parlour while he perched on the edge of his bed. As the conversation turned to that winter's hay stocks, it reminded him of something which still rankled.

He had left behind 200 horse-loads the autumn he left for Copenhagen, he told them. Some of it, he conceded, was perhaps a little old (er, twelve or fourteen years, to be honest), but he had had it re-baled and re-covered. There was plenty of hay stored elsewhere to tide the Laxamýri beasts over the winter; this was extra and he wanted it kept safe till his return. It was the one and only thing he asked Snjólaug to remember before he went on his way.

Jón reports him as saying: 'After I left the house, I rode out to see the hay. There was no hole in it. It was the most beautiful hay I had ever seen in my life.

'But that winter there was a Viking sea-ice all over the north, from the end of February to the start of summer. No ship could sail to or from Iceland. So it wasn't until the middle of June that I arrived back. I had a feeling things would be bad here, so I made no inquiries at Húsavík but hurried straight home. Everything was growing and greening. A warm breeze brought the scent of birch trees, birds were breeding and summer was on its way. Dust rose under the horses' hooves. I was glad to be home.

'But what was this? Where was my old hay? I rode over to where the hay had been stored, but it had been so swept and scraped that not a wisp was to be seen. Well, I didn't wait. I rushed into the house. Snjólaug was in the kitchen, as I knew she would be. I didn't waste any time greeting her, just asked, "Well, my good woman, where is my hay – the big hay, remember, which I left out there and asked you to look after?"

'She turned to me and smiled and said, "So you're back at last."

' "Yes," I said, "but the big hay? The hay! What's happened to it?"

'She wasn't taken aback in the least. She started filling the coffee pot, saying, as if she were talking to herself about something of no importance, "Oh, the hay. Yes, that went to some hard-pressed people in Reykjahverfi, Aðaldalur, Reykjadalur, Kinn and Húsavík – yes, and a little out at Tjörnes, a little went there too. And now it's fine. The first boat has arrived with supplies, thanks be to God." She said nothing else.'

Sigurjón's guests looked at one another with raised eyebrows. And what, one of them asked mischievously, had he said to that? The old man told them at once.

' "To hard-pressed people?" I said. "To that useless rabble! May God Almighty forgive you, Snjólaug." '

And she? What had she said?

'Oh, she smiled at me with that tolerant smile of hers and said, "Wouldn't you like a cup of coffee? I think you're in need of some refreshment. I've just been filling the coffee pot." '

By this time, Sigurjón reported, he had been practically hopping with rage; but she had merely leaned against the kitchen range, not disconcerted in the slightest. The guests watched now as the old man stood up from his bed and stared over their heads at a picture, hanging on the wall behind them, of a woman. When he next spoke, it was quietly, as if he were speaking to himself.

'I never saw a wisp of that hay again,' he said.

Sigurjón's anecdote is as hilariously self-revelatory as a Browning monologue. No wonder the tale came to be written up by a neighbouring farmer, Guðmundur Friðjónsson, as a thinly disguised short story entitled *The Old Hay*. Jón

Haraldsson's account, suspiciously fluent in its recall of a thirty-year-old conversation, appeared in a 1951 newspaper article. A safe source is hard to come by in Iceland, since stories are there to be embellished, but this one has the ring of truth all the same. The master and mistress of Laxamýri were two contradictory personalities whose union yet endured with much mutual contentment for almost fifty years. As the Bishop of Akureyri would put it at her husband's funeral, Snjólaug had 'an equilibrium of the soul', which anyone would need to live in harmony with the excitable Sigurjón. But it is clear that throughout their marriage she operated a policy of velvet resistance which successfully undermined her husband's will when it mattered.

Equally, his agitation at the folly of her giving away their long paid-up insurance policy against future bad winters shows exactly why Sigurjón made such a success of farming. He may sound almost laughably mean, but this is a man who could remember the so-called Blood Winter of 1858–9, when hundreds of sheep starved to death for want of hay. He was never going to win any awards for social conscience, but Sigurjón knew the wise farmer always kept more than he needed.

At dinner last night my father and I had learned that Sigurjón paid for that trip to Copenhagen in gold, after amassing a hoard of coins from his foreign trade in smoked salmon. Gold coins? The two of us had looked at each other across the table with a silent 'Aha!' Could these have been the fabled gold coins of my Aunt Didda's smuggling anecdote – the coins slipped out in secret to Sigurjón's allegedly banished daughter?

At the other end of the table Árni Sigurjónsson, my great-uncle's youngest son, had snorted at the suggestion.

'Look, several of Sigurjón's children and grandchildren inherited those coins. I now have one myself, come to that,' he said. 'It's like the gold of the Nibelungs. This family would make a myth out of anything.'

Nibelung fantasies or not, my father continues to be heartened by the evidence that the occasional anecdote he and his sister have told me may at least bear some passing connection to fact.

First the Danish gold, then Sigurjón's dramatic conversion to abstinence.

'You see,' he says as the plane swoops in to land. 'There is usually something there in the stories, some small grain – all right, some very small grain – of truth. It's all most encouraging.'

I have to remind you that we did not know then about King Christian IX not being responsible for the first road in Iceland. Nor did we know about my dad's grandfather, Magnús the Carter, not being Magnús the Carter at all. We were about to find out about that one.

Akureyri

'*Góðan daginn*, Magnús.' The man at the Hertz rental counter in Akureyri's diminutive airport looks up eagerly when we stroll over to collect the car keys. 'Welcome home.'

He and my father chat animatedly while I sign the papers.

'Who was that?' I ask as we head outside into an overcast morning; we have left the glittering sunshine in Reykjavík.

'Haven't a clue,' beams my father. 'Nice chap, though.'

I wonder if this is what it is like to walk around Edinburgh with Sean Connery. Icelanders everywhere recognise my father. They greet him with the shy affection you might offer a long-lost relative, which, come to think of it, is probably what he is in a country where every second stranger you meet turns out to be a third cousin. But up here in the north they welcome him with an even more easy familiarity than elsewhere. He is still Magnús son-of-Sigursteinn here, a local boy done good, even if the full eight months of his infant tenure in Iceland were spent in the capital.

We are directed towards a small white car, which by virtue of having a discernible colour at all is a welcome improvement on the family Beetle of yore. I wonder idly where the jack is, but the Hertz man is nowhere to be seen and my father has adopted the airy 'Don't bother me with your technical problems' demeanour which he keeps for computers, video recorders and potential punctures. Hey ho. The roads are better these days anyway.

He waves me cheerfully towards the driving seat. Due to an over-indulgence in refreshments on the London–Glasgow shuttle last year, followed by an encounter with an eagle-eyed police officer on the drive home, he is currently not at liberty to take the wheel himself. However, he professes himself delighted to be relieved of the responsibility of negotiating the mountain roads of north Iceland and settles himself contentedly in the passenger seat, fishing in a tweedy pocket for his pipe. He ignores the seatbelt, which he has always considered a flagrant violation of his liberty to kill himself, but can't resist a twitchy glance at the speedometer. In fact, he is too busy eyeing the gauge to notice that we actually sail blithely down the wrong side of the road most of the way to town. Once the approach of a sole car from the opposite direction has alerted me to the problem, he relaxes enough to fill the car with pipe-smoke, and we have a chance to look around.

Akureyri was started by a king of Denmark, something the Icelanders would prefer not to remember. It is much more romantic to be able to claim an intrepid Ingólfur Arnarson, like Reykjavík, than to have to admit that the most important town in the north was set up as a trading station to swell the royal coffers in Copenhagen. Fortunately, they can always call on the neighbourly services of Helgi the Lean, who was the first permanent inhabitant of the land around the fjord Akureyri rests on, Eyjafjörður, making his home a few kilometres up the valley around the year 890. Helgi, the son of a Viking adventurer and an Irish princess, was a quintessentially Icelandic bet-hedger who is said to have believed in Christ but invoked Thór for sea voyages and other hardships. After he had reached Iceland safely and collected his household pillars (tossed overboard to parley with local spirits in the usual fashion), he reverted to the new faith and piously named his farm Kristnes, Christ's Ness. The site of his homestead is now a geriatric hospital.

Akureyri itself came into being when the Danish crown began leasing natural Icelandic harbours to Danish and German merchants in the sixteenth century. It was Danish traders who later built the first houses around the harbour, while the Icelanders continued to live in their stone and turf homesteads up and down the fjord. By the time the settlement received its

Jóhannes
Kristjánsson
(Laxamýri patriarch)

M

Sigurjón Jóhannesson
of Laxamýri

Snjólaug Thorvaldsdóttir

Two countries, one flag.
Magnus and Mamie Magnusson in 1989.

municipal charter in 1862, it still boasted a population of only 286. Even now, for all that it likes to be known as the capital of the north, the population is less than 16,000.

As we approach the town, the cloud is drifting so low that it is shredding against the mountains which rise sheer behind it, and the breeze blasting in through my father's open window is sharp. Akureyri is famous for revelling in sunshine when Reykjavík is moaning about the weather, but today it is the other way round. Not that it matters; it takes more than a few clouds to take the shine off Akureyri. It always looks lovely on its perch near the head of the fjord, encircled by sea and snow-encrusted mountain, the air clean and bitingly fresh. We are only about 60 miles south of the Arctic Circle here, but it is a jewel of a place.

In summer the sun never sets. It streams down the fjord long after midnight, inviting you to do all sorts of things by its disconcerting light, not least, my father is telling me as we buzz along the waterfront, play golf. The Arctic Open is held here every midsummer, he says, and they always play under the midnight sun.

'Really?'

'Um, well, I think so.'

My father is generous enough to concede that he is not, at this or any time, to be relied on for facts about golf. But I checked up later and it is true about the Arctic Open. The novelty of playing in the middle of the night on the world's northernmost golf course, a position Akureyri vigorously defends against a few upstart fairways in Norway and Finland, does indeed attract enthusiasts from across the globe every summer. There cannot be many competitions where you tee off in the evening and are still striding the links under a tangerine sky in the small hours. Showing off its mild climate and profusion of most un-Icelandic blooms, Akureyri turns the whole event into a sleep-defying party, and for that one summer solstice weekend boasts of rivalling Reykjavík as the hip place to be.

Golf may not have been introduced by Ingólfur Arnarson, as my father's old friend Jökull Jakobsson would have had us believe, but it has become massively popular in Iceland.

'I'm told you're allowed one extra club when you play on an Icelandic course,' adds my father, not to be denied his pennyworth.

'A hammer, by any chance?' I hazard.

'Exactly. A mallet for any lava which spoils your lie.' I think that's a joke and I suspect it came from Jökull, too.

It is too early in the season for golfing revellers today. Akureyri feels empty. Where *are* all its 15,000 souls at 9 a.m. on a Friday morning? Perhaps they have been up all night and have only just gone to bed, as Icelanders are wont to do in the summer. There is barely a car to be seen. Nothing moves in the streets plunging down to the harbour except an occasional solitary shopper. Hunting coffee, we find those streets full of bookshops and small art galleries with windows displaying dazzling paintings in the flamboyant pinks, reds and violent oranges which the landscape seems to bring out in its artists. There is that distinctive Icelandic feeling of civilised backwater about the place, big culture in a small town, Bond Street meets Auchtermuchty. I like it.

Akureyri requires of us a temporary shift of family focus. It is where my grandfather's family came from, the 'non-Laxamýri side', as my grandmother might have put it if her English had been up to it. Since he grew up hearing as little about this side of the family as his mother could arrange, my father is just as keen to track these ancestors down as he is to follow the Laxamýri trail. More so, perhaps, if I read the hint of mischief in his enthusiasm correctly.

His father's father, Magnús Jónsson, was a smallholder whose main claim to fame (so my dad had always told me) was that he started the first carting business in Akureyri with a four-wheeled horse-drawn cart, so that he became known ever after as Magnús *keyrari*, Magnús the Carter. So delighted was my father in his youth with the idea that his humbly born paternal grandfather had invented a carting business, that he gave this unremarked clan a name calculated to exasperate his mother. When Ingibjörg was trilling about her famous, well-off, talented Laxamýri forebears, the *Laxamýrarætt*, he baited her with the boast that he belonged to the *keyrarætt*, the carter dynasty, and was proud of it.

'At that time, remember,' he had told me, 'we were still a colony of Denmark and so Magnús was a peasant. But he was a peasant who was moving himself up by his own efforts. He built his own house, for instance, and he started a little business. My father used to describe running along behind the cart when he was a boy, nicking the occasional apple from the gardens where the bourgeosie were trying – rather unsuccessfully on the whole – to grow them. I'm afraid my mother did look down on that side of the family a bit.'

Imagine, then, my father's delight when we pop in to visit one of his Akureyri relatives and discover right away that the carter dynasty is related to kings. I knew a king or two was bound to heave into view eventually on this trail, but how satisfying to find them in the Other family tree. And not through some nebulous kinship by way of Ingólfur Arnarson at that, but through all sorts of intricate, proven links via a fellow called Ketill Flatnose, which are laid out in baffling detail on the coffee table in my father's cousin Hallgrímur's flat.

Hallgrímur Aðalsteinsson produces his family tree with the same casual pride as you might air the family seaside snaps. He is an elderly man with thinning grey hair and a look somewhere about the eyes which reminds me of my *afi* Sigursteinn, who was his uncle; Magnús Jónsson was Hallgrímur's grandfather too. Leafing through his large book of immaculately inscribed names, I can see that it goes right back to the settlement of Iceland, and then beyond to the said Ketill Flatnose, along with what appear to be several kings in Norway.

Since the conversation is in Icelandic, I have to this day only the haziest notion of what this impressive series of royal connections is actually all about. I was banking on my father understanding it, but he has either forgotten or (perish the thought) had no more of a clue at the time than I, although he made all the appropriate noises. It seems to involve a Norwegian princess, Thóra Magnúsdóttir, daughter of King Magnús Barelegs of Norway (so-called because he had a fine pair of knees and a predilection for the Scottish kilt). She married an Icelander and, er, Bob's your uncle. Real genealogical anoraks can produce such complex and far-reaching royal connections that it will come as no surprise to me if Queen Elizabeth of Windsor herself is one day knocked off her throne by an Icelander. But we in the carter dynasty are quite content with Magnús Barelegs, as long as this particular scion does not have to explain to anyone how she got there. Seated around Hallgrímur's coffee table with the book spread in front of us, we exchange complacent smiles.

Once again it is strange, if not downright perverse, that such passionate republicans as the Icelanders should be so keen to prove their descent from kings. Look at the pair of us, all but skipping down the road a few minutes later because we turn out to be related to some petty ruler with nice knees. It seems especially odd when you remember that Icelanders believed until quite recently that their country was founded by freedom-loving individuals who chose to sail off into the unknown rather than knuckle under the tyranny of a Norwegian monarch. This was a notion put about by the sagas and eagerly snapped up by patriotic Icelanders campaigning for independence in the late nineteenth and early twentieth centuries. It has now been discovered to have about as much historical validity as William Wallace, aka Mel Gibson, yelling 'Freedom!' with the last beat of his Brave Heart. But the idea has had a powerful grip on the national imagination for centuries.

The opening pages of *Laxdæla Saga*, for instance, describe our ancestor Ketill Flatnose as a powerful and well-born lord who found he could not prosper in Norway under the rule of King Harald Fine-Hair. When he learned that the king was intending to make him a vassal, Ketill called his kinsmen together and said they were either going to have to flee Norway or stay and be hounded off their lands and perhaps put to death. Two of his sons announced that in that case they would go to Iceland, where there was rumoured to be excellent land for the taking, an abundance of stranded whales, plenty of salmon and good fishing grounds all year round.

Ketill himself is reported to have been rather rude about the new island's attractions, calling it 'that fishing station' and insisting that it would never see him in his old age. He sailed off instead to stir up trouble in Scotland, but two of his sons and a daughter set out for Iceland. Since Ingólfur had already staked his claim to the south-westerly Reykjanes peninsula, Ketill's kin took over land in the west, south and north. (In case you were wondering, the husband of Ketill's daughter Thórunn was Helgi the Lean, who started our line of northern Icelanders at Eyjafjörður.)

It was this account in *Laxdæla* and elsewhere of noblemen choosing to leave Norway rather than live as slaves to a king, which gave rise to the appealing theory that Iceland was colonised by heroic republicans. It was an idea disseminated far beyond the country by Victorian medievalists like William Morris, a man of scholarly but hopelessly romantic Norse enthusiasms, who translated the sagas into English with his Icelandic friend Eiríkur Magnússon.

Iceland was extremely popular with the Victorians. They not only travelled there by the boat-load, but also appropriated its mythology and its saga-heroes for all sorts of crusades of their own at home. The right-wing essayist Thomas Carlyle was as attached to Óðin as my father, the poet Matthew Arnold was wistfully inspired by the fair-faced young god Baldur, and Morris the socialist had his political ideas bolstered by the founders of the old Icelandic commonwealth. Morris's admiration for those settlers was boundless, men who had turned their backs on a despotic king to hold aloft the dream of freedom and start their own brave experiment in democracy at Thingvellir. When he arrived off the coast of Iceland in 1873 Morris asked himself, in typically plonking verse:

> Why do we long to wend forth
> Through the length and breadth of a land,
> Dreadful with grinding of ice
> And record of scarce hidden fire,
> But that there 'mid the grey grassy dales
> Sore scarred by the ruining streams
> Lives the tale of the Northland of old
> And the undying glory of dreams?

For Morris, the reality of backward, foreign-dominated, nineteenth-century Iceland fell all too short of the old dreams. How much more disillusioned would he have been to learn what modern scholarship now suggests: that the sagas were actually engaged in an effective public relations exercise on men who, in their own way, had been just as ruthless in accruing land and stifling freedom in ninth-century Norway, and who left for Iceland because they were reluctant to pay taxes for the privilege.

My father and I discuss this on the way back from Hallgrímur's flat. For a man given to bouts of hero-worship himself, my father is unflinchingly clear-eyed about the men who settled Iceland.

'Oh, the Norwegians who sailed off to Iceland had treated their own neighbours with scant respect, I can tell you,' he says, striding off down the road to the car. 'They subjected others to exactly the kind of oppression they were unwilling to accept from Harald Fine-Hair, who was out to unify all the petty kingdoms of Norway under a single crown and demanded total acceptance of his authority. Of course this meant taxation on their lands, which they didn't like at all.'

Poor William Morris. I have long felt a comradely sympathy for the Icelandic love affair which left him struggling to separate fact from fiction. It happens to the best of us. I offer him up a small, apologetic smile as another myth crumbles in the keen Icelandic air.

My father and I are on our way now to the town library, where we have arranged to meet an obliging young local historian by the name of Jón Hjaltason, to see what he can tell us about Magnús the Carter. He is waiting for us in a minute paper-laden office at the back of the library, from which he emerges, blinking, to take us to the two houses where Magnús brought up his children at the turn of the century.

My grandfather Sigursteinn was the third of Magnús's seven children with his wife Margrét. The eldest was Hallgrímur's father, Aðalsteinn, who in later life managed the State liquor store in Akureyri. My father stayed with him after the war when he went to work on the herring boat, the *Snæfell*, during an Oxford vacation. 'The hardest work I've ever done, that herring boat,' he had been telling Hallgrímur.

Sigursteinn was bright. At secondary school he was talent-spotted by the Icelandic co-operative movement, which was recruiting likely lads to train up for the future. The first of these co-ops (formed, if you remember, at Húsavík in 1882 to a resounding silence from the area's biggest landowner) had led to the creation of others across the country. In 1902 they all joined to form the Federation of Icelandic Co-operative Societies, known as *Samband Íslenskra Samvinnufélaga.* By the time it approached my grandfather, the *Samband,* as they called it for short, was on the way to becoming the largest economic concern in the country. It needed Icelanders trained in business to take it forward, and youngsters like Sigursteinn, schooled in the north where the movement was strongest, were just what the umbrella body was looking for.

He was sent first to technical college in Copenhagen and then on a course of business studies in Hamburg for a year, before returning to start work with the *Samband* in Reykjavík. There he strolled into the town's largest department store one day with money in his pocket and a swagger in his step, and was instantly smitten by the dark-haired girl with blue eyes who sold him a bottle of eau de cologne 4711 at the perfumery counter. His studies abroad had leant him a man-of-the-world air, which he played to the hilt. With his dapper suit and rolled-up umbrella, Sigursteinn was every inch the image of an Icelander going places, although he was actually feeling rather deracinated in the capital, far from his family. Confident but vulnerable – it's always a winner with the girls. As she would breathlessly recount for years to come, Ingibjörg Sigurðardóttir, granddaughter of Sigurjón of Laxamýri, was swept off her feet.

The house where Sigursteinn was born in 1899 is just up from Akureyri's harbour at Lundargata 2. The chalet-style villa in natty two-toned lime and pale green which Jón points out to us has obviously been extended, but even so it is bigger than I expected. Sigursteinn used to remind his children every Christmas, when they prepared for the lavish Edinburgh present-giving around the tree, that his family in Iceland had been so poor that he and his siblings received only one Christmas present every year. This was sometimes an apple or, if the right boat were in, perhaps an orange. Nothing else.

He told the story to remind his children how fortunate they were, and I have found it useful to pass on myself when my own brood have pored too greedily over December's Argos catalogue. I had imagined Sigursteinn's family in something smaller than this. How strange to find the past bigger than you imagine.

The family's next house, which Magnús built for them in 1902, was larger again, although still far from palatial. Leading us up the hill to the place where it used to stand, Jón Hjaltason drops his bombshell.

'Actually,' he turns to my father with a flicker of hesitation, 'I have to tell you that Magnús was not known as the Carter here in town.'

Not Magnús the Carter? Not the founder of the *keyraraætt*? My father smiles weakly across at me. Jón offers a grimace of apology.

'It was Magnús's brother Jósef who was *keyrari*, the main carter in Akureyri. Jósef was so strong that he claimed he could carry three times as much as anyone else. He charged three times more than anyone else, too – and they paid him. He was the father of Jóhannes á Borg, your kinsman who built Hótel Borg, you know, the strongest man in Iceland. Your grandfather might have helped his brother with the carting, of course, so he would be a carter in that sense, but Jósef was the one who ran it.'

'So did they call my grandfather anything?' my father asks, a shade nervously.

'Yes indeed. He was known as Magnús *stúdent*.'

My father takes the polite dismemberment of another small saga on the chin. At least the idea of a carter dynasty is intact; he would not have wanted his mother to have the last word on that one. We agree right away that Magnús the Student has a resonance we can live with. Perhaps he had studied at the new secondary school, Möðruvellir, which was still enough of a novelty in his day to earn its pupils a name. I am already adjusting the story for my own children.

'Once upon a time,' I will tell them, 'there were two brothers, Jósef and Magnús. One was strong and the other was brainy. The strong one had a son who could lift a horse on his shoulders and went round the world being an Icelandic Strangler. The brainy one had a son who went to school, just as he had done, and studied so hard that he was asked to help his countrymen sell their fish in Britain. And that is how you come to be here today.'

Yes, it has possibilities.

We are on a grassy hillside now, with a flattened patch in the middle where Magnús's new house and outbuildings used to stand. A clump of wiry trees grows here still. This is where young Sigursteinn and his brothers and sisters grew up, and where his mother Margrét nursed herself and some of the children through the frightening tuberculosis which visited the house ten years after they moved in. I wonder how often she looked out of the window at the point where we are standing now, over the harbour and across the fjord to the mountains which never lose their snow, and worried about what would become of them all. She succumbed to tuberculosis herself on 2 June 1912, and her youngest daughter Unnur, the four-year-old baby of the family, died ten days later.

Jón says there used to be a stream running down the hill and past the house, which would have been ideal for the family's water needs. In 1906 Magnús was annoyed when the town fathers dammed the stream further up the hill to make a swimming pool. He complained it was slowing down the flow into his well, but the council told him that was just too bad. Clearly, councils don't change.

'This house was relatively small,' Jón is telling us as we potter about the slope. He has been studying the records for us and has scribbled down the dimensions.

'It was built of timber and with an iron roof, one floor and a basement underneath. The roof came up in a peak. Magnús also built another house nearby for his animals. This is quite funny because it's nearly as big as the house itself. The house was 7.5 metres by 6.3 metres and the shed was 7.5 by 5.6, which is almost the same size. He had some sheep and probably one or two cows; after all, he had to have some milk for all those children. And perhaps you know that Akureyri was the potato capital of Iceland?'

I didn't. Akureyri, bless it, is always trying to be the capital of something.

'Yes, we started to grow potatoes here about 1800. It was, of course, a Danish merchant who began the practice' (jovial grimace) 'but we took it up. Magnús had his potato garden, as nearly everybody had.'

He talks about the past in a typically intimate Icelandic way.

People who lived a couple of hundred years ago are 'we' not 'they'. Magnús Jónsson planting his potatoes at the turn of the century sounds like an old neighbour of his. I could listen all day.

My father has gone wandering about the slope with his pipe in his left hand and a concentrated, reflective look on his face. There is not much to see but plenty for him to imagine on this hill where his dad grew up. For this alone, I suspect, our trip has been worth it. Whatever we discover about Laxamýri, the carter dynasty still takes precedence in my father's heart.

The Next Generation

While Magnús the Student was digging his potatoes and driving his brother's wagon around town, the most famous landowner in the north was having another fine house built for himself, complete with cowshed and barn, just down the road by the harbour. Perhaps it was Magnús who delivered the timber. This was 1906, and Sigurjón of Laxamýri was retiring to Akureyri.

He hit the town running. At the age of seventy-three, as lithe and active as ever, Sigurjón had sold Laxamýri to his sons and was planning to see out his days with Snjólaug in the closest the north could boast to a metropolis. The herring industry had boosted the population well beyond a thousand and Sigurjón relished the bustle of town life. The trotting figure with the hooked nose and groomed beard was soon a familiar sight in the sparse streets of Akureyri. Retirement was, naturally, a misnomer. He rushed about as if his life depended on it, collecting gossip, cultivating contacts and tirelessly working to sort out the tangled financial affairs of his sons.

My father and I walk up the steps to the front door. The house which Jón has brought us to see in the area of town called Oddeyri is in the chalet style popular at the time in Iceland, with cute attic windows and a Tyrolean air which fit happily into this most alpine of Icelandic towns. Owned now by the town for rental, it has been painted a bluish grey and even now looks handsomely expensive. Sigurjón, who thought it the best house in town, paid a small fortune for it, although he wrote triumphantly to his youngest daughter that through rigorous supervision of the materials and workmanship, he had managed to have the price reduced from 22,000 to 16,000 *krónur*. He had certainly not lost his nose for a bargain.

These days the harbour is at the far end of the road, built, like so much of modern Akureyri, on land reclaimed from the fjord. But when Sigurjón and Snjólaug opened this door in the morning, they would have seen the sea lapping at the shore just a few yards away. Lingering at the top of the steps, I notice a plain white card attached to the door, bearing the name of the house. My father and I peer at it, and then look at one another.

'They called it *Laxamýri*,' my father says.

So who were these sons to whom Sigurjón consigned his blooming Laxamýri and then spent his retirement worrying about? Oh, that's easy. Drunkards. Gamblers. Ne'er-do-wells who let Laxamýri go to the wall as soon as their father was off the premises. That was the picture which had flickered down to me through the generations. No longer the exuberant anecdotes of larger-than-life success which clung to old Sigurjón, these were the Chinese whispers of failure.

Who, then, would have believed that the sons of Sigurjón Jóhannesson were actually exceptional men in their different ways, talented men, popular in their communities? It was a revelation. Drinking? Yes, some of the brothers were partial to a drink and one or two definitely overdid it, but this was a weakness shared with many Icelanders. Jóhann was forgiven his fondness for the golden glass because he became a famous writer, but his brothers were not so indulgently remembered by Laxamýri's dispossessed descendants. Gamblers? Yes, but not in the way I imagined at all. Ne'er-do-wells? Hardly. The more I consider the sons of Sigurjón, the more I think the misfortune of all but Jóhann was simply to have ended up in the wrong job.

There were five who reached manhood, as well as three daughters of whom my great-grandmother, the second Snjólaug, was the youngest. Judging from the photographs, those boys had looks as well as talent. They remind me of America's Kennedy clan, not in any detail of the features so much as in a shared handsomeness which held something akin to glamour. They had long, slim faces, aquiline noses, dark hair combed off the forehead, and usually a moustache of varying degrees of extravagance – although Jóhann is clean-shaven in portraits.

The four we know about, Jóhannes, Egill, Lúðvík and Jóhann, were all in their way creative spirits, a softer breed than their father, with considerable personal charisma. Their mother was a cousin of Iceland's finest lyric poet, Jónas Hallgrímsson, and some of that artistic sensibility seems to have rubbed off on her sons. Most of them also shared their father's interest in making money. If even one of them had inherited the business acumen to achieve it, the history of Laxamýri might have been very different.

They all grew up at Laxamýri, where Snjólaug, the second youngest, played childhood games with Jóhann, the baby of the family, in the meadows above the river, which she talked about to the end of her days. But only Jóhannes and Egill devoted their lives to the estate, at first helping their father to run it under a joint leasing arrangement and then buying it together on his retirement. Lúðvík settled in Akureyri as a teacher, although he continued to influence the fortunes of his old home through hapless meddling in the herring business. Jóhann left for Copenhagen to train as a vet and stayed on to pursue his vocation as a playwright.

Thorvaldur, the second eldest, farmed for a while at Saltvík, one of the small properties on the estate, but committed suicide at home in Laxamýri in 1896, at the age of thirty, leaving only silence. It is strange that in a family as close and anecdote-rich as theirs, his tragedy should have left no story to be frenziedly spun from Reykjavík to Edinburgh in years to come. Only one whisper has crept through the generations, the rumour that *ástarsorg*, the sorrow of unrequited love, was to blame for the death of this young farmer. So simple and unadorned an explanation. Perhaps that means it is true.

Jóhannes, the eldest, named after his grandfather, is the one whose acquaintance I found it easiest to make. His last surviving daughter, Líney Jóhannesdóttir, was still living in Reykjavík.

She had written a book about her childhood at Laxamýri, in which she described her father as 'a lonely thinker with a child's heart'. Through her memories I pictured a dreamy soul, a lover of books and plants, a boy with a wanderlust his father used to dread. In his teens it was Copenhagen to which Jóhannes disappeared, after hunting cormorants to earn a passage against his father's express wishes. Later he sailed off to the United States to study botany. Sigurjón, who knew how seductive the New World was proving to Icelanders, was terrified he would never see his eldest son again.

'I am convinced, my dear Jói, that you can have a better life at home,' Líney quotes him writing to Jóhannes from Laxamýri in 1891. 'I don't like the idea of life in America at all, especially in the United States where you are always fearing for your life . . . If you were to seek education over there, then it would be certain that I should never see you again in this life, because, as you know, I have never been keen on going to America and will not go there either, no matter what happens.'

Jóhannes's first adventure in the United States can only have confirmed his father's fears. Before he left on his travels, he had managed to collect a specimen of every plant in Iceland, except one which grew too far away for him to reach at the foot of the Vatnajökull glacier. He packed this treasured collection into an iron box and took it with him to the States, where he hoped it would help him secure a place at university. But the box was stolen on the way and every single plant lost. Much later he sought out the remaining plant at Vatnajökull and kept it with him until he died, a telling indication of how much the lost collection had meant to him.

Arriving in Seattle without his passport to university, his chance of becoming a botanist lost with it, Jóhannes turned to the sea. Stuffed with salmon, the Pacific straits north of the city were already providing immigrant Icelanders with an excellent living. Jóhannes took out a loan on a fishing boat and for the next four years drifted contentedly up and down the coast in the sunshine.

In years to come Jóhannes would tell his children that Laxamýri was the most beautiful place on earth, except for Seattle. Then he would laugh, so that they were never sure if he was joking or not. He enthralled them with the sights he saw on his travels across the continent: sights as strange to Icelanders as trees a thousand years old, trains, casinos, bars where the women danced on tables, black men who were treated like dirt and executed without trial, Indians who had come to Seattle to settle in tents on the riverbank. He learned to imitate the sounds of the Native American language, and many years later, when Laxamýri was gone and he was an old man washing bottles in the state liquor bottling plant in Reykjavík, he would still jump around doing manic 'Redskin' dances to entertain the children in the street.

Shortly after the trip to Iceland with my father, I returned to Reykjavík alone to visit Líney, who has since died. She looked instantly familiar, a watery-eyed woman of eighty-eight, with an aquiline nose exactly like the one sported by her Uncle Jóhann on the Laxamýri memorial.

'Have you noticed it?' her son, a Reykjavík banker, whispered proudly as he introduced his mother. 'It's the Laxamýri eagle-nose. She has the real thing.'

Here, too, to have Laxamýri-anything was to be blessed indeed.

Líney Jóhannesdóttir reminded me of my grandmother and her sisters: small, a little inclined to dumpiness, with hair that had barely turned grey swept back in a bun of the kind my Great-aunt Snjólaug wore at my wedding. She had an engaging smile and the sort of mesmerising memories which the very old sometimes retain for times long past. Behind her on the wall of her son's living room hung her portrait as a young woman, the long nose inhibiting beauty, but slim and attractive with troubled eyes.

She still remembered the mannerisms of Sigurjón, her grandfather. ('He ran everywhere,' she said in her quivering voice. 'No one could keep up with him.') Laxamýri itself she talked of with an anger which was still raw more than seventy years after she had left. And she remembered Jóhannes, her father, with tearful affection.

'Do the Indian noises for her, Mamma,' urged her son, also (brace yourself) a Jóhannes.

Without a moment's hesitation, the old lady launched into an alarming sequence of gurgles, grunts and clicks. She said it was the language her father had taught her, recalled from the days he lived among the Indians. Any self-respecting Native American would have been mystified, no doubt, but I was entranced. It brought the past exhilaratingly close that evening – to be sitting in a modern Icelandic house in the twenty-first century, listening to the sounds a son of Laxamýri had learned on his American travels in the 1890s.

Jóhannes came home at the behest of his father, who was tireless in his efforts to entice his first-born away from the dangerous enchantments of the New World. Sigurjón fired off persuasive letters with every passing boat, trying as many ruses as he could think of to bring Jóhannes home. He warned him that his fingers would catch a disease from the poisoned skin of American salmon, mocked the salmon over there as being no bigger than herring anyway, and promised to guarantee personally any loan required for the passage back. In the end, he offered Jóhannes Laxamýri itself.

Líney was convinced that Sigurjón omitted to tell him he would be sharing the farm with his brother Egill; otherwise, she could not believe he would ever have come back. Whether that is true or not, Jóhannes gave in at last. He abandoned the life of a Pacific fisherman and any remaining scientific aspirations, and returned to become a farmer.

Egill must have been even more disconcerted to find himself sharing Laxamýri with his older brother. The most natural farmer among the sons and the most obvious successor to his father, he was already farming Laxamýri when the prodigal son swanned back to divide the inheritance. The brothers remained close, but it must have been hard for Egill to swallow.

Egill, too, had talents which could have served him well in a different life. He could do anything with his hands. He had trained as a silversmith and made silver sockets for whip handles and delicate ornamental clasps for the black head-pieces women wore with their traditional costumes. He carved the figures of saga-heroes out of wood with a knife, produced fine carpentry and was a clever metal-worker, as his father had also been. Later he learned to be a goldsmith, fashioning jewellery and watches for clients.

It may have been in these pursuits that Egill's heart really lay. At one point he certainly considered making a career out of them. While Jóhannes was still in America, Egill wrote to ask whether there might be any openings out there for someone with his skills. But nothing came of it, and he remained a Laxamýri farmer.

Their younger brother Lúðvík was the family eccentric, a teacher by trade but a gambler by instinct. Not, I now realise, a gambler in the sense my father believed his mother had meant when Ingibjörg talked about the Laxamýri brothers; he imagined some rakish roulette wheel, or a softly lit, green baize table on which decadent card games were played late into the night while the estate expired through neglect. But it was speculation my grandmother had meant, rather than cards or casinos. The mistranslation of the Icelandic only added to the general murkiness of a story which I doubt anyone who came after really understood.

Gorgeous, dreamy-eyed Lúðvík's big idea was to make money out of fish, by investing in an industry which was dangling the prospect of quick bucks as it began to undergo dramatic changes at the turn of the century. Rather late in the day, motorboats and trawlers were ushering the industrial age into Iceland. The first 2-horsepower paraffin motor was installed in a six-oared Icelandic fishing boat in 1902, and three years later the first Icelandic trawler, bought from Scotland, began operating from Hafnarfjörður. The new technology made extensive cod and herring fishing possible. Lúðvík, with his share of the Laxamýri inheritance in his pocket, was determined to be in on the boom.

He was not alone in seeing the chance for profit. This was Iceland's future, the industry which would drive the transformation of the country into the advanced modern civilisation it is today, and many did become rich on the vastly improved yield. Between 1902 and 1930, annual fish catches multiplied five-fold, the number of people out at sea doubled, and the numbers engaged in fish processing tripled. However, buying into that future required huge injections of capital and considerable luck. The flighty herring created a Klondyke situation in Iceland: when they were plentiful, people could become rich;

when they were absent, it was a disaster which bankrupted investors and ruined livelihoods right down the chain.

Boom and bust, the Icelandic addiction – and Lúðvík was in the thick of it. One by one his entrepreneurial ventures crashed, until eventually they sucked in Laxamýri itself.

My father has come over all nostalgic about the herring. The visit to Hallgrímur has revived memories of a Klondyke summer of his own in 1949, which he spent as the *Snæfell*'s junior deckhand. He earned so much money at sea that at the end of it he was able to start buying the collection of Icelandic books which now lines three rooms of his home in Scotland.

'Akureyri looked a bit different then, but I think we tied up somewhere down there,' he says, waving vaguely in the direction of the harbour. 'Best herring boat in the north of Iceland.'

We have strayed into a grey-looking café for lunch. It possesses all the intimate charm of a Moscow canteen, but breakfast was too long ago for us to care. My father is reminiscing thoughtfully, over a redeemingly tasty plate of fish pie.

'It was skippered, this boat, by a fellow called Egill Jóhannesson, the herring king of his day. He was a little man with spectacles, enormously energetic, who would go stark-staring bonkers whenever herring were around.'

Lúðvík Sigurjónsson might have dreamed of such a summer. The herring turned up with a vengeance. Catches came so big and so fast that the crew of the *Snæfell* barely had time to sleep. Long experience had taught the skipper exactly where to find them.

'It wasn't just a question of throwing out a net and hoping for the best,' says my father, lowering his voice and starting to measure his words, a sure sign of a story on the way. 'You had to wait until you could see them breaking the surface in a huge rippling mass, moving slowly with the current.

'The secret then was to get to the herring before the shoal submerged again. Two boats were dropped unceremoniously from the stern of the ship, carrying between them a long purse-net. Then the boats would be cast off and race away to intercept the shoal. Before they reached it, they would separate and move off in a wide circle to get right round the shoal.'

I love him when he gets into his stride like this, organising a memory and making pictures. It's like being back on his window-sill again.

'Speed was now imperative. The moment the leading fish touched the net, the whole shoal would submerge, so the net had to be closed on the surface and pulled tight at the bottom to form a purse. All the herring were trapped now and we could lift them from the water at leisure.'

He laughs. 'But not much leisure. At any moment another shoal might appear on the surface, and the skipper on the bridge would go mad again, screeching at us to get on with it, get on with it, and go after the next one.

'Have I ever told you how I nearly drowned once? It was my job to cast off the two boats from the mother-ship once everyone was on them, and then jump down myself into a pile of netting on one of them. Only one day I missed the boat and plunged right into the middle of the sea.

'"Leave him be! Leave him be!" bellowed the skipper. "Just get the herring, for God's sake!"

'So there I was, floundering away, until luckily the cook, Eggert, who was the only other person left on the ship, saw what was happening. He reached down with a gaff, hooked my oilskins and hauled me back on board.'

'Surely the skipper didn't really mean to leave you there?' I say, mildly shocked. Never mind his life; this was my existence hanging in the balance, too.

'Of course he meant it. He couldn't hang around to rescue junior bloody deckhands. The man had his reputation as the herring king to keep up.'

At the comfortable distance of more than half a century on dry land, my father smiles fondly at the thought of this hero of the seas who would not limp while his outboard motors were the same length. Sounds like a madman to me, but maybe you needed that kind of fanatical drive for success as a trawlerman in Iceland.

Young Magnus spent his few free moments on the trawler scribbling stories in notebooks, a pastime which the rest of the crew regarded with some bemusement. What kind of stories, I ask him?

'Oh, ideas for poems, novels, plays. Nothing ever came of them. I wanted to be the next Jóhann Sigurjónsson, of course.'

I suppose it's just as well he wasn't aiming to be the next Lúðvík Sigurjónsson. That great-uncle was not the safest of role models for a chap who wanted to keep his herring earnings safe in his pocket.

In the big town-house on the shore, Sigurjón was pacing up and down his room, dictating a letter to one of his sons. It was 1910. Laxamýri was constantly on his mind and, as usual, he was worried.

Egill and Jóhannes were not running the business as he would have wished. Jóhannes, the thwarted botanist, was more interested in admiring the birds rioting among the islets than watching the accounts. Egill held the business reins, but too loosely for his father's liking. At times it seemed he was spending more time making those gold watches of his and riding about the district on official community business than he did on the farm. Some of the loans he had taken out were, in Sigurjón's view, unwise.

Nor did he feel Egill was dealing with people as cannily, or firmly, as he himself would have done. The pair even gave away hay in winter with as deplorable a wantonness as their mother; they never seemed to understand when it was time to bang a fist on the table and just say no. All in all, there was a lack of his own singleminded farming focus in both these brothers which bothered the old man.

He was also worried about Lúðvík, who seemed to be perpetually in financial trouble. Who knew where that was going to end? And there was Jóhann, still trying to sting him for money from some artist's garret in Copenhagen. When on earth was that young man going to get a proper job?

Sigurjón had been venting his frustrations in unfailingly loving but persistently concerned letters to his sons ever since he moved to Akureyri. He dictated them to his daughter Soffía mostly, who worked nearby as a masseuse, and sometimes to Egill's teenage son Sigurður when he was in town. There are 173 of them collected in the county archives at Húsavík Museum, each one dense with farming instructions and urgent admonition.

Most of the letters are to Egill and are full of forthright advice about every aspect of the business: the eiderdown and the salmon fishing; how to deal with neighbours ('You have to find this chap, and in a quiet manner let him know what's what'); how to sort out the tenants of the smaller farms on the estate; how to manage the finances ('Have a care that you take better care of your financial affairs than your brother Lúðvík'). The tone is affectionate, but you sense the increasing agitation of an elderly man whose mind is still active, as he tries to steer a path for two middle-aged sons in a job to which neither is completely suited, through a world which is fast slipping out of his grasp.

Iceland was changing. Sigurjón had been able to run his empire like a lord of the manor, running lives as well as a business. But increased commerce and industry in the coastal trading settlements were creating different possibilities for work, which meant that people stopped contracting themselves to farms like Laxamýri for a whole year at a time. At the same time new laws, long resisted by big landowners like Sigurjón, introduced greater freedom and rights for workers. The farmers who once had total control over their labour found it was not as available, compliant or cheap as it had been. Already the methods of control and influence which Sigurjón keeps urging on Egill in the letters – putting the screws on someone here, squeezing a bit there – are starting to sound like an anachronism.

The development of the co-operative company at Húsavík had also changed the area's commercial dynamic. The brothers fell out with the new owner of the Danish trading depot, whose father had been a close friend of their own father, and dealt with the co-op instead. But it was precisely by playing the old Danish trading game that Sigurjón had obtained the best deals. His sons were never as crafty at seeing on which side their bread was buttered.

The economic pressures mounted as the new century progressed. Salmon prices were hit by a depression between 1907 and 1909 and later by the First World War, causing Laxamýri's profitable smoked salmon market to collapse. The salmon catch had already been badly affected by laws stipulating that no one could set traps for fish across more than one-third of the breadth of a river, laws which set Sigurjón's blood pressure rocketing every time he thought about them.

So there was plenty to agonise over in his retirement. The letter he was writing from the Oddeyri house on 23 February 1910 was a rare one to Jóhannes, apologising for always writing to Egill when he really meant whatever he said to be for both of them. He starts by commiserating on the news that whooping cough has reached Laxamýri and hoping the children will survive. Jóhannes had already lost four sons in babyhood (another would be born and die within a month that same year), and the grandparents in Akureyri were fearful about the health of his young daughters.

He goes on to offer advice about the Laxamýri hay (naturally), which someone has told him just this morning is looking good. Then he turns his attention to a fishing boat Lúðvík has invested in, for which he is now desperate to find a buyer. 'I asked Egill to sell Lúðvík's boat if possible,' he writes, adding plaintively: 'It has a very good engine in it.'

This boat had long been the bane of Sigurjón's life. Three years ago he had told Egill that the fetters were tightening around Lúðvík, and his own responsibility as guarantor of the loans was frightening. 'I have put myself into terrible responsibility for him,' he wrote, 'and how I'll get out of it, I do not know.' By 1910 he was worrying that a friendly bank manager who had been giving Lúðvík loans without collateral had died, and a harder breed of businessman was likely to take over. He was afraid that Lúðvík would get next to nothing for the boat, because at this stage of the boom and bust cycle everyone was trying to sell. The financial problems went on and on, year after year.

My Great-uncle Sigurjón in Reykjavík remembers Lúðvík himself later in life as an engagingly eccentric uncle who always seemed to be either a millionaire or a pauper. But Lúðvík's father and brothers saw few signs of the millions.

In 1916, still following the dream of great enterprises and quick profits but with no obvious signs of expertise to support it, Lúðvík launched himself into herring salting. He acquired land on the seashore at Siglufjörður, at the head of the peninsula north-west of Akureyri, which the herring industry was transforming from a tiny shark-fishing village into what would become the northernmost, and one of the largest, towns in Iceland. With Siglufjörður exporting 200,000 barrels of salted herring in that year alone, it made good sense for Lúðvík to set up his own plant there. Or rather, it would have made sense, if he had put it in the right place.

But according to an unpublished paper stored at Siglufjörður's Herring Museum, he could hardly have chosen a worse position for what became known as Lúðvíksstöð (Lúðvík's Place). The site he picked at the north end of the point had no defence against the northerly winds or the heavy seas and ice-floes these encouraged. At least twice he had to rebuild the plant after it sustained massive damage, and there are no records of much salting activity there at all.

In 1925 he acquired an 18-ton motorised fishing boat which he named the *Sigurjón* (his father, birling in his grave at the prospect of more boat problems, would not have been flattered), which started herring and cod fishing from Siglufjörður the next year. In the summer of 1927 his bank in Akureyri foreclosed on a loan in the middle of the herring season and Lúðvík had to stop the salting which, ironically, had for once been going well that season. In a gesture which was considered exceptionally scrupulous for a herring speculator, he gave his workforce pledges for their unpaid wages to cover the salting which had already been done, and rented or loaned the *Sigurjón* to the crew for the rest of the season. It was sold the following February and Lúðvík was left penniless.

It may be that Lúðvík also did his best to shield his backers from other losses along the way, which were many. But the people who supported him were still hurt, not least his brothers at Laxamýri. It is hard to establish exactly when and how Egill was drawn in, but Laxamýri was certainly used as collateral for loans. When these were called in, it seems that Egill and Jóhannes had to raise capital by selling off many of the smaller farms which their father and grandfather had added to the estate. Eventually they mortgaged the farm of Laxamýri itself.

Whatever the details of the family's involvement in Lúðvík's adventures, it is certain that Laxamýri was left badly equipped to withstand the other pressures facing it in the new century. One thing is clear above all: wagering your all on the herring, economic saviour of Iceland or no, was a bigger gamble than any roll of the dice.

Perhaps Lúðvík should have stuck to teaching. If he had been a more competent, or perhaps even a more ruthless, business-man, we might be remembering him today as a trawler tycoon, one of the tough entrepreneurs whose gambles paid off and who drove the Icelandic fishing industry often mercilessly forward in the twentieth century. But whether in the business of the sea, or on the land bequeathed by their father, the Laxamýri brothers were never quite skilled or ruthless enough.

'Quite the most beautiful little town in the whole world,' declares my father, never one to stint on superlatives where Iceland is concerned.

We are driving out of Akureyri, along the bridge over the fjord, squinting in the afternoon sunshine which has nudged through the clouds just in time for our departure.

As the road rises into the mountains and briefly curves back on itself, I snatch a final look at the town where old Sigurjón thought he was going to end his days. There it is, reclining in a bowl of sunlight beside the water, beguilingly beautiful.

'You're right,' I say.

'Well, that must be a first. What am I right about?'

'Akureyri. Quite the most beautiful little town in the whole world.' He beams. Another twist in the road and the home of his forefathers is out of sight.

We are climbing eastwards through the mountains towards the next indentation in the northern coastline, Skjálfandi Bay, on which lie both Laxamýri and the town of Húsavík, where we are planning to spend the night. I wonder if this precipitous road, smoothly surfaced now, follows the same route as Sigurjón took when he finally left his house on the harbour and made his way back to the family estate in 1916. Probably not. It would have been a long ride on horseback for an elderly man. More likely he went by boat, taking with him whatever he felt he needed to see out the rest of his life, along with one possession which had been specially commissioned to see out his death.

His beloved Snjólaug had died in 1912. He had buried her on a hill high above the town, in a stone chamber with space for two, and asked the carpenter who had made her coffin to hammer up a matching one for him. He tried living without her in the Oddeyri house, but in the end the loneliness was not to be borne. He missed Snjólaug's serene presence around the place, quelling him with a look and giving away his worldly goods with every knock on the door. It was time to go.

'I will never return to Laxamýri,' he had written emphatically only a few years before to his daughter, my great-grandmother, Snjólaug, when he was trying to persuade her and her husband to move from Reykjavík to Akureyri, buy his house off him and look after him there in his old age. Sigurjón had couched the plea in his usual persuasive style: 'I recall that you mentioned once that you would count yourself lucky to be able to take care of your parents during our last days'. But his daughter, who had a touch of her mother's steel about her, resisted the pressure. So here he was now, off instead to the place he thought he had left for ever.

What Egill and Jóhannes thought of the idea, with two big families already squashed into one household and the business accounts in a state they might prefer their father not to see, can only be guessed. But perhaps they understood that here, in the end, was where he belonged.

In any event, the time had come for Sigurjón of Laxamýri to take up his coffin and return to the house he had built the year the king visited Iceland.

10

The Road to Laxamýri

The road is high and winding and we meet next to nothing on it. I do wish my father wouldn't grip the door handle like that on the bends.

'I know you're keen to get there, dearest, but please don't feel you have to take every corner as fast as that one,' he observes at one point, mildly enough. The rest of the time he puffs quietly at his pipe beside me, and we drive on through a landscape of grass, rock and dawdling mountain stream in companionable silence.

I had forgotten how comfortable we are with silences, he and I. Neither of us is as adept at chattering as my mother, who if she were with us would be offering a running commentary on whatever popped into her head, with a song or two for good measure, doubtless topped off with the heretical suggestion that no matter how imposing this landscape might be it really is not a patch on the Scottish Trossachs. (Icelanders should not be offended: she thought the Sea of Galilee a poor exchange for Loch Lomond and would doubtless consider the Great Wall of China an extravagant variation on Antonine's efforts in Scotland.)

No, when we are on our own my father likes to expound, I to listen, and in between we are happy to be quiet. I haven't a clue what he is thinking about right now as he sits there smoking, eyelids drooping. He is probably wishing he was dozing at home in front of the television cricket, instead of careering up and down some interminable mountain with a daughter who he clearly feels has regressed to an age too young to be trusted behind the wheel of a car.

He would be glad to know that I, for my part, am extremely wide-awake, more alert than ever before to the vast emptiness of Iceland, even of the parts like this which are lived in and cultivated. The scale of what the Icelanders have been up against in developing their extraordinary land-mass is in evidence wherever you look. Just think of where we are now. It's Route 1, the ring-road around Iceland, the weather is perfect, and all we have passed is a couple of red-roofed farmhouses, a few sheep and one of those lumbering four-by-four giants, squatting on tyres as big as elephants, which the Icelanders love. The statistics parroted in the guidebooks are as starkly meaningful in this desolate, hill-farming landscape as when we flew over the glacier: a total area of 102,819 square kilometres, of which 52,000 square kilometres is wasteland, 12,000 is covered by ice-fields, 11,000 by lava-fields, 4,000 by sand deserts and 3,000 by lakes. That leaves only 20,000 square kilometres which can be used for pasture and a mere 1,000 square kilometres under cultivation. Every time I consider it I am impressed all over again by the victory of the Icelanders, so very, very few of them, over this stroppy landscape.

'The welfare of nations does not depend on the size of populations or on their possessions,' said Jón Sigurðsson, the man who led the struggle for home rule in the second half of the nineteenth century and whose birthday was chosen for the declaration of the republic on 17 June 1944. 'A nation is successful if it is capable of seeing the advantages of its country and using them in the manner they should be used.'

It is a maxim with enormous resonance in the successes of modern Iceland, from the fish-processing factories to the Blue Lagoon, the pop music innovations of Björk to Reykjavík's world-renowned gene bank, the geothermal plants in their clouds of billowing steam to stained glass art so lovely it makes you shiver. The sadness – and I feel it keenly out here – is in how long it took the good times to come and how many people left these mountain valleys before the tide began to turn, often the most enterprising and adventurous whom Iceland could ill afford to lose. Sigurjón's own widowed sister, Sigurveig, emigrated to Argyle, Manitoba, with her three daughters; seeing them off on the boat at Húsavík, he gave each of them a gold coin for the journey.

Iceland's emigrants did well in the New World, but the desperation which drove many of them there is still remembered, not only here but in the communities in Canada, with resoundingly Norse names like Gimli in Manitoba, where they settled. There you will find Icelandic still spoken, *hangikjöt* served on rye bread just the way my grandmother did it, and a lingering third-generation homesickness among these 'Western Icelanders' for the old country which found it so difficult to support their ancestors.

Yet the way the Icelanders emerged in the end from hundreds of years of natural catastrophe, recurring epidemics, famines, under-nourishment, colonial neglect and deep cultural lassitude is as impressive as any of the watersheds in world history. The effects were not felt quickly enough for those who left, but looking back now on the later nineteenth century you can see the signs of a nation starting to believe in itself again. You watch as writers forge a literary renaissance by celebrating the heroic ideals of the old golden age, kept alive from one generation to the next but now seized on as a tool of nationhood. Poets like Snjólaug's cousin Jónas Hallgrímsson encourage their countrymen to be proud of the physical beauty of the land, not merely daunted by its power. Scholars such as Jón Sigurðsson turn politician to start the process of wresting home rule from the Danish government. Decked fishing boats and, later, trawlers begin seriously exploiting the Icelanders' biggest natural advantage, the sea, as towns are built on cod and herring. Free trade with other countries at last encourages enterprise, with the co-operative movement gradually boosting the economy. Institutions of all sorts are founded: an agricultural school, a navigation college, the first newspaper, a theological school, a medical school, the National Museum, the Museum of Natural History, the Reykjavík Theatre Company. Eventually even the ferocious heat under the ground, source of so much grief over the centuries, is turned to the Icelanders' advantage.

I disturb my father's reverie to ask him how it was they started to harness the elements, and he swings instantly into lecture mode.

'Ah, that was Erlendur Gunnarsson, of Sturlureykir, near Reykholt. About 1911, I think. Let me tell you about him. An excellent fellow.'

According to my father, Erlendur was the first man to harness geothermal energy for heating his home and cooking his food. Since the *reyk* part of his address means smoke, he must have been well placed to observe the behaviour of the hot-springs hissing into the sky in a whoosh of steam below his home.

'It was ingenious. Ingenious,' my father enthuses. 'Erlendur had never been to school, never learned physics or engineering, but he made the crucial observation that although water doesn't rise, steam does. Farmers in Iceland had always built their homesteads on high ground, above the hot-springs, and they had no way of pumping the hot water up the hill. But this guy found a way of piping the steam up to his farm, and then he designed a cooking range to utilise it. Sheer genetic resourcefulness.'

He rushes on, warming to his theme, just as Erlendur's house did. 'It had its drawbacks, of course. Steam leaked out at every joint and the whole house smelled of brimstone. His wife rebelled, I'm afraid, which is perhaps why no other farmers followed his example for several years.'

This is a suspiciously good story. I am just opening my mouth to skewer him with a razor-sharp interrogation about his sources, when he spots something out of the window.

'Look down there,' he says, his voice suddenly soft. 'Slow down a minute, will you? Isn't that a wonderful sight?'

A herd of Icelandic horses is idling along the banks of a broad stream in the valley below, shaggy manes flopping over their eyes. They look like mythical golden creatures from up here on the road, and my father's eyes are shining at the sight of them. He adores the breed, mainly, of course, because it is Icelandic and has been here since the first nimble pioneers ambled out of the settlers' ships in the ninth century, but also because hardy, sure-footed horses like these were long what bound Icelandic society together. They brought the family chieftains to Thingvellir from every corner of the land, across mountains, rivers and lava plains. They kept people in touch over vast distances, in winter as well as summer. With the exception of the boat, a perilous option at the best of times, they were Iceland's sole freight and transportation system until well into the twentieth century. As heroes, I dare say they even outdo Iceland's fêted moss.

Since they have always borne my own attempts to ride them with the sweetest of tempers and a discerning disregard for anything I have instructed them to do, I too hold Icelandic horses in the highest regard. I can see why William Morris became so attached to the patient beast which carried him on his travels that he insisted on taking it back to England with him.

For years my father gave a home to two elderly members of the breed in a field next to his house near Glasgow. They were called Skími and Bleikur, one dark as chocolate, the other pale beige, and they played and nuzzled and ran in the wind until each died and was buried with due ceremony within sight of my father's study. As the herd recedes into the distance, a blur of unkempt mane and shiny summer coat, he gazes back through the car window with delight.

Before my father went and spoiled it all by marrying my mother, his own mother had high hopes of an alliance between the House of Laxamýri and the royal House of Norway. It was a great disappointment to Ingibjörg that my father's student friendship with Princess Astrid of Norway did not lead to the altar. My father tells me (with that curious, eye-avoiding demeanour which parents adopt when discussing affairs of the heart with their offspring) that, contrary to the mythology he allowed to grow up around it, the relationship did not even lead to a kiss. But his mother was convinced it was a grand romance in the making.

Ingibjörg met the princess when she travelled to Oxford with my grandfather in 1950 to watch an Icelandic play which Magnus was producing (in English) for the Jesus College dramatic society. Hearing the applause for her son's production of playwright Davíð Stefánsson's *The Golden Gate* was cause for pride enough, but to take coffee in his college digs afterwards with the King of Norway's daughter brought fluttering joy of an even higher order. Her hopes soared further when a box of chocolates, chosen with exquisite taste, arrived in the Edinburgh post from Astrid some days later.

I suspect my father did nothing to disabuse her. For a young Oxford man-about-town to whom image was everything, a princess on the arm was not to be cast lightly aside. His look at the time consisted of a blazer, yellow pig-skin gloves and a rolled-up umbrella carried so exclusively for effect that, when asked by my mother on a later date to shield her from a shower on Cathkin Braes, he had to admit shamefacedly that the umbrella was full of holes and useless in the rain.

By the time I remember my father, the blazer had been usurped by the ubiquitous tweed jacket, and the princess by the real love of his life. Mamie Baird was a merry tomboy of a reporter from Glasgow whose only acquaintance with royal residences was the bell on the front door of Birkhall House, Princess Elizabeth's honeymoon retreat on Deeside, in which she once got the finger of her glove stuck for several uproarious minutes in pursuit of a newspaper scoop.

Swallowing her disappointment, Ingibjörg had to acknowledge that the usurper was a likeable girl, able to charm Sigursteinn at his grumpiest and gratifyingly keen on Iceland, with which she had been hastily familiarising herself. But the fact remained that she was no princess. Her late father, a passionate Labour man, had worked as a school janitor rather than a king and she lived with her mother and twin sister in a council house in the burgh of Rutherglen, near Glasgow. Mamie will doubtless have assured Ingibjörg that Rutherglen was a *royal* burgh which had received its charter as far back as 1126 from no less a monarch than David I of Scotland himself. This is something Ruglonians love to boast about because it puts them one up on Glasgow, their upstart neighbour along the Clyde, but it is just possible that Magnus's mother was less impressed.

When Ingibjörg went to Rutherglen to meet her son's prospective mother-in-law for tea, it was probably the first time she had been inside a council house. It might even have been her first exposure to a working-class high tea, a knife-and-fork meal of cold meat and salad followed by buttered bread and toasted scones. In Edinburgh, one had dinner. Mamie ensured there was no social embarrassment by swiftly removing the teacups which her mother, in the finest traditions of a Scots high tea, had set at each place. She knew society folk in the capital liked coffee served after the food, not tea with it.

Despite the ocean of life experiences between the two mothers, the occasion passed off with genuine warmth. If Ingibjörg's thoughts ever flickered from the spotlessly plain Rutherglen living room to the Norwegian royal palace, she was much too well-bred to let them show. My unassuming maternal grandmother likewise found her guest charming. My father adored his new mother-in-law whom he promptly dubbed Weeskin, from the affectionate Icelandic term, *litla skinnið*, for anyone small.

Mamie had no qualms about marrying into a bourgeois Edinburgh family with posh Icelandic roots. With a Scottish grammar school education behind her, a steady Burnsian conviction that 'a man's a man for a' that' and a Highland grandmother as proud of her descent from clan chieftains as any Icelander of his kings, my mother had self-confidence enough to have taken on Buckingham Palace with equanimity. It helped that she was earning far more than my father by the time they met anyway. He was an impecunious postgraduate student, penning Edinburgh Festival reviews for the *Scottish Daily Express* in his vacation to fund the next term's study in Denmark; she, having started in newspapers as a seventeen-year-old because the family could not afford university, was their chief features writer.

They met in the cramped Edinburgh office of the *Express*. Aged twenty-four, Magnus was scanning the files with urgent concentration to see if his six or seven lines of polished prose had made it into that day's edition; he was paid by the line, so his solvency at the end of the week depended on a good showing. Mamie, fresh in from Glasgow to cover the annual arts festival herself, spotted him at once. In an office of shabby hacks, it was hard to miss this exotic figure with the blond hair and red-tinged beard, immaculate in blue blazer, grey slacks and tie (though without the umbrella today).

'Who's the character with the beard?' she whispered. On being informed that his name was Magnus Magnusson, she giggled. No one seriously had a name like that. Told that he was an Icelander, she immediately thought of igloos (an impression which, thankfully, would be well corrected by the time she met his father). But she took an instant liking to the soft Oxford accent, and when she left for lunch that day, he raced to join her. By the time she returned to the office he had also secured her company at a Greek restaurant in Rose Street that same night. Towards the end of the meal she noticed him in earnest conversation with the proprietor, asking if payment of the bill could be delayed until the end of the week, when he would receive his vast lineage fee from the *Express*.

By the end of that summer, he had decided to marry my mother and make a career in journalism. It meant giving up his studies in Denmark, for which Mamie always felt obscurely guilty. But Sigurður Nordal knew he was a story-man at heart and probably expected it. At least the ambassadorial lawn was safe now.

The couple married in June 1954, with the sweetly resigned blessing of his mother. The disparity in their backgrounds never mattered a whit to my father. Sartorial affectation was one thing, but he found all real social pretensions ridiculous. Besides, he was a carter dynasty man himself.

They settled in Rutherglen, which turned him overnight into a west of Scotland man, and my mother threw herself enthusiastically into the Icelandic traditions he brought with him. Every 17 June for many years she would hang an Icelandic flag from the window to celebrate Independence Day, noting wryly that by the time my father rolled home after a night spent toasting the republic, it had invariably drooped to half-mast. She quickly learned how to cook *hangikjöt* and enough Icelandic to greet relatives with a *'Gleðileg jól'* at Christmas and wave them off with a hearty *'Bless bless'* at the front door. She made us all chant *'Takk fyrir matinn'* when my father wasn't there to enforce the mealtime rituals. To this day she will phone up after a family occasion at my house to say *'Takk fyrir síðast'*, because there is no phrase pithy enough in English to convey the 'thank you for the last time' sentiments of the Icelandic.

Soon after she met my father, she elevated Iceland to second place in her firmament of nations, which was as high as it could possibly go and well ahead of England, and there it remains to this day. The country even became a useful source of material during her time as an after-dinner speaker. An expatriate Icelander once rushed up to congratulate her on a talk she had given in Edinburgh. 'I never knew my country was such an interesting place,' he said admiringly, pumping her hand. No wonder, if her material was based on my father's stories.

My grandparents grew as fond of her as Ingibjörg's own parents had become of Sigursteinn who, as Ingibjörg did her best to forget, was himself the son of a peasant. The leavening of the Laxamýri lineage with some down-to-earth lower-class grit was something of a tradition on our side of the family, and a successful one at that. The first to do it was Ingibjörg's mother, my great-grandmother, Snjólaug, in 1899.

What is it that suddenly reminds me of Snjólaug? My father and I have turned left now on to Route 85, heading north towards Húsavík, and it may be the sheer immensity of barren emptiness on either side of the road that does it. This is the sort of landscape into which I used to imagine Sigurjón's youngest daughter being 'cast out' from Laxamýri, as my Aunt Didda had so enticingly put it, banished by a cold and unfeeling father for daring to fall in love with her social inferior.

When Didda told me the story, I had dreamily imagined Snjólaug's horse picking its way across the cold moorland until her childhood home was only a pinprick of light behind her. I saw the family servant chase after her in a clatter of hooves to hand over the gold coins, smuggled out by her mother. I saw her turn the horse's head to the south and ride away, broken-hearted, from the childhood home she would never see again.

I saw a lot of codswallop, frankly, but that is the way with family legends. Offered a hint, you snatch a story. Ingibjörg must have done this herself in passing on her mother's vague suggestions of a troubled courtship to Didda. Didda probably stirred in some colouring of her own. I went mad with the icing. Perhaps story-telling is always like this: a handed-down recipe, in which indulging the palate is so much more important than worrying about whether you have the ingredients right. The trouble only comes when you call this entertaining mish-mash history. Or when you do what I did last night and put it to your great-uncle that the legend of his mother's courtship might actually be true.

'Sally *mín*,' Uncle Sigurjón had said, holding me in such a steady gaze across the table that I felt like one of his suspects under deceptively gentle police interrogation, 'you really must understand that this whole thing is *alveg fráleitt.*'

I had to look it up in the dictionary later and I think the word 'preposterous' covers his point adequately. But, believe me, you don't need fluent Icelandic to understand when your wicket is looking overwhelmingly sticky.

How, my uncle asked politely, could Snjólaug have been banished for ever from Laxamýri when she was still there delivering her babies a year or two later? Ah, yes, good point. And what was old Sigurjón doing inviting the pair of them to move in with him in Akureyri in 1908 (and here was the letter to prove it) if he didn't want his doorstep ever darkened again? Hm, got me there, too. Toying uncomfortably with my fork, I wondered if Didda had simply been reading too much Mills and Boon.

The lava-plain we are driving through now goes on and on, grey and lumpy. Plenty of moss, too, of a hue verging on the sickly, I would have said. But I don't. My father is smoking too peaceably for me to do it to him, and anyway I really must set this story straight.

This much seems clear. When Snjólaug Sigurjónsdóttir was visiting her married sister Líney one autumn in the fishing village of Sauðárkrókur, away to the west of Laxamýri, she met a schoolteacher by the name of Sigurður Björnsson, whose brother Árni was the local pastor. They were farmer's sons, brought up by their widowed mother. Árni, as the elder son, had been sent to the grammar school in Reykjavík and then to university in Copenhagen to study for the ministry. But the money did not stretch to an education for Sigurður. He had to take work where he could find it, on fishing boats and as an itinerant farmhand, before raising enough money himself to enrol in 1888 at the area's new secondary school at Möðruvellir, many days' walk away from his home in Skagafjörður.

After leaving school he worked as an itinerant teacher, travelling between farms where the population was too sparse to maintain a permanent school, and then started a new job in the primary school at Sauðárkrókur, at the foot of the Skagafjörður fjord. His brother Árni had already settled there with his wife, who happened to be Líney Sigurjónsdóttir, eldest daughter of the most famous landowner in the north.

Sauðárkrókur had few diversions for a lively bachelor in his thirties, so Sigurður's prospects brightened considerably when Líney's quiet young sister stepped off the boat from Húsavík that autumn, at the beginning of a visit which was to last right through until the spring. Dark-haired like her brothers, Snjólaug had a soft, round face and a pert nose (no sign of the Laxamýri hooter here), and Sigurður was smitten.

Far from the gaze of the girls' sharp-eyed father, the romance flourished. So much so that by the time Snjólaug had to return home, Sigurður was emboldened to follow her. He moved to Húsavík, handy for courting at Laxamýri, and took a job as an assistant in the Örum and Wulff store.

If those are the facts, here comes the speculation. There is a letter printed in Jóhann Sigurjónsson's *Collected Works*, in which he wrote to their eldest brother Jóhannes in November 1898: 'Thank you for your letter and pictures, my brother. You write to me that Sigurður and Snjólaug have got their way and that truly gladdens me, as I know it will have gladdened you.'

Got their way. The phrase suggests a clash of wills which may just be enough to vindicate my romantic Aunt Didda. And there is another clue. Jóhann went on to write a play called *Lava Farm* about the owner of a large and wealthy farm who wanted his beloved daughter to marry the prosperous young man of his choice, only to be thwarted by her love for a visitor to the area. Evidence, or what?

'So how about this?' I suggest to my father who, with the merest hint of an eye-roll, drags his attention from the hypnotic nothingness outside the window to the intricacies of his grand-parents' courtship. Maybe this is a girl thing, but reputations are at stake here. Mine and his sister Didda's, for a start.

Imagine, I say, that Snjólaug's father was not easily persuaded that a shopkeeper was any better husband material for his youngest daughter than an impecunious teacher. A letter from the time lightheartedly suggests that Sigurjón might have preferred the local magistrate. Not only was this fellow not a magistrate, but at thirty-two he was much older than her and had clearly lived a bit; not unusually for Iceland, there was already a love-child in the wings.

Sigurjón's natural inclination to consider no man good enough for his youngest daughter can only have been bolstered by his habit of organising his life around strategic alliances. Someone whose whole *modus operandi* was based on knowing the right people would undoubtedly feel that little Snjólaug could do better for herself: if not the magistrate, then perhaps another churchman like Líney's husband, Árni. I imagine Sigurjón scanned the horizon hopefully for bishops, checked out the marital status of the Akureyri bank manager, and told Snjólaug bluntly that she should aim higher.

Snjólaug, who later became a stalwart of the Icelandic suffragette movement, will certainly have mounted a quiet resistance, and her father was not a man to be resisted easily. So let us assume that Snjólaug and Sigurður had a battle on their hands, covertly egged on from the sidelines, as Jóhann's letter suggests, by her brothers and sisters. However, since everything I have learned about Sigurjón of Laxamýri suggests a deep and abiding affection for his children, as well as a particularly fatal weakness where his wife was concerned, let us imagine that the paternal front was always vulnerable to collapse. In the end I wouldn't be surprised if mother and daughter together succeeded in persuading Sigurjón that this union had been his most excellent idea in the first place.

'It all fits, doesn't it?' I say. 'Sigurjón puts his foot down at first, but then he gives way because he's dotty about his daughter anyway. Then, when he gets to know his son-in-law, he discovers him to be a perfectly fine and rather well educated man after all. Just like your mother fell for your own beloved after she got over her own disappointment about the princess.'

My father blinks. The analogy had not occurred to him. Ignoring it completely, he draws on his pipe, watches the smoke curl out of the slit in his window and then sums everything up with magisterial eloquence.

'Didda's story was such a curious one,' he says. 'It's clear the facts don't support the suggestion that Snjólaug became a Laxamýri outcast in any way. And yet that one letter from Jóhann, and perhaps the play too, indicate a little ripple in the river, suggesting there is rock underneath it which divided the water and made it a little unruly in places.'

The man mints metaphors like 1,000-*krónur* notes. No wonder I have always believed every word he ever told me.

I should add that after Snjólaug and Sigurður married, just before the turn of the century, their first two children were indeed born at Laxamýri. Then they moved south to Reykjavík, attracted by the new opportunities in the fledgling capital on the eve of home rule. Ingibjörg, their fourth child, was born there in 1905, a girl after my own heart who will have squeezed every drop out of anything she heard about the ups and downs of her parents' courtship. Once you add Snjólaug's own nostalgia for Laxamýri and later confusions over the share-out of the old man's gold, you have the genesis of Didda's story.

My grandmother's own love affair had its travails, too. Ingibjörg's father did his best to make history repeat itself by evincing considerable suspicion of Sigursteinn Magnússon, the debonair carter's son from Akureyri, when he came calling. Sigurður promptly sent Ingibjörg away to Denmark, in the hope that a year's study at the domestic college in Søro would cool the temperature. The course did wonders for her cuisine, but nothing for her ardour. Once again, the lovers prevailed and the two men went on to become friends.

Sigurður Björnsson opened a shop in Reykjavík, before becoming an estate agent and later going into the fire business. My father, that fount of dodgy information, assured me he was the fire chief of Reykjavík. I used to picture this great-grandfather of mine in a shiny yellow fireman's helmet, wielding a long hose and dashing about in manly fashion rescuing maidens from the blazing timber houses of 1920s Reykjavík. But it turns out that his job as *brunamálastjóri* actually means director of fire affairs – something else I discovered last night. It was an insurance assessment post which did not, alas, require the brandishing of a hose or the donning of a helmet of any kind.

Visiting him as a child in the 1930s, my father remembers Sigurður as a kindly widower, affectionate with children although he could be stern. He was stout by then, with spectacles and a little toothbrush moustache. At that time he was living in a fine house which he had built for himself in Freyjugata Street. There he took porridge every morning, lashed with sugar in such mountainous quantities as his young grandson had never dreamed possible and which he considered the greatest luxury he had ever known.

My father is dreaming less of sugar right now than of the smoked lamb which he has been hankering after ever since we landed in Iceland. *Hangikjöt* (literally 'hung meat') is a speciality which graces all the traditional festivities along with any other occasion my father can contrive to get his hands on it. Back home we crave it so much that no returning suitcase is permitted to leave Iceland without a pack of *hangi* tucked in with the smalls, along with a loaf of rye bread and enough packets of dried fish to make their pungent presence felt the length and breadth of the house.

'I'm going to order it for dinner as soon as we get there,' he announces, with his first spark of animation in a while. This lava-plain is becoming tedious. 'Most of it is produced in Húsavík so they're bound to have it at the hotel.'

We continue to drool over our ideal dinner, barely noticing that the landscape is changing and the rearing lava has subsided into exposed heath and pasture land. Out of the corner of my eye I spot the Laxá river rushing under the road and away to the sea.

'I wonder if they'll serve it with white sauce,' I muse.

'Certainly,' says my father briskly, as if he were taking the order personally. 'And there'll be small boiled potatoes in butter, of course.'

'And green peas mushed into the sauce the way your mother used to do it. And how about . . .'

Jóhann's memorial is suddenly there at the side of the road and we have almost missed it. I brake abruptly and we skid into the lay-by with a scrunching of stones, a less dignified approach to Laxamýri than either of us would have wished. My father bolts out of the car and into an unexpectedly sharp breeze. Whatever delights the sun is performing in sheltered Akureyri, it has not mustered much of a show here yet.

We linger by the entwined letters J and S long enough to satisfy the formal requirements of the moment: a photograph, a grave scrutiny of the plaque and a glance across the moor in the direction of Laxamýri, which is still out of sight down the road.

There is a quote from Jóhann's poem *'Sorg'* (Sorrow) on the memorial:

> *Á hvítum hestum hleyptum við*
> *upp á bláan himinbogann*
> *og lékum að gylltum knöttum.*

My father and I translate the lines together:

> On white horses we raced
> up to the blue vault of the sky
> and played with golden spheres.

Here Jóhann's real childhood playground is all around us, his white horses beating along the surf-tossed shoreline just beyond the moor, his vaulted sky a great dome over our heads, as big as you could hope but not as blue today as the one I woke up to this morning. The hopeful flirting of one solitary ray of late afternoon sunshine is making little impression on a gang of sallow clouds. My father is pretending not to be cold.

Listening to the flurrying wind and the frustrated click of his lighter, I find myself wondering if there are ever days so still that you can hear the waterfalls from here. I had read about them in the memoirs of Líney Jóhannesdóttir – not Snjólaug's eldest sister, but the old lady in Reykjavík who lived here when she was a girl. Where the Laxá river spills over in its headlong rush for the sea, she writes, the waterfalls were never quiet. They were loudest in the stillness of winter, on the days when the roar of the surf was quiet and you could hear the falls thundering behind gigantic icicles. You noticed them especially on those days when the rest of the world went silent, when something was inexplicably wrong, like the August day in 1919 when the news came about Jóhann.

Líney says she would at one time have sacrificed anything to be able to live here again, listening to the waterfalls and gazing at the Kinnarfjöll mountains rising, white with snow whatever the season, out of the black sands.

'Such is the power of the land's pull,' she writes, adding unexpectedly sharply, 'And it doesn't always appeal to the best parts of one's soul.'

Hauling my Arctic anorak off in the car, I wonder aloud, above Velcro rips, which parts of my own soul Laxamýri is appealing to now, three-quarters of a century later.

'What do you think?' I say, tossing the jacket on to the back seat and vowing to go without tomorrow, as befits a Viking's daughter.

My father has not read Líney and says he hasn't the faintest idea what souls have got to do with anything. The only appeal being made right now is to his stomach and could we please get a move on for the hotel.

He is definitely cold.

Jóhann the Poet

Jóhannes was working in the meadows when the messenger arrived with the telegram about Jóhann, and his children knew at once that something was wrong. He came running in his white shirt over the home fields and back to the house, and never went out again all that August day. In the hush that fell over Laxamýri, all you could hear were the birds and the distant complaint of the waterfalls.

In Reykjavík, Snjólaug too was distraught. Jóhann had mentioned in a letter from Copenhagen only a fortnight before that he was unwell, but nobody had realised how ill her brother really was. Her daughters wept. Ingibjörg, at fourteen, had idolised her glamorous uncle and could not be comforted.

Iceland mourned a man who had brought renown to the nation with his success as a playwright, a man who had entranced them from afar with his lyrical flair and poetic lifestyle. The youngest son of Sigurjón of Laxamýri was dead, and a new legend was already born.

My father grew up with it. Jóhann's meteoric career, so tragically grounded, came to symbolise for him everything that was beautiful and wasted and irretrievably lost about Laxamýri itself. In this he was encouraged not only by his mother, but by the finely wrought sadness of Jóhann's verse. The poem he loves so much that his book falls open at the page (*Einn sit ég yfir drykkju* ... Alone I sit with a wine-glass/the long afternoon of winter) threw a slightly maudlin haze over his view of both Jóhann and Laxamýri.

I inherited it. When your grandmother pounces on your early feats of newspaper reportage with the ecstatic declaration that the literary blood of Jóhann Sigurjónsson is running in your veins, then naturally you are disposed to think well of your great-great-uncle. I'm not sure that 'Edinburgh Zoo Loses Cockatoo' entirely merited the comparison, but who was I to argue?

The truth is, I have happily boasted in days gone by of being related to Iceland's Shakespeare, Burns and Byron rolled into one, an unequalled giant of Icelandic letters. On this trip to Iceland, I was determined to find out at last who and what our celebrated kinsman really was.

Here I must skip forward in our journey to the final evening in Reykjavík, when my father and I returned to Hótel Esja for one night before leaving for home. There we invited the literary historian Jón Viðar Jónsson to come and give us a detached view of Jóhann's achievement. I tossed my Shakespeare/Burns/Byron theory at him, and he winced politely.

'Well, I am not so sure about that,' he began, stirring his coffee carefully, very carefully, at a low table beneath the picture window in my father's room. Perhaps he sensed the ghost of my grandmother's eagerness in the question.

'Jóhann was the first real modernist of Icelandic poetry,' he said at last. 'He was not a prolific poet, but his poems have survived and are certainly among Iceland's best. And although his plays have certain failures alongside their great qualities, he was absolutely the greatest playwright of Icelandic letters during the first half of the century.'

He eyed me over his coffee cup with a twinkle. 'Which is not to say, of course, that he was exactly a Shakespeare.'

On behalf of my grandmother, I accepted the judgement with a regal nod.

My father was listening intently. He looked rather serious. In fact, he was taking this conversation altogether less frivolously than I was – I who was enjoying our game of knock-the-legend and would have accepted even the Fall of Jóhann with a resigned shrug. In that moment, though, I realised how much the reputation of the family *skáld* genuinely mattered to my father. It was fine to play skittles with the myths as long as we were only bowling over firemen's helmets, banished daughters and the honour of being first carter in Akureyri; but Jóhann was different. It mattered that the author of a poem he had revisited restlessly over his lifetime, altering a nuance here, an alliteration there, in order to ease his translation ever closer to the original, should still ride high in the minds of those he respected most in modern Iceland. I detected relief and something akin to gratitude in his eyes.

Laxamýri meant different things to the sons of Sigurjón. For Egill it was a farm to be harvested and, progressively, a financial headache. To Jóhannes it represented nature to be studied, eiders fondled and the return of the arctic terns in May admired from the window with bursting heart. But Jóhann found there something else again: lifelong poetic inspiration and a huge mountain-ringed theatre for his earliest attempts at playwriting. These childhood efforts, acted out on long summer days to the insistent beat of the surf, usually starred himself and Snjólaug. Just two years older, she also supplied a gratifyingly rapt audience for his first poems.

At fifteen Jóhann was sent south to the prestigious Latin School in Reykjavík, where he continued writing and even managed to have a few immature verses published in the newspapers. He also developed a talent for mathematics and natural history. 'I have used the two months I have been in Reykjavík rather well in the main,' he wrote to Jóhannes in 1896; the brothers, for all the eighteen years between them, were much alike, and maintained a close, long-distance friendship to the end of Jóhann's life. 'I have been reading up a bit on my subjects, but often I couldn't be bothered doing that, and have been reading about zoology, botany and dogmatics by Ingersoll. There are only three subjects which I never neglect, and those are zoology, English and maths.'

The interest in zoology took him to Copenhagen in 1899 to study veterinary science, a development encouraged by his father. There was only one trained vet in the whole of Iceland and Sigurjón was looking forward to having his own on hand at Laxamýri. If he could have read Jóhann's confidences to Jóhannes in June 1900, he might have been less hopeful: 'This uncontrollable desire to do something great hardly ever leaves me in peace,' Jóhann wrote, in terms which his father would have found alarmingly airy-fairy. He had a great leap to make, he said, and drew on images of Laxamýri to explain it: 'Just think of standing on a drifting piece of ice and having to jump across a great fissure, or else be carried along with the strong current towards the cold blue edge of the waterfall and then disappear like a sick duckling into the dark opening of the whirlpool, to have to jump and have doubts about your strength.'

The first Sigurjón knew about any leap was when Jóhann dropped out of his veterinary studies in 1902, only months before his finals, announcing that he planned to be a playwright and earn a living from his pen. His father was appalled by the notion that writing plays could be considered a proper job (no one in Iceland had ever done it professionally) and tried to entice him home with the offer of the smallholding at Saltvík which Thorvaldur had briefly farmed. Jóhann, however, could not be moved. He wanted to be a great writer. It was an ambition so all-consuming that it had become an obsession. He believed that only by staying in Denmark could it be fulfilled.

In Copenhagen he joined a self-consciously arty circle which specialised in turning night into day and striking romantic poses, both in their lives and work, in all sorts of fairly ridiculous ways. But Jóhann had an energy and a bubbling love of life which transcended the bohemian affectations.

The future saga scholar Sigurður Nordal was dazzled. When they met in 1906 Nordal was only twenty, newly arrived in Copenhagen to study Old Norse at the university. 'After sitting with Jóhann for only a single evening, it seemed to me he was born to become a great poet,' Nordal wrote more than thirty years later, in an essay to commemorate the sixtieth anniversary of Jóhann's birth. 'He had to be a poet, and could not be anything else. His appearance drew people to him at once. His face was so beautiful that even men could not help looking at it, just for pleasure, as changes of emotion flashed and flickered across his features – I am tempted to say, sounded in his face, as if it were a musical instrument in the hands of a maestro.'

Obviously there is some serious hero-worship going on here. Nordal was an ardent romantic as well as a budding intellectual, and he adored Jóhann. He found his conversation scintillating. Jóhann 'had an overwhelming need to tell his companions about whatever works he was engaged on, expatiating on their themes and the changes they were undergoing, quoting passages of dialogue, explaining what he had in mind and what he was aiming at, reciting old and new poems. Even when he was talking about something totally different, his poetic imagination was always awake, his creativity ceaseless, his choice of words enchanting. There was unbelievably much he was interested in and fascinated by.'

What we are seeing is the birth of Jóhann Sigurjónsson's mythic status as the quintessential artist. 'When I was with him,' says Nordal, 'I often felt that he was The Poet, in the way a poet should be.'

Yet even allowing for youthful idealisation, a singularly attractive personality emerges from this and other portraits. Surrounded by all kinds of drunkards and hangers-on, Jóhann was the king of the court, funny and ironic, infinitely charming and, like so many of his family, able to talk anybody into doing almost anything at all. 'His moods were rich and his temperament generous, vibrating from one string to another,' wrote Nordal, reaching again for the violin. 'His face expressed both vehemence and arrogance, humility and gentleness, sincerity and sensitivity, exuberance and melancholy, sorrow and joy.'

You can imagine the effect that sort of description would have had on my impressionable grandmother. She and Sigursteinn were close friends with Sigurður Nordal, who used to visit them often in Edinburgh (until Nordal temporarily blotted his copybook with my grandfather by announcing that the sagas were partly fiction). It seemed to everyone that the wavy-haired academic was just a little in love with Ingibjörg, with whom he could linger over a chaste coffee for hours, his face crunching up into his familiar pixyish smile as they talked. I have no doubt that, at least some of the time, they were basking in memories of her Uncle Jóhann.

Nordal the student was not alone in being enchanted by Jóhann. There is nothing like dying young and handsome for ensuring a good write-up from your friends, but everyone agrees that the young Icelander was an exceptionally charismatic figure in Copenhagen café society. Unexpectedly, I find myself reminded of his father in the picture that friends draw of this thin, stoopy-shouldered young man with his long curved nose and grey-blue eyes, who walked everywhere fast and was always on the look-out for money. I doubt if Sigurjón's face was ever thought as beautiful, nor his company remotely as seductive, but he and Jóhann shared a vigour and purposefulness which people found infectious.

What Jóhann was attempting to achieve in Copenhagen was something no Icelander had managed before, which was to forge a career as a professional playwright, operating out of Denmark in a bid to win a larger public than the 80,000 souls at home could possibly provide. It was a formidable ambition for a young man alone in a foreign country without a national tradition behind him, and he knew it. But Ibsen in Norway had won fame and fortune from his plays, so why not an Icelander with poetry in his head and a thirst for greatness?

He found it hard going at first. Although he wrote excellent Danish, it was difficult to get his plays staged in that country. The early ones lacked emotional maturity and, to the increasing detriment of his pocket, were slow to find a publisher. By the time he started writing his masterpiece, *Fjalla-Eyvindur* (*Eyvindur of the Mountains*), during the winter of 1909–10, his father's liberal subsidies had dried up and he was stinging everyone in sight, as well as his brothers and sisters in Iceland, for money to keep himself in the convivial style to which he would have liked to become accustomed.

A young Icelandic writer by the name of Gunnar Gunnarsson arrived in Copenhagen that winter and attached himself to his compatriot, who was then living in an attic at 30 Silver Street. Gunnar was envious of these digs, both for the view over the Royal Gardens and for the fact that the room boasted furniture. As long as Jóhann was in funds, there was a bed, a rocking chair (handy for homeless friends to sleep in), a table and chair, and a mirror on the wall. The mirror came and went depending on the pawn cycle. When you met Jóhann, Gunnar reported, he would either offer you a drink or ask if you were buying one. If the answer were no and the pockets empty, he would laugh and say, 'In that case I have a mirror to offer.' And off he would go with the mirror under his arm to hunt down the wherewithal.

Finishing the Danish version of *Fjalla-Eyvindur* took longer than it might because Jóhann was also busy trying to get rich quick. Like his brother Lúðvík, he always had an eye open for new business opportunities; and also, like Lúðvík, his efforts met with little success. He produced dust lids for beer mugs in outdoor pubs, which mostly rusted away in a warehouse in the suburbs. He also came up with a brilliant device to protect moustaches from getting wet when you were drinking, which sadly also bombed. When he wasn't poring over his patents, he was dashing off to a chemistry laboratory for bizarre experiments which never saw the light of day either.

It is a wonder Jóhann managed to write anything at all. But in the summer of 1911, he handed in the completed Danish manuscript at last and turned his attention to rewriting his play in Icelandic. He hired his young friend to help him at a crown a day, with breakfast and coffee thrown in, and the penurious Gunnar clocked in at Silver Street at nine every morning bearing his worldly possessions in their entirety: one thick quill pen. Sitting opposite each other at the small, rickety table, they reworked the Danish into Icelandic, taking turns at writing. When it was Gunnar's turn, Jóhann would pace around the room, smoking cigarettes. They played with every sentence several times before it was accepted by both and committed to paper. Even so, the manuscript was a mess of insertions and deletions.

Jóhann found writing singularly more taxing than talking, at which he was effortlessly fluent. Sigurður Nordal noticed how indecisive he was when it came to putting words down on paper. 'In conversation, sentences could be born from his lips fully formed,' he said, 'but when he was starting to compose, Jóhann could be groping around for ages for his theme, letting other people tell him what to do and always changing the central subject. He pored over every sentence for hours at a time, with constant strikings-out.'

Nevertheless, *Eyvindur of the Mountains* gradually inched towards completion. At midday Jóhann and Gunnar staggered out for lunch (a plate of beans each was often as much as they could stretch to) and then worked on until they were too tired to continue. Their finances deteriorated with every page, due in large part to their habit of ending the day in the pub, where Jóhann was immediately surrounded by a crowd of hopeful cronies. His capital was running out fast and the room was being steadily emptied around them. The bedspread had disappeared off the bed, the mirror was no longer on the wall, and Jóhann's silver cigarette case had also been removed, gone – in a favourite euphemism of his – to visit his 'cousin'. But the harrowing dynamics of *Fjalla-Eyvindur* so absorbed them that they didn't care. By the time they finished the work, their waistcoats too had gone to visit the cousin.

To Jóhann's relief, the play's publishers liked it. They gave him an advance of 300 crowns, 50 of which were owed to Gunnar. Unfortunately, Jóhann was incapable of having 300 crowns in his pocket without making a night of it. By the time he had taken his friends out to dinner, satisfied those of them who sidled up in the course of the meal for a quiet word about their own finances and redeemed his pawned goods, there was so little left of the advance that Gunnar suggested his own 50 crowns could wait. So Jóhann pulled from his pocket instead a Roman coin on which, according to Gunnar, he 'put a spell', assuring his friend with grave levity that while he had this coin in his possession, he would never want for cash.

'It never leaves my pocket,' Gunnar wrote many years later, without revealing whether the spell had by any chance worked. 'It is a precious memory of a summer and of a friendship that I would not trade for anything.'

Eyvindur of the Mountains received an ecstatic reception when its world premiere was held in the pioneering Reykjavík Theatre Company on Boxing Day, 1911. Snjólaug and Sigurður will surely have been there in the pretty playhouse by the lake to see him acclaimed as a theatrical sensation with a play which began a new tradition of Icelandic drama. The future Nobel prize-winning novelist Halldór Laxness went to see it in the same place a few years later. He was a boy of twelve at the time and could barely sleep afterwards for thinking about it, an effect he said no other literary work ever had on him again. Over the next few years the play was translated into nine languages and performed all over Europe.

It also earned a place in film history a few years later when it was turned into a Swedish silent movie by the actor-director Victor Sjöström. By introducing landscape for the first time as an active agent in the drama, *Berg-Ejvind och Hans Hustru* (*Eyvindur of the Mountains and His Wife*) proved to be a milestone in the development of film language. Charlie Chaplin is said to have been much impressed by it. Jóhann, who must have been disappointed that it had to be shot in Lapland rather than Iceland because of the First World War, attended the premiere in Stockholm in January 1918.

The play, based on folk-tales about a famous Icelandic outlaw, is a *tour de force*, pulsating with passion and torment. It is a big play with big themes – love, sacrifice, the helplessness of human beings crushed by the forces of nature – and a haunting lyricism. Critics have ranked it with the works of Strindberg and Ibsen as one of the great Nordic plays. I have never seen it performed, but the effect of reading it in translation stayed in my mind for days. It is strange, powerful, disturbing and extremely low on laughs. You would never guess from reading it that Jóhann could keep a room in fits of laughter telling a story. But there is a lot of him in it, none the less, and perhaps a hint of Laxamýri too.

'He has loved you for a long time without knowing it,' the outlaw says of himself to Halla, a tragic heroine in the unflinching saga mould, who makes the fateful decision to follow him into the wilderness. 'But until this evening he never saw how beautiful you were, like a blue mountain rising up out of the mist.'

And so Jóhann Sigurjónsson found the success he had been pursuing. It arrived at the same time as another auspicious event in his life: the death of the husband of his long-time lover, Ingeborg Blom, which allowed the couple to marry in 1912.

It goes without saying that Jóhann was attractive to women. If men like Sigurður Nordal gazed on his dark, mercurial face for sheer pleasure, you can be sure the girls did too. He already had an illegitimate daughter, Gríma, born in 1906 from a liaison with a girl called Elenor. He had also been engaged in Iceland to Sigurlaug Elísabet Björnsdóttir, the sister of none other than Sigurður and Árni Björnsson, who had married two of Jóhann's own sisters, Snjólaug and Líney – a tantalising triple romance with the humbly born family from Skagafjörður, which must have given their father a few sleepless nights. But Ingeborg Blom was Jóhann's lasting love.

Ib, as he called her (after her initials I. B.), has suffered a cruel fate from our family myth-making machine, for the rumour was that Jóhann had married the ugliest woman in Denmark for her money. It is a story bearing the hallmarks of gossip over a silver Reykjavík coffee pot, but that didn't stop my father passing it on with his usual hearty authority. This was one I really had to check.

I doubt if my father has learned to blush. In fact, I don't think I have ever seen him look even slightly embarrassed. So you have to consider other aspects of his demeanour in Hótel Esja that evening to gain a clue to his feelings when I asked Jón Viðar about Ingeborg Blom.

Ugliest woman in Denmark? Our scholarly guest looked taken aback. Jóhann's beloved was perhaps no great beauty, to judge from pictures, but hardly that plain. 'She was a lively and charming woman,' he said, 'who no doubt loved poetry, which I suppose was not the least important factor in their relationship. Her memoirs show that she had a natural gift for story-telling.'

They had conducted a long and, as far as anyone could judge, genuinely passionate affair until she was free to marry.

'Ah yes,' beamed my father, as far from blushing as it is possible to imagine, but taking refuge in a quick puff of the pipe, one small cough and an unnecessary glance out of the window, all of which clearly signified Guilt. 'Is that so?'

'But she did have money?' I press, keen to salvage something from this tale, even if my father has surrendered without a fight in most un-Viking-like fashion.

'Yes, she did,' Jón Viðar conceded. 'Possibly rather a lot, after her husband died.'

Well, there you are then. Jóhann did not exactly marry for money, but money may have been a useful part of the package. Perhaps the legend has merely pressed its finger on a slightly tender truth about Jóhann, which is that money was rarely far from his thinking about anything.

My father has now decided on reflection that he may have confused Jóhann's story with that of Árni Magnússon, the eighteenth-century saga collector who is said to have taken a rich but elderly Danish woman as a bride to finance his manuscript purchases. If my father is going to admit a mistake, he would rather it was born of high-minded literary confusion than gossipy whispers from his mother and aunts.

Personally (and without a shred of evidence) I prefer to think that Ingibjörg and her sisters were motivated by the fate of Sigurlaug Elísabet, the fiancée Jóhann left behind in Iceland, who was their own aunt. The *Íslendingabók* web database records that after her broken betrothal to Jóhann, she lived out her days, unmarried and childless, with Líney and Árni. How was a wealthy Danish widow ever going to measure up to that story for pathos and romance?

Whatever the rumours back home, Jóhann and Ib proceeded to set themselves up in a finely furnished home with a big, tree-filled garden in the suburb of Charlottenlund, a far cry from the previous year's attic with the pawned mirror. Jóhann set to work on more plays, but nothing else he wrote was considered as good as *Fjalla-Eyvindur*. Certainly nothing achieved the same popularity. As easily wounded by the critics as he became elated by success, Jóhann was often depressed. He wavered over the importance of his vocation. 'Sometimes I feel it is a great role to be a writer,' he wrote to Ib. 'But sometimes I feel it is no role at all and that mankind can very well be without it and I am unnecessary in this world.'

Perhaps he was conscious that for all the sparky youthful genius of *Fjalla-Eyvindur*, he still had considerable maturing to do in his playwriting. Perhaps he realised that even the greatest of his poems – and some, like '*Sorg*', from which the quotation on his Laxamýri memorial is taken, or the exquisite '*Heimthrá*' ('Homesickness') are very fine indeed – were still less than he had the potential to create.

'If he had lived longer,' Gunnar Gunnarsson said of Jóhann Sigurjónsson, 'there is no doubt that he had his best years as a writer ahead.'

However, towards the end of his life, Jóhann found writing difficult. He was drinking heavily and socialising hard, waiting for the capricious Muse. With cash in short supply again, he threw himself into a project to build a harbour for herring fishing at Lake Höfðavatn in the north of Iceland, labouring to raise investment for the digging of a canal through the isthmus which divided the lake from Skagafjörður. Once again the herring adventures which shaped the whole of Iceland's destiny in the twentieth century were about to play their part in a single Laxamýri one.

Jóhann believed passionately in the potential for a processing facility at Höfðavatn. The herring in Skagafjörður were so abundant that they were sometimes being fished as far as the shore; the boats would run aground as men scooped glistening net-loads from the sea right up to the shallows. Perhaps if he had lived, Jóhann's sheer determination would have seen the project through. But with Lúðvík already trying to launch his doomed salting plant further up the peninsula at Siglufjörður, there is a sad familiarity about the sight of another brother dashing around those Icelandic fjords in 1918 and 1919, indefatigable in his enthusiasm for a scheme which was also fated to come to nothing.

Jóhann was there in May 1919, when an agreement was signed for the purchase of three Höfðavatn farms for development, and he spent some time walking in the area, which he loved. But it was clear to those who met him then that Jóhann was ill. Twenty-year-old Björn Jónsson, son of the farmer at Bær whose land was being purchased, was impressed by Jóhann's passion for the project and by his eyes, which 'seemed to look right through me and read my thoughts'. But he noted that Jóhann was under the influence of drink most days and was quite evidently unwell.

The previous year Jóhann had suffered from Spanish flu. Then he contracted TB, which cannot have been helped either by the alcohol or by hurtling around breezy Höfðavatn when he should have been resting at home.

He left the area at the end of May and returned to Denmark. Three months later, on the last day of August, Jóhann Sigurjónsson died in Copenhagen of acute pulmonary tuberculosis. He was thirty-nine.

The way Jóhann planned it, he was going to be buried in a glacier. Alive, of course. He wanted to be put to sleep just before he died and then lowered gently into an icy fissure. The cleft would then be filled with more ice, providing an air-tight chamber for his unspoiled flesh to rest and his soul to sleep until, in a few hundred or thousand years' time, mankind would find a way of dissecting the glacier and waking him up. Long preoccupied with death in the themes of his verse, the eternity-obsessed poet and the crackpot inventor came together in a plan which, like many of his ideas, was ahead of the times and not so silly. But what it crucially depended on – just ask the millionaire Americans who are trying to arrange much the same thing today – was having the funds to execute it. Jóhann did not.

As the month of August 1919 drew to a close, he knew he would not be spending eternity in a glacier, waiting for the future to wake him up. The best he could arrange was that death should at least not overcome him in a hospital. In the days before he died, he was up and about at home, occasionally walking slowly with Ib to the small garden he loved by the Royal Library. Close to the end he was sitting up in bed doing card tricks, until he began to feel faint. Ib sat up with him all that night and talked to him about the Icelandic glaciers, which she had never seen and he never would again. His last words were to ask her to open the window, so that his soul might fly free.

Vestre Kirkegaard in Copenhagen was packed for the funeral. Among the onlookers was Halldór Laxness, now seventeen years old, who was standing outside in the sunshine, hoping for a glimpse. He listened to the murmur of the Danish pastor's oration from inside the church and then watched as the coffin was carried out to the grave and two Danish poets stepped forward to bid a formal farewell.

Laxness was moved by the scale of the funeral. As an aspiring writer himself on his first trip outside Iceland, he felt an affinity with Jóhann Sigurjónsson, although he wished the Laxamýri man had stayed at home to develop his talent instead of copying third-rate Danish *brennivín* drinkers. Still, no writer in Iceland had ever been accorded such a fine funeral, and he could never have imagined that so many people would mourn the death of a lone Icelander in another land. Such an unlikely variety of people, too: national leaders and academics, artists, street-sweepers, washer-women.

For a moment, as the funeral addresses of the two poets came to an end, there was silence in the churchyard. The only sound was the birds in the cypresses. Laxness thought it was all over. But at that moment four Icelandic students stepped forward from the crowd, took up position in a semi-circle by the graveside, and began to sing. In the calm of the late-summer afternoon, they sang in harmony the hymn-writer Hallgrímur Pétursson's elegiac meditation on death, which is heard at every Icelandic funeral: '*Allt eins og blómstrið eina*' – 'Just as the fragile flower blooming in the field yields its fragrance and falls to the ground when the scythe so chooses, so too does the life of man come to a sudden end.'

It sounded, thought Laxness, as if the song had sprung unbidden from the depths of the mind.

More than eighty years later, the Danes struggle to remember Jóhann Sigurjónsson. Outside his homeland he is largely forgotten, and even in Iceland it has taken time to dissociate the delightful image of the *skáld* from the quality of his work. Just as I am doing on this trip with my inherited family sagas, Icelanders have had an eventful journey of their own to make in modern times, reassessing the myths which this inveterate story-telling nation has passed down to itself. But they do seem to have arrived at a fair and thoughtful conclusion about Jóhann. As their pioneer playwright he is respectfully remembered; in fact, in a recent poll in Iceland he was voted the greatest Icelandic playwright of the twentieth century (with my father's old friend and foster-brother Jökull Jakobsson coming second). As a poet of rare emotional power he lives on, as far as I can judge, as freshly as ever.

A young Icelandic student told me she thought *'Sorg'*, with its stark first line – 'Woe, woe, to the fallen city' – and its profound sense of urban and emotional collapse, was the finest poem she had ever read in Icelandic. A publisher friend of my own generation says that every now and then, when he has had his fill of manuscripts from would-be writers, he takes out the poetry of Jóhann Sigurjónsson to remind himself how words can truly be made to sing and to weep.

My grandmother would be as proud of that as she would of the elegant memorial on the road to Laxamýri.

Húsavík

My father grasps the proprietor of the homely, white-painted Hótel Húsavík urgently by the hand and asks whether by any chance *hangikjöt* is on the dinner menu this evening. The man looks anguished.

'I am so sorry. We have none in the kitchen. None at all. If I had only known . . .'

He trails off. I am standing there with the luggage, willing my father to say, in best British fashion, that it is quite all right, anything will do.

'Oh dear,' I hear instead. 'That's a pity. I've been thinking about it all day.'

A long-forgotten sensation of teenage embarrassment sweeps over me. Please, Dad, let it drop. Please let's make do with steak and chips, or maybe battered whale, grilled horse, fried reindeer, or who knows what delicacies may be on offer. Just don't go on about *hangikjöt*.

But to my father's delight, the proprietor is offering to go out personally, buy some from . . . well, I've no idea where at this time in the evening, and have it cooked for us specially.

'I'm afraid you may have to wait a little longer for dinner,' he says on his way out of the door.

My father smiles broadly. 'No problem at all. Thank you very much indeed. It'll be worth the wait. Sally can go and find out where the graveyard is in the meantime.'

What? I had been looking forward to a hot bath and some satellite telly. But as the result of an earnest conversation my father had been conducting in the lobby before I came in, the local verger has declared himself most willing to show us where Jóhannes Kristjánsson, the Laxamýri patriarch, is buried. Now that dinner has been satisfactorily organised, my father is in his briskest, let's-get-on-with-the-business mood.

One of us, he says, should certainly go and see Jóhannes's grave. No time like the present. Can't be far. Bound to be worth a look. But really, on balance and all things considered, he personally would prefer a smoke in his bedroom. He waves me airily off the premises.

I am driven through the streets fanning out from Húsavík harbour by an elderly man with a wide smile and, alarmingly, no English. It takes me the length of two streets to construct an enquiry in Icelandic about whether he expects it to rain tomorrow. He says he doesn't know. 'Ah,' I say. He nods. I nod. We drive the rest of the way to the old graveyard in shy silence.

Only a few graves are there, sparsely dispersed around the edges of a small field, among a smattering of fir trees. A metal cross with strip lighting towers incongruously in the centre. Jóhannes's grave is easy to spot in an overgrown corner directly opposite the entrance: it is so much grander than the others. Not ostentatious exactly, although it might have looked so once, it is enclosed by a wrought iron railing, with a broken alabaster cross crowning a stone which dwarfs most of the others in the graveyard. Stained white fragments of the cross have spilled drunkenly over the weeds. The only other fine grave is the one next to it, also separated by a railing, with a Danish name engraved on the flaking stone. It is a measure of how far Jóhannes, the illiterate peasant, had progressed in this life, that he should rest in death next to the Húsavík aristocracy.

More accurately, it reflects the wealth of the son who erected the tombstone: Sigurjón of Laxamýri, who buried his father here beside his mother and three of his own small daughters who did not survive childhood.

Grey-white lichen is obscuring the names. Scraping it away, I read a simple tribute in Icelandic, containing a hint of earthly pride: 'Here lie the notable couple Jóhannes Kristjánsson (1795–

1871) and Sigurlaug Kristjánsdóttir (1800–1859). And with them Snjólaug, Kristrún and Snjólaug Kristín, daughters of Sigurjón Jóhannesson who placed this stone in memory of his late loved ones'.

Three little girls. Three Laxamýri daughters born in 1863, 1864 and 1869 whom I had no idea existed. Few people could afford to mark the graves of the infants lost as a matter of course in those hazardous times, but here you catch a fleeting glimpse of the pain of their passing. Snjólaug, Kristrún, Snjólaug Kristín. Sigurjón did not have much joy with the passing on of his wife's unique name; all the gold coins in the country could not guarantee his children safe passage through the disease minefield of nineteenth-century Iceland. But at least the couple had one Snjólaug to keep in the end: my great-grandmother, born in 1878.

An oyster-catcher rises suddenly from the long grass with a piercing whistle, startling me, and I turn to rejoin the verger in the car. We drive slowly back through Húsavík, grinning dumbly at one another until he offers to show me inside Húsavík Church. This exotic timber construction, designed at the beginning of the last century by Iceland's first indigenous architect, Rögnvaldur Ólafsson, has been likened, not unkindly, to a gingerbread house. When it was consecrated in 1907 it managed to seat practically the town's entire population of 450. The artist Sveinn Thórarinsson used some friends of his from nearby Kelduhverfi as models for the altarpiece painting of Lazarus' resurrection, just as Berkshire's Stanley Spencer did with the villagers of Cookham in his religious paintings – and apparently with equally mixed feelings about the result.

I ransack my Icelandic vocabulary for expressions of appreciation for the verger's gesture and the impact of the building, settling in the end for 'Wow!'– which delights him and saves me a lot of trouble.

Húsavík is quiet this evening. When the poet W. H. Auden passed through on his 1936 tour of Iceland, herring gutting was in full swing on the pier. His eye was caught by 'great beefy women standing up to their ankles in blood and slime, giving free demonstrations of manual dexterity'. Fishing is still the mainstay of the town, along with whale watching, which attracts shoals of tourists in summer, and a big meat-processing plant which I dread to think may be handling an emergency *hangikjöt* order from the hotel even now. These days the processing of saltfish and shrimps at two factories in the town is carried on in less picturesquely robust style than was on display for Auden. There is little going on in the harbour at the moment. The sun has returned to gleam on the mountain-ringed bay and the wind has dropped. It is more sheltered here than up on the Laxamýri heath.

Húsavík, which has grown from a hamlet of 300 people at the beginning of the last century to a major service centre for the area with a population of almost 2,500, is the site of Iceland's very first settlement. It even beats Reykjavík, something no visitor to these parts would be wise to forget. Around 870 another of the great Nordic explorers, this time a Swedish Viking by the name of Garðar Svavarsson, went looking for a country which a passing seafarer had earlier dubbed Snow Land. He landed and then spent the summer sailing right around the country, a historic achievement in itself, thereby establishing that it was a large island which he modestly renamed Garðar's Isle. Rather than risk a return voyage home through the autumn storms, he decided to winter on the island at a place which has been known ever since as Húsavík (Bay of Houses).

However (and this is the important part), according to the oldest preserved version of the tale in *Landnámabók*, Iceland's Domesday-like Book of Settlements, a tow-boat broke away from Garðar's ship when he was setting sail in the spring, and three people were left behind – a man named Náttfari, along with a male and a female slave. They settled down at a place now called Náttfaravík, on the other side of Skjálfandi Bay. What happened to them afterwards is not clear, but there are suggestions that they were unceremoniously elbowed out of the way when the main stream of immigrants started arriving later on.

This all means that technically (and I can assure you they are very technical about it indeed up here in the *Thingeyjarsýsla* area), Iceland's first settler was not Ingólfur Arnarson at all, but this Náttfari. Reykjavík has always argued loftily that Náttfari doesn't count because he was left behind by accident and didn't *intend* to settle; they note that in another version of *Landnámabók* he was actually (whisper it) a slave himself. But don't say that to the people of Húsavík, or to the old Icelandic socialists who used to denounce this settlement 'takeover' as an example of how chieftains like Ingólfur were always trying to steal the political honours from the real workers.

Ah, but it's a tricky business, history in Iceland. My modest family researches are nothing compared to the fastidious mining of ancient sources, often later versions of a lost original, which goes into supporting whichever view of the nation's history you care to side with. Thus Húsavík was pointedly celebrating Garðar, Náttfari and the eleven-hundredth anniversary of the settlement of Iceland in 1970, four years before the rest of the country held the official commemoration of Ingólfur's arrival in 1974.

This is the wonderfully prickly, argumentative, human dimension to the ubiquitous sense of connection to the past you experience right across the land. Halldór Laxness may be right to argue, through Pastor Jón in *Christianity at Glacier*, that 'the closer you try to approach the facts through history, the deeper you sink into fiction'. But it is precisely the fictions, if such they are, which provide this country with its tangible aura of historical continuity. Naturally this is a dangerous principle to espouse in other contexts. Historical fictions cause trouble enough in the world. But in Iceland – where battles are fought with words, not bombs, within a peaceful commitment to one small nation – long, disputatious memories do tend to invigorate rather than poison the present.

Húsavík wears its settlement colours on its sleeve. The main thoroughfare is called *Garðarsbraut* (Garðar's Street). One shop calls itself by the name he gave the island, *Garðarshólmi*. There is a club named the *Náttfari*. No names derived from Ingólfur here, for sure. It feels like a plucky sort of place, this home town of my ancestors, proud of its links to the settlement, proud that 70 per cent of Iceland's *hangikjöt* is produced here, proud of the electricity being generated just south of the town and the potential for more in the hot-springs nearby, proud of its role in the founding of the co-operative movement which employed my grandfather. It has been hard for the town to watch big brother Akureyri seduce some of its industrial clout away in recent years. The Co-op sold off its assets in 1999 and the new merged company set up in the northern capital. The dairy factory moved there, too, leaving Húsavík without its celebrated yoghurts and cheeses. It is the fate of many small towns to lose out to bigger urban centres, but here at the heart of an area famous for knowing its own worth and stalwartly blowing its own trumpet, it hurts.

I join my father in the hotel restaurant later in the evening, when two steaming plates of *hangikjöt* are placed before us. I dare not ask our host how much trouble it took to procure this feast; I only hope he didn't have to bang on the door of the slaughter-house personally. Fortunately my father is effusive in his gratitude and declares himself well content. But he has other things on his mind now.

Ever since we sat down at the table he has been tut-tutting softly over the English on the menu. Now he quietly suggests to the proprietor that he might like to alter a few of the spellings before some smart-assed travel writer comes along and laughs at them. This immediately plunges me into another lather of embarrassment. What if his motives are misunderstood? What if this accommodating man, who has all but recreated the menu for us already tonight, thinks my father is an interfering Colonel Blimp? Can he possibly realise that what we are witnessing is merely another tender manifestation of the Blue Lagoon Flags Worry syndrome? It seems he does understand. At any rate he joins us graciously at the table and the pair of them pore over the menu together with a pen.

I know what my father is thinking. He is afraid that spelling mistakes might blind visitors to the dignity and the quality of the efforts being made in this small family hotel. He is profoundly solicitous of the Icelanders' reputation in ways I am just starting to understand as I watch him in action on this trip. Iceland is more than just a homeland to him; it is a crusade. He is a man of many deep and consuming passions: for words and literature, for history and education, bird-watching, the environment, good journalism, big families and large vodkas when my mother is not looking. So multifarious are his enthusiasms that when the family designed him a coat-of-arms for his birthday

once, it was a taxing proposition to represent them all on one
jokey shield. We settled in the end for his old Labrador dog,
Lucy, a book, a swirl of pipe-smoke, a castle turret, a flight of
birds and the Mastermind chair. But flouncing over the rim of
the shield was the most potent symbol of all: the flag of Iceland,
abiding passion of his life in which all the others are subsumed.

To feel that he has contributed to the world's appreciation of
Iceland, through his translations of Laxness and the sagas, or his
books and television programmes, gives my father a satisfaction
which transcends his pleasure in other achievements. I doubt if
even his KBE from the Queen, welcome though it was, meant as
much as his Order of the Falcon from Iceland. When he was
presented with the prestigious Edda statuette in 2002, an award
similar to a BAFTA recognition of lifetime achievement, he was
more moved by the spontaneous standing ovation from youngish
Icelandic movers and shakers than by just about anything else
in his three score years and ten. It was not so much the honour
of the award itself as the palpable affection welling up from the
audience which almost rendered him incapable of delivering his
thank-you speech in Icelandic.

A friend of mine who watched it on television said it was an
astonishing phenomenon that this man in his seventies, who
had lived all his life abroad, still meant so much to so many
generations of Icelanders. 'I think your father is a national hero
here,' she added, matter-of-factly. Him and the moss, I thought.

He will hate to read this. Enticing my father to come with me
on our family quest proved, in the end, much less difficult than
persuading him to let me write about him afterwards. In the end
it was agreed that I could write what I liked as long as there
were no compliments. Oops. But the truth is that he is the
lynchpin of this saga and I can't do without him. He has ever
been my way into Iceland. Even attempting to peel away the
layers of legend and taste the country fresh, I still need him to
compare flavours.

The bonus of the exercise is the understanding I am gaining
of him in the process. I am beginning to discern in clearer out-
lines the Icelandic-ness of the man, starting to see where so many
of the character traits and apparent contradictions originate: the
touchy pride; the hospitality so expansive that my mother used

to suspect that at least half of Iceland had passed through their house; the all-or-nothing approach to life which earned him a rumbustious reputation as a young newspaperman and, in his more sedate later years, has manifested itself in a perfectionism as dementedly unflagging as the skipper's on the old herring boat; the lifelong engagement with the past which does not preclude a surprisingly modern mode of thinking about education, art (he's all for the Turner Prize) and his grandsons' hairstyles; and, above all, his joy in the vagaries of story, which manages to coexist with pure academic pedantry when it matters.

Add in the saga aphorisms and the fondness for elves, and you have a man who, as I now see, could be nothing but an Icelander. 'Scots by adoption and Scotch by absorption', is how he jokily describes himself. If he were being serious he might add, 'And Icelandic to the soul.'

Here in Húsavík I am still learning about my father. The menu correcting reminds me of our punctilious labours over the Laxamýri book. If our host, nodding patiently and doing his best not to look like a man with a hotel to run, were rash enough to suggest speeding the process up, my father would doubtless say to him, too, 'It really is important to get it right.' Just how viscerally important, I had not appreciated before. Watching him sitting there, hunched over the list of desserts, I realise that to feel he has pre-empted even one sneer, one patronising comment, with his efforts tonight will make him profoundly content.

You only need to dip into the writing about Iceland over the years to understand why Icelanders are so touchy about how others see them. They have been picked over and gazed at by the David Attenboroughs of the travel world more times than any nation minding its own business could possibly deserve. Visiting in 1862, the year Sigurjón began farming Laxamýri, the odious Reverend Sabine Baring-Gould from Devon opined that Icelanders (all of them) had no sense of smell, which he reckoned was just as well given the stench from some of the houses. He thought it might be down to the enormous amount of snuff consumed. 'Nature has made a mistake in forming Icelanders' faces,' he went on. 'She should have inverted their noses, so as to facilitate their plugging them with tobacco.'

Now I will grant you that Icelanders were fond of their snuff.

I can see my *afi* Sigursteinn now, standing straight-backed and shock-haired in front of our mantelpiece while he felt in his pocket for the polished silver box in which he kept his snuff. It was a riveting ritual. He would pinch the tobacco between thumb and forefinger, pause for a moment as if to weigh up the angle of projection, then toss his head back and let fly a volley of snorts at a sound level no child in the house would have dared attempt in company. The climax was a theatrical nose-blow into a large white handkerchief which he kept in his top pocket. Although the point of the exercise entirely eluded me, it never failed to captivate. Baring-Gould, for his part, was clearly driven to teeth-grating distraction.

Even the fairest-minded among the many Victorian travellers could not resist a jibe. Elizabeth Jane Oswald from Fife took exception to the turnips, potatoes and cabbages which the inhabitants of Reykjavík insisted on growing in their gardens with, she sniffed, 'a complete disregard for appearances. How I longed often to do a little gardening, and square things up, for the Icelanders have no ideas about out-of-doors amenity.' Let us assume, in charity, that she had not stopped to consider the effect that a howling winter, leavened with the occasional passing earthquake, would have on anyone's enthusiasm for pocket handkerchief gardens.

Earlier the botanist William Hooker, travelling the country in 1809, had been particularly and somewhat lasciviously annoyed by the way the women dressed. 'The remarkable tightness of their dress about the breast where the jacket is, from their early infancy always kept so closely laced as to be quite flat, is a practice which . . . entirely ruins their figure in the eyes of those who come from a more civilised part of the world,' he harrumphed. Writing up his recollections in 1811, after a fire aboard the ship had destroyed both his notes and his entire natural history collection, Hooker was no more pleased with the faces of the women he saw about their work in the fields. 'As to the features of this groupe [*sic*] of ladies,' he noted crisply, as one inspecting a particularly ill-favoured slug, 'the generality of them were, assuredly, not cast in nature's happiest mould, and some of the old women were the very ugliest mortals I had ever seen.'

These days foreign travellers are not so quick to believe that their own neck of the woods is more civilised than Iceland. They tend, on the whole, to be impressed by a country which finally gained its independence in 1944 and then managed to cram 200 years of lost development into 50, without losing its soul. Modern Iceland is as different from backward nineteenth-century Iceland as the fresh-faced beauties strolling the streets of its towns are from Hooker's ill-nourished field workers.

The changes which began with the developments so keenly affecting my forebears – the founding of the co-operative movement, the industrialisation of the fishing industry, the movement of labour and burgeoning of towns – accelerated furiously after the Second World War. Neutral Iceland had spent the war under pre-emptive British occupation. Troops took over a number of buildings in Reykjavík and requisitioned our strong-armed kinsman Jóhannes of Borg's smart town-centre hotel for their headquarters. The German consul was caught in the act of burning documents in his bath tub and promptly arrested. In the days that followed, the soldiers built barracks all over town and constructed the airfield from which we took off for Akureyri this morning. They hired so much local labour that most of the residual unemployment from the Depression disappeared and Reykjavík became flush with money.

When the Germans reached the English Channel in 1940, the British started to worry about having 25,000 men tied up so far to the north and the United States then took over the protection of Iceland. The Americans in turn built the airport at Keflavík, along with the large military base. Since then, although subject to anguished bouts of heart-searching, the foreign presence has been edgily tolerated under the NATO banner.

Over in Edinburgh my father's family escaped being packed off to wartime internment in the Isle of Man as enemy aliens, by virtue of Sigursteinn's role as Icelandic consul. The Samband offered him a rise in salary, plus what is described in family lore, thriller-fashion, as 'danger money', for continuing to mediate the trade in fresh ice-packed fish to Britain, which war had suddenly made extremely profitable. My grandmother was delighted.

'A rise at last, *Sigursteinn minn*,' she was heard to murmur, clapping her hands together happily.

But she had reckoned without my grandfather's steely patriotism. He refused any further payment, on the grounds that not a single extra penny of Iceland's precious foreign currency should go in taxes to a government currently occupying his country. As Gunnlaugur could have told her, men do not limp while their legs are the same length, nor accept money when their country has been, however benignly, invaded.

Postwar Iceland, having won back its full independence while Denmark was still occupied by the Germans, surged ahead with astonishing speed in the second half of the twentieth century, metamorphosing into a country where the standard of living became so high that when my husband and I took our children there a few years back, we spent most of the *krónur* we had optimistically set aside for an entire week's maintenance on one round of hamburgers and Coke at a service station on the way to the first stop.

Modern technology has been embraced with the unremitting fervour of a people long starved of luxury and innovation. The telephone, which had been received with only cautious interest in Britain and the United States, was instantly seized upon, superseding the letter at once – which could only be a relief since Icelanders had always been so slow at answering them. The fax machine was leapt upon with glad cries, and e-mail has now all but wiped letter-writing off the face of the island. Visitors can only whistle admiringly at a population of 284,000 which boasts at least 210,000 mobile phones and near enough 200,000 internet users.

No gadget is too silly to race out and buy in case you become the last person in town to have one. Who knows how many foot spas are still lurking sheepishly at the back of cupboards after a particularly effective sales drive one Christmas? They are now a national joke, although one relative told me defensively that she still used hers all the time; there was nothing like giving your feet a jacuzzi after a long day at the office.

Politics is as fractious, bitter and personal as you would expect in a highly educated, multi-party and very small society. A country which can engineer a political issue out of its own settlement 1,100 years ago can get exercised about just about anything. Having said that, even I was taken aback when Icelandair's inaugural Scottish–Icelandic Burns Supper in 2003 was denounced by one of the guests for allowing subversive socialist propaganda to contaminate the Immortal Memory.

'But Robert Burns did, er, lean to the left, you know,' I explained to the well-oiled and very excitable man who had approached me afterwards to complain. 'And this was, you know, a Burns Supper.'

He was not mollified. 'It's nothing short of a disgrace and I shall inform the Prime Minister,' he spluttered, red in the face. 'You must realise that we have elections coming up soon in Iceland.'

It was a maverick response which his fellow guests found hilarious, but I doubt if it could happen anywhere but Iceland. Meanwhile, the genuinely political issues – whether to join the European Union, how much of their unique wilderness should be sacrificed to the energy industry – are debated with all the zest and vitriol which Icelanders have devoted to their affairs from the day they first won their Parliament back from the Danes. It is bracing stuff.

The arts are flourishing as never before in this brave new Iceland, and the evidence is everywhere: in homes, bookshops, theatres and studios, in the casual elegance of the roadside sculptures and the voluptuous colours of the landscape paintings. Writers receive a decent government grant to pursue their craft, with the result that books continue to flood the market. Artists complain about not attracting subsidies themselves, but the art, both modern and traditional, keeps coming all the same. Most Icelanders have travelled extensively, many of them spending long periods of study abroad, and this gives social intercourse a cosmopolitan air which lightens the introspection. Perhaps all this is why Iceland often feels like a rather civilised place to be.

Let me not become sentimental, though. It helps that there is high employment, no social underclass, a strong family structure to balance Icelanders' relaxed attitude to marriage, and a relatively low crime rate. I remember my father maintaining airily when I was young that crime was so negligible in Iceland that there was only one person in jail in the whole country. Who was this poor fellow, we wondered? It was father-speak, of course, to be taken with the usual sack-loads of salt. He was right to the extent that despite their fondness for the bloodthirsty sagas, Icelanders show little inclination to murder or maim each other nowadays, preferring to work off their antisocial impulses on a wall, with spray paint. But there is nothing saintly about Icelandic society when it comes to evading taxes or pursuing complicated business scams, the latest of which I am invariably regaled with in eye-popping detail whenever I visit the country.

As for history and culture, I doubt very much that all Icelanders care about the past the way my father does. Although many do, there are others who seem exclusively concerned with racing forward, making money and grasping at modernity with a gizmo in both hands, as the Icelanders are so good at doing. I imagine, too, that there are plenty more who respect their history without making as much of a song and dance about it as past generations did. There cannot be many now who would advertise their Viking descent quite as obviously as my father does, although I'll bet anyone could tell you why Gunnlaugur refused to limp. Yet most Icelanders still consider it an article of pride to remember. The extraordinary self-confidence of this nation is based at least as much on their literary heritage as it is on their thrusting achievements from the last century to the present day.

You see evidence of that pride in their insistence that the language is preserved intact and no foreign words be allowed to pollute its purity. A committee of academics has been entrusted with the task of inventing words for new objects and concepts when they come along. Naturally, this being Iceland, everyone chips in with a view and hot debate ensues until a consensus emerges. Thus the word for telephone, *sími*, was cunningly adapted from an old word for thread. Computer is *tölva*, an inspired joining of *völva*, a sibyl who foretells the future, and *telja*, to count or reckon. The disease which the world knows as AIDS is *eyðni*, which sounds like AIDS, but was created from the word *eyða*, meaning to destroy or lay waste.

But a society as deeply in the thrall of English global communications as Iceland cannot avoid some linguistic pollution.

175

Visitors passing a park these days are likely to notice boys playing a game which sounds very much like football (*fótbolti*) and shouting a suspiciously English '*Jess!*' after a goal. Turn on the radio and you might hear a trawler fisherman talking about his 'job' (or *djobb*, as an Icelander would write it). Even older people are not immune. An elderly acquaintance was recently heard to mutter, on reaching her apartment, '*Nú er ég* safe' ('Now I'm safe'). Although it sounded like one of my grandmother's more catholic sentences, this old lady knows no English. '*Seif?*', she said when quizzed (already the word has acquired an Icelandic spelling). Oh, that was just a word she kept hearing these days.

Some people worry that the encroaching tide of easy anglicisms will engulf Icelandic in the end. But if that happens, it will not be without stiff resistance. New coinages from Old Norse roots continue to be forged, and each act of communal word-creation encourages Icelanders to keep thinking about their language in ways all too alien to native speakers of lazily triumphant English.

Unlike Hooker, visitors nowadays also tend to be somewhat overwhelmed by the female of the Icelandic species. After paying a memorable visit to a Reykjavík nightclub, the journalist A. A. Gill announced that Iceland had 'the most groin-throbbingly, pulse-revvingly (drop a gear) beautiful women in the world. Not just one or two, not a handsome few, not a judicious nubile sprinkling, but flocks, shoals, herds, coveys and prides of the most stunningly direct and confident, perfectly formed women.'

Either the gene pool has picked up since Hooker was here or Gill was having a good night. But it is interesting that for all the genuine admiration which visiting foreigners seem to feel for modern Iceland, still the historical tendency to condescend is seldom far beneath the surface of visiting lap-tops. Even Gill, who I think would count himself among the admirers, could not resist adding that the men of the species were 'universally, unremittingly hideous'.

I can reassure the travelling sisterhood that he was either very drunk or very, very jealous. But let me offer this warning to any journalists who may follow: my father is manning the barricades. If any should weave their way north to Húsavík, they will have no scope for mocking the menu of the town's eponymous hotel.

It is after eleven o'clock and the late sun is slanting through the windows and glancing off my wine glass. People are still wandering in and out of the restaurant as if it were the middle of the day.

A relative of ours who lives locally has arrived to join us for coffee. Björn Sigurðsson is a grandson of Egill, a smiling coach driver who has lived all his life right next to the land which once belonged to his grandfather and to his father.

As he and my father talk in a dense Icelandic which I am beginning to find impenetrable this late at night, I look out of the window at the mountains and allow the conversation to drift over my head. Egill. Jóhannes. Recriminations among their descendants. Difficult decision for everybody. Siblings. Lots of siblings. Dividing the estate. Debt. Despair. Something about an uncle of Björn's hurling Líney Jóhannesdóttir's book across the room when it first came out, because of her failure to understand how difficult it had been for Egill to keep things going.

After this I let it go completely and concentrate on the mountains, washed in the soft, improbable light of the midnight sun. I am trying to remember a quote from W. H. Auden, one of the most affectionate and perceptive of Iceland's travelling band, an Englishman for whom the country became nothing less than sacred soil.

'It is different from anything else,' he told Iceland's main daily newspaper, *Morgunblaðið*, in April 1964. 'It's a permanent part of my existence, even though I'm not continually harping on it . . . Iceland is the sun colouring the mountains without being anywhere in sight, even sunk beyond the horizon.'

I wonder if this is what Iceland is for me, too. Not sacred soil, by a long way, but as permanent a part of my existence as ever it was Auden's, colouring my life from far across the sea and offering a perspective more valuable than I have sometimes allowed.

Thus you watch Britain struggling to remind itself what nationhood means when the Queen Mother dies, and you think of Thingvellir. You observe the birth-pangs of devolution and wonder how long it will take Scotland to learn what Iceland had to learn: how to define itself in the modern world without an enemy to rally against or a big brother to run to. Among the touchy Icelanders, to look at it the other way, you suddenly appreciate the urbane irony of the English and the pawky self-deprecation of the Scots. In the depths of an Icelandic winter, you recall wistfully that no Glasgow rain was half as wild as this. Then again, in the middle of Heathrow you wonder why design can't be beautiful as well as utilitarian. On it goes, the one country colouring the other, like Auden's sun on the mountains.

Perhaps I was wrong to feel uneasy on our way over in the plane. The truth is that hybrids can have double, rather than half, the fun. It certainly multiplies the real riches we are able to pass on to our children. My own five – each of them half English, a quarter Scots and a quarter Icelandic – have a smattering of Icelandic names among them, an impressive grasp of '*Takk fyrir matinn*' and a gratifying inclination to support Iceland in the Eurovision Song Contest. When I took the four oldest there in 1993, they were too young to appreciate much more than the delight of discovering hot open-air swimming pools in the middle of the lava. But they did at least come away with a sense that they belonged.

The occasion which really brought it home to them happened on a sunlit day near Thingvellir, when the mentor from my student days, Vigdís Finnbogadóttir, gave us lunch at her summer chalet overlooking the Thingvallavatn lake. She was in the last term of her sixteen-year presidency by then, the Queen of Iceland as my husband dubbed her, which was a constitutional whopper but thrilled the children. Playing along with the royal theme, she said there was something she wanted to do before we left. She gathered all except the baby on the verandah and announced that she was going to make them knights of the Queen of Iceland.

One by one, they strode forward and knelt before her, knowing it was only fun, and yet something more.

'Jamie Magnús, I name you a knight of Iceland,' intoned the queen, looking most acceptably like one in her long white coat and regal blonde hair-do. She tapped him on the shoulder. 'May you remember this land of ours.'

'Sigurður Gordon, you too I name a knight of Iceland. Arise and go forth and do not forget.' The five-year-old arose and marched off with a grin as wide as his face.

My plump three-year-old daughter nearly toppled over trying to kneel, and settled in the end for a rakish bow. 'Arise, Dame Anna Lisa, knight of Iceland,' said Vigdís, keeping her face straighter than I was managing. 'Remember this is your country.'

The children re-ran the video for years afterwards and the one-time baby still nurses a grudge that he was not invited to the ceremony. When I asked Vigdís in a radio interview some time later what she meant by it, I already had an idea what she would say.

'I did it so that they would remember, as I always wanted you to,' she said, effortlessly eloquent as usual. 'And so that you would be able to remind them that their forefathers lived here, and that their forefathers created all these stories that are worth remembering. And so that they might want to come back now and then, to stand on the soil that is the soil of their ancestors.'

I hope they do remember that they were once made knights of Iceland. I hope they wonder about their names, their Christmas Eve feasts, their *afi*'s stories, their mother's *Complete Icelandic Course* by the bedside opened at Nouns, Irregular Declensions, so that she can answer her friend Marta's e-mails. I hope they feel the tinge of Auden's sun as they grow older. Actually I hope they ask about Laxamýri, too, although things will be different there. For a start I'll be able to tell them a kind of truth instead of a mish-mash of myth. It may mean that the birds they hear in the trees, to adapt Laxness's strange image, will chirp more prosaically for them than for me, but it will do them no harm to learn that history is nearly always less simple and more human than we like to imagine.

At the very least I'll have a more complex and humane story to offer my children than was ever told to me.

Sigurjón of Laxamýri Returns

One of Sigurjón's first tasks on moving back to Laxamýri was to hang his coal-black coffin in the storehouse next door. There it hung from the ceiling like a squat cockroach, suspended above the reeking supplies of salted meat and smoked trout, waiting for the day he would join his wife in the churchyard high above Akureyri.

Not that Sigurjón behaved like a man who was hankering for the grave. He still skipped everywhere and the house shook with laughter early each morning when he came downstairs. The old housemaids puffing and blowing on the fire abandoned their yawns and coughs, and the children drowsing in their beds could hear them giggling like girls as Sigurjón rushed around making his coffee and getting in their way. Even in his eighties, he was an unstoppable life-force, not above cheerfully pinching a pretty young maid who came to work there for a time and doing his best to shock her.

The young families of Egill and Jóhannes were fond of their grandfather. He took time to play with them, although not always in ways of which his sons approved. A crying baby would be silenced with whatever came to hand, and if that happened to be one of Jóhannes's finest volumes in English from the bookcase, then in it went to the cradle as a toy. Sigurjón, who never cared much for books, considered the contented infant gurgles a job well done, but Jóhannes was beside himself with irritation. He had collected these books on his travels and treasured them; he had enough to do fending predators off the eider ducks without having to mount a rearguard defence of his bookcase as well.

After Sigurjón's return, the 1874 house was straining more than ever at the joists. Two families were living cheek by jowl in a household which, even by Laxamýri standards, was enormous. Egill and his wife Arnthrúður had four sons and two daughters. Jóhannes's wife Thórdís bore eleven children in all, although only the six daughters survived. Alongside them lived maids, farmhands and guests.

It was a difficult situation for the wives. Arnthrúður and Thórdís were discordant personalities thrust together in a crowded house with, worst of all, a shared kitchen. The way they worked it was that the two families ate together, with one mistress dishing out the soup and the other the main course of fish or meat. They shared equally the costs incurred by feeding and boarding the visitors who, then as before, used Laxamýri as a stopping-off point on their travels. But private clients, such as those of Egill's who came to see him about having a watch made or to consult him as district administrative officer, were provided for separately.

It all sounds like a nightmare student flat-share, exacerbated by the difficulty the two women had in getting on with each other. Thórdís was for giving things away to the needy at every turn, an admirable quality if they had belonged entirely to her, but irritating to Arnthrúður who preferred a more businesslike husbanding of the shared resources. Even Thórdís's daughters were aghast when their mother gave away their own prized possessions, a soft sealskin for making shoes and a decorative kettle which bleeped when the water boiled, to a poor woman who arrived to stay. Yet, although the heart quails at the thought of the tensions in that crowded household, the two families continued to rub along together, sharing each other's joys and bereavements, for more than twenty years.

During the day the brothers worked the farm as a team, looking somewhat alike with their long, slim faces and drooping moustaches, their interests and temperaments dictating the division of labour. Egill, always more robustly engaged with the world, ran the business and initiated the investments. He also saw to practical tasks like the carpentry. When they hunted seals together, it was he who wielded the fearsome four-gauge shotgun. When the salmon catch came home from the river, Egill did the filleting and Jóhannes washed and salted the fillets and prepared them for smoking. When they went out to check the lumpfish and seal nets, it was Jóhannes the fisherman, ever quick with his hands, who retrieved the catch and mended the nets.

Haymaking they tackled together, standing side by side in the fields to turn the mown grass. So also the drying of the eiderdown, which they joined forces to spread in the sun and then move to an enormous hearth in the storehouse. Jóhannes's particular duties were to collect the driftwood and attend to the nesting grounds, where his pleasure was to stroll the banks of the river in the spring, stroking the eiders as he looked for eggs; at those times he was as content as he had been once on his drifting boat.

But in general Jóhannes seems not to have been particularly happy. A farmer with no feel for farming, an instinctive scientist with few outlets, a frustrated intellectual who loved to read and discuss ideas, he found that the one person who could understand the limitations of his life was his youngest brother, far away in Denmark. A surviving letter from Jóhann back to him as early as 1901 hints at the older man's regret at the turn his life had taken since returning from America. 'I am often thinking about you, brother,' Jóhann wrote from university in Copenhagen, in typically poetic vein, 'thinking about everything which I know you have dreamed, but which has never come to pass; thinking about that ice-cold hand which life proffered you when you asked for a warm hug. It is sore to ask for bread and receive a stone.'

Not surprisingly with all those people living in the house, Sigurjón quickly decided he needed a granddad annexe. An old hand at house building by now, he commissioned an extension, comprising two rooms upstairs and two off the kitchen below. One of these became his living room, where he sweltered beside a stove which gave off such an intense heat that the rest of the family nearly expired. He would not let anyone open a window.

There was a small ventilation hole in the sill, with a stopper which he would take off to feel what the weather was like. If the weather was fine, he left the hole open. If it was rough, back the stopper would go.

He liked to stand at the window, checking what his sons were doing as they moved about the land. He could see right across the home fields from here to the river where the eider nested. He was also in the habit of posting himself and his telescope outside the west door and gazing down with narrowed eyes and suspicious frown at these nesting grounds. He had been looking out for these ducks since he was eleven years old. Woe betide any predator – bird, animal or human – spotted by him now.

According to his grand-daughter Líney's 1975 memoir, *There Is Something No-One Knows*, he was particularly incensed at the liberties being taken by local men who rowed out towards the cliffs at night, lying in wait to shoot the flocks of eider as they flew past at daybreak. The old man used to rise at dawn himself, she said, and stomp down to the cliffs with a shotgun, giving the men a shock as he loomed into sight on the skyline above them, shouting and shaking his gun at them.

Her picture of the poachers, bobbing about in their boat and looking up in alarm at this gun-toting dance of rage on the clifftop, had me convinced that some of the inhabitants of Húsavík must have been sleeping less easily in their beds after the return of Sigurjón to Laxamýri. I was wrong, as it happens. Again.

The curator of Húsavík Museum permits himself the merest hint of a sigh. It is Saturday morning and Guðni Halldórsson has opened up specially to let us have a look around on our way to Laxamýri. He is a fair-haired, bushy-bearded bear of a man who greets my father with warm respect and me with distinctly stern politeness. I have a discomfiting sensation of having wandered into the headmaster's study to find that Professor Dumbledore has somehow read my guilt before I have even committed the crime. I know with sinking certainty that under these beetling brows Guðni has me sussed. I might as well be wearing a placard:

'Dangerous romantic on loose. Keep under surveillance. Re-educate if possible'.

He puts me (and Líney) briskly right on Sigurjón and the poachers. Although killing eider-ducks was illegal after 1847, the birds did continue to be poached well into the twentieth century, mainly by the use of special nets into which the eider were lured with cod- or lumpfish roe mixed with sand. But any such poachers were certainly not near the cliffs north of Laxamýri, either with their nets or shotguns; they would have been further along the coastline. And, since we are on the subject, Icelanders had never used guns to threaten one another; Sigurjón was probably just strolling with his four-bore in case he spotted a fox or a bird of prey endangering his eider, or happened on something he might prey on himself for the family dinner, like a seal, ptarmigan, razorbill, black guillemot or cormorant. Nobody feared Sigurjón or slept uneasily after his return. In fact, Guðni would like to assure me that he was well liked in the area.

'Líney was a writer and needs to be taken as such,' he says, a mite gruffly. 'One has to be aware of how fact and fiction coalesce.'

Oh, no. Not fact and fiction coalescing again. Can somebody in this saga-soaked country not just tell me a story straight for once? No colour, no exaggeration, no artfully reassembled direct speech, no birdsong, pleasant or otherwise. Just tell me what happened. Please.

And that is when Professor Dumbledore smiled his wise smile and revealed himself to be a kindly cove after all, who could help Harry understand his complicated past. Step forward Guðni Halldórsson, former international shot putter and athletics administrator, now historian and county archivist, a man who embodies the feisty pride of this area and is quite as dedicated to Getting Things Right as my father in his non-fiction moments. To the accompaniment of the benign ticking of a seventy-year-old grandfather clock, we sit in his office listening to the first measured, dispassionate account of the fall of Laxamýri I have ever heard. It is a long time since anyone has mentioned the estate in my company without the words 'beautiful', 'bounty' or 'wasted'.

The three of us are sitting at a table in the centre of the room, on which Guðni has laid out Sigurjón's letters to Egill from Akureyri between 1906 and 1916 in piles, each folded in a neat rectangle, many written on square exercise-book paper. Lúðvík's boat, Jóhann's debts, Egill's arguments with the Danish merchants, the drop in smoked salmon prices, the wranglings over fishing rights, the exasperated tenderness of an old man for his sons even as he was bailing out their mistakes and watching his life's work unravel slowly in their hands: so many seeds of Laxamýri's fate are already there.

But Guðni has no time for sentimental conclusions. 'The way the loss of Laxamýri came about has been a family secret, a family tragedy,' he says crisply. 'But here in the letters we see that it was simply financial misfortune and miscalculation.'

Later he leads us out of his office, past a striking Norwegian oil painting of Jóhann Sigurjónsson, looking sad and Byronic, and round some of the collections. There are Laxamýri mementoes everywhere: Sigurjón's beard brush with a little mirror inside, a silver-mounted bamboo cane for his whip, his mighty black telescope, a massive shotgun for shooting seals. The artistic leanings of the family are in evidence, too, although I only have time to note the rulers carved by Sigurður Egilsson and some fine embroidery by Líney's sister, Soffía Jóhannesdóttir, before my father whisks us off to the basement to admire a stuffed polar bear captured on the island of Grímsey in 1969 and a monster salmon caught in the River Laxá in 1998.

The museum offers an intimate glimpse of the social and maritime history of a large swathe of the north, far beyond Húsavík itself. Guðni looks pained when I refer to it tactlessly as 'little', without realising how far it extends and how hard he has worked to nurture its growing reputation across the country. 'Two thousand square metres in total,' he says, in a strained sort of voice. I am humbled. This is worse than insulting the moss.

He shows us a replica of the living room where the first farmers' co-operative met to plan their economic revolution in 1882. This I think I really might be permitted to describe as tiny. The bed set into the wall is so small that it is hard to imagine anyone spending a comfortable night in it. But history was made in this room, the watershed in Icelandic commerce which would one day direct my own grandfather's fortunes to Scotland.

Wherever we go in the museum, this powerful sense of connection persists. It is strange to turn a corner and come across a tombstone engraved with the Danish words: *DIGTEREN JÓHANN SIGURJÓNSSON OG HANS HUSTRU*. It is Jóhann's original gravestone from Vestre Kirkegaard. 'And his wife' is a literary reference to the Danish title of his masterpiece; when a new one was commissioned for Copenhagen in 1969, it was thought more tactful to include Ingeborg's actual name.

Outside, the family theme continues with a little timber house in the grounds. It was built of driftwood in 1872 by Sigurjón's brother Jónas Jóhannesson, one of the oldest preserved timber buildings in the county. Jónas connected it to his own turf house at Thverá, not far from Laxamýri, and called it his 'guest-house'.

Some time after this visit, I sent Guðni my conclusions on what we had learned, and begged him to comment. I could sense the beetle-browed frown as he drew my attention to a few residual threads of romantic interpretation, but each point was covered in patient and thoughtful detail. In a tape recorded in his office, marked by the sounding of the great clock on the hour, he summed up the family epic which had played itself out just a few kilometres up the road.

'The Laxamýri family is classic Thomas Mann in *Buddenbrooks*. The first generation builds up, in the second generation everything blooms, the third generation divides the wealth and it withers away.

'If one needs to find out the truth – and I think it is very, very hard to find the whole truth in this respect – it seems to be a number of different things working together. Not just the collateral for Lúðvík's loans, not just the Depression from 1907– 9, not just the new laws on workers' rights, or the effect on prices of the First World War, or the personalities of the brothers. A lot of things combined to make it wither away gradually. And then after it had withered away, the only thing left standing was the legend.'

A heavy pause on the tape. I felt as if he were looming over me, stabbing his finger at that placard. 'But I'm also warning you about legends, Sally,' he said. 'They can be dangerous.'

The winter of 1918 brought an enemy to Laxamýri which old Sigurjón was powerless to threaten with his telescope and (peacefully inclined) shotgun. No weapon of his could fight frost and pack-ice and a cold so terrible that many of his precious eider perished. Did the old man see their fate coming and give up, deciding that Laxamýri would have to handle this latest blow without him? Or perhaps he himself was overcome by the cold, huddled in his room beside the big stove with the ventilation hole closed tight. Who can say? As Guðni would doubtless prefer me to state, Sigurjón was eighty-five years old and he died.

In any case, he was ready to go. He had written up his memoirs and settled his affairs. Nothing was left to chance. He had left instructions that his body was to be taken to Akureyri and laid alongside that of his wife. The wooden cover over Snjólaug's grave was to be replaced by a stone one bound with iron, locking them together for all time.

The black coffin had long been ready for the call. On 27 November it was lowered to the floor of the storehouse and carried into the house to receive his wiry body, uncharacteristically still at last.

In the November snow, Sigurjón left Laxamýri roped to a sledge for his final journey to Akureyri. As the horse was harnessed and Ponni, an old retainer who had served the family for years, settled himself on its back with a generous supply of liquor to sustain him, nobody would have been more than averagely astonished if Sigurjón had popped up to direct the departure himself. It was just the sort of operation he would have relished masterminding. Ponni, his face red in the cold and shiny with pride, clicked the horse forward and the sledge began to ease silently over the deep snow. Young Líney watched as the dark horse lifted its feet high and then slid them back into the whiteness, so quietly it looked as if it were tiptoeing. As Sigurjón glided away from Laxamýri in his black coffin, there was nothing to be heard but the surf beating unnaturally loud in the stillness, and the waterfalls murmuring like music.

There were many deaths for the household to cope with in those years. Jóhannes and Thórdís lost five young sons between 1898 and 1910: twins who died within hours of each other the day after birth, two more who each lived less than a month, and little Sigurjón, namesake of his grandfather, who survived long enough for Jóhannes to dare hope he might grow into manhood, only to die twenty days after his first birthday of a stomach disease. The sisters born later were told that the child cried ceaselessly, calling out for *mamma* and *pabbi* long into the night. Jóhannes could never bring himself to talk about this son.

In 1919 Jóhann's death, nine months after his father's, came as a hammer-blow to the household. Then, a few days before Christmas 1921, it was Thórdís who lay on the bier in the living room, only forty-six years of age, her thick black hair spread around her like a dark cloud. Jóhannes thought she looked so pale and beautiful that he summoned their daughters into the room to see her. He did not cry in front of them, then or ever, but they knew he lay awake at night, bereft.

Egill was ill himself now and his eldest son Sigurður had taken charge of the business. Jóhannes was weary. With the farm mortgaged and the financial prospects dire, with no sons of his own to farm after him and no wife to run his share of the household, he found the situation increasingly oppressive. In the spring of 1922, he assigned his half of the farm to Egill and, to the anguish of his daughters, moved them away from Laxamýri for ever.

14

Laxamýri

The morning is wearing on, crisp but still overcast, as we drive back up the road we travelled yesterday. We are looking out for the modest wooden signpost marked Laxamýri we had passed just beyond the memorial. Over to our right the gaunt cliffs are busy with birds, the sea colliding with the rocks below in a foaming white beard of surf which reminds me bizarrely of the portrait of Jóhannes the patriarch.

A few minutes ago my father and I had looked at each other outside the museum and said, 'Right, shall we go, then?' like soldiers preparing to hazard no-man's-land. And here we are now, driving down a bumpy track past a clutch of black hens pecking in the dust by the side of a barn.

Hens? Nobody mentioned hens. Sleek fat salmon and eider with down as soft as a baby's head are what the script specified here. Winding river and roaring waterfalls. A mouldering Nordic Brideshead with just a touch of Wuthering Heights, in which my father might murmur about being alone with a golden goblet while the ghosts of Jóhann and Snjólaug flit up to the blue vault of the sky on white horses and play with golden spheres. But really, not hens.

We learn later that these birds are descended from the Vikings, *la crème de la crème* of the chicken world, if you please. But even the most high-born of hens cannot scratch any other message on God's earth than one. The F-word. The word I realise

I have always avoided when thinking about Laxamýri. Go on, hens, don't spare me. *F-a-r-m. F-a-r-m.* This is a *farm*.

I suppose I should have prepared myself better. Of course Laxamýri is a farm, and always was. These days it is one of the most successful producers in Iceland. But it is one thing to know the facts and another to meet head-on an idea which has been swelling in the collective imagination of at least six generations, growing more perfect as it has become less reachable. I am the woman who understands perfectly that history's William Wallace was actually a thug and yet managed to emerge from a showing of *Braveheart* whooping 'Freedom!' with the rest of that benighted Scottish audience. I may yet discover that Christian IX of Denmark grew a large posterior and died of gout, but in some tiny cavern of my imagination I will love him still.

But hens? How ridiculously, deflatingly real can you get?

As we negotiate the track between long, whitewashed buildings noisy with shuffling beasts and mysterious clankings, and breathe in the pungent aroma of dung, I think about asking my father if 'romantic farm' is an oxymoron. But this is not the moment. He is straining to see round the corner of the last barn to where – and suddenly I see it, too – a neat, wooden farmhouse stands looking quietly out to the mountains. And that is when my heart turns over.

Sigurjón's mighty house is so very small. Not mundane and disappointing, like the hens, but so little and vulnerable in the great space which is opening before us as we drive, that I feel I could rush over and scoop it into my arms. This is not the castle of dreams my grandmother's sighs evoked, but a spruce farmhouse utterly dwarfed by the landscape which once cast such a spell on those who lived here that they could not let it go. I find it achingly familiar, which is strange. Nothing in my hope of romance and fear of anticlimax has prepared me for such a different emotion altogether – a rush of pure, unproprietorial affection.

The house isn't frail at all, really. I can see that as we draw nearer. It is the landscape which is big and overwhelming, the endless sky and the moorland, the *mýri* which my grandmother used to dwell on so lovingly when she was speaking its name. It undulates off in every direction, wide and bare, halted only by mountains which rise blue-black (Jóhann was right) and snow-fingered in the west and by the ocean crashing against dizzying cliffs on the other side. Out there beyond the meadows the bluest river I have ever seen is racing towards the sea. Somewhere along there will be the waterfalls which Líney loved and where Sigurjón twice nearly met his Maker. I can hear them now through the window, rumbling faintly on the breeze.

As we draw up outside the house, I can see the date 1874 plainly visible on the wall. I can make out Sigurjón's extension – the place must have been small indeed before that was added – and the storehouse still standing a few feet away. Before we are properly out of the car, the front door opens and a tall, ruddy-faced man in his early forties shoots out, hand outstretched.

'Welcome to Laxamýri,' beams Atli Vigfússon.

Within minutes Laxamýri's latest owner is showing us eagerly around the farmhouse, which he has not long finished renovating. The old homestead had been suffering from subsidence and was in need of a fresh touch inside, but he has kept what he could: two gnarled oak doors, the original ceiling beams, the two bedrooms built by Sigurjón when he returned from Akureyri, and his own grandparents' kitchen, complete with shiny milk churns and stove. The rest he has modernised into an elegant, art-filled home, with interior walls taken out to create a spacious sitting room. He leads us straight through this to a rectangular area by the window.

'This was Sigurjón and Snjólaug's bedroom,' he says. 'Here is where Jóhann the poet was born, and your grandmother Snjólaug, Magnús. Jóhannes and Egill were born before this house was built, of course.'

We can still make out the shape of the small bedroom. I wander over to the window and look out at the scene Sigurjón would have peered at every morning after hurtling out of bed. I wonder whether it was Egill or Jóhannes who inherited this room later.

'Here,' says Atli, knowing how keen we are to feel the past and doing his best to help, 'we can look over at the mountains and the garden and the meadow down there by the riverbank where Sigurjón made his hay. Further along are the waterfalls. We call them the Eiderduck Falls.'

He senses our impatience to be out there. 'Perhaps you would like to see around for a short while before lunch?'

I am on my way at once, my father strolling behind with as contented a look as I have ever seen on his face. It is the expression of a man who has not only been invited to inspect a dream, but who has just caught the unmistakable aroma of *hangikjöt* drifting down from the new kitchen on the floor above.

'See Laxamýri,' I whisper to him, 'and eat.'

As eight-year-old Líney walked away from Laxamýri, she noticed that the golden plover had arrived and the whimbrel was calling. Beside her Jóhannes, his face looking even longer and more haggard than usual, was driving some hundred ewes and three cows from their home pastures towards the family-owned smallholding of Saltvík down by the sea, their big, equable horse Lýsingur plodding alongside. Líney listened to the retreating rumble of the waterfalls, clutching at the last whisper from beyond the hill until all the sound had gone.

Above the bay, she ran to throw a stone on a cairn which old Ponni had once told her about as they drove a cow past it. He said there was a spell on this cairn and you had to toss a stone on it whenever you passed or else a dreadful fate would befall you. She threw one for her father as well, and hoped she had done enough to appease the restless spirit they said was buried here, a woman too guilty to lie in a churchyard. Then she and her father walked down the hill to their new home.

Various members of the family had farmed at Saltvík from time to time. Now it was Jóhannes's turn to rent it from the estate. The property consisted of a turf house and assorted huts huddled together close to the sea, their green roofs sloping so low to the ground that a curious cow actually wandered up one of them and was surprised to find itself hurtling straight through to the floor below in a thunderous crash. All the buildings were in a state of some disrepair, although possibly not as dramatically derelict as Líney describes in her memoir. Her anguish at being 'torn', as she puts it, from Laxamýri may well have magnified the contrast between the comfort and spaciousness of the home she had left and the leaky, old-fashioned dwelling waiting for her over the hill.

As the sheep pottered around the field and started grazing, she and her father made a heart-sinking inspection of their new home. She describes old rags plugging the crevices where the door hung, a leaking roof, the long corridor from the door through to the living room at the back, damp and musty. Into it they moved their household effects, including the family organ which had come in part exchange for the hay-machines which Jóhannes would have little use for on such a small farm.

Living at Saltvík (Salt Bay) was an adjustment none of them found easy. The sisters hated having to rush round catching rainwater in pots and pails as it leaked through the roof in a symphony of drips. They did not much enjoy sharing their kitchen with the cows, either, although these hulking companions did give off a useful heat in the winter. Jóhannes worked morning to night in the fields and out in his small rowing boat to provide for his daughters, but he worried about the difficult life he had brought them to.

Young Líney helped him with the haymaking and the fishing, holding the boat steady while he pulled in the catch. At the start of each trip he liked to enthuse her with wild visions of the monsters they would catch – sharks and whales and 300-pound halibuts – and she never doubted that sooner or later they would catch all these. Drifting in easy silence close to the shore, she sensed his contentment out here at sea. She wondered if he was musing on his years in America when he had been free and happy.

Other days she explored far and wide on the sturdy Lýsingur, and sometimes rode towards the hill which represented her greatest temptation. There were a few big boulders at the top. Climb one of these and she knew she would be able to glimpse Laxamýri again in the distance and listen for the waterfalls which pounded in her dreams. Just once she wanted to do it, but always she stopped herself. Instead she would prop herself against a boulder while her horse grazed on the hill and think about her six-year-old sister Sigurjóna, who had been sent away to live with a foster family rather than face the rigours of their new life without a mother.

Young enough not to be troubled by the discomforts at home, Líney found life at Saltvík an adventure. Not so her father. Continually anxious that this was no place for a motherless child, he decided at last that she too would be better off with foster parents in Reykjavík. After two summers at Saltvík, Jóhannes took her south on the boat from Húsavík and she went to live with strangers. They were good to her, these new parents, but she felt for a long time that she didn't have any home at all. Rootless and disoriented, she lay in a fine house in Reykjavík, missing her father and dreaming about Laxamýri.

Within a year, Jóhannes too left Saltvík. He remained in the north for a while as a teacher and then moved to the capital himself, where his married daughters looked after him until his death in 1933. The man whose joy had been to stroke the eider-ducks on one of the greatest estates in all Iceland ended his days washing bottles for the State liquor and tobacco company.

His family have carried a great hurt about Laxamýri ever since. Jóhannes gave up his birthright and theirs, they say, and for what? For Laxamýri to be lost to the family six years later, sold for thirty pieces of silver? The trauma the daughters suffered in being snatched from their childhood idyll was intensified by bitterness over its ultimate fate. When Líney married, her husband Helgi complained that she could talk about nothing else. Her book is shot through with an almost incoherent nostalgia. She passed on that sadness, and a resentment which it was clear to me when I met her had not healed in nearly eighty years, to her own son, Jóhannes Helgason the banker.

This Jóhannes is a big, bluff man who told me straight away on the evening I visited that for him Laxamýri would always be special and he remained angry that it had been lost.

His wife Anna chipped in: 'For many years Jóhannes wouldn't go to Laxamýri. I was begging him to go, because I was so curious to see the place after all those stories, but he wouldn't go in, although he passed it by on the road many times.'

'I wouldn't go because I felt the family there now were trespassers.' Jóhannes was blunt, but a little shame-faced. 'That's what I was brought up to believe. I couldn't help it. Then in

1997 I saw an article about the renovation of the old Laxamýri house and I wrote a letter. I got such a kind letter back from Atli that I swallowed my pride and went there for the first time.'

'And what did you think?' I leant across in my armchair in front of the wide picture window to catch his answer, a fellow pilgrim confronting reality.

'I should have visited sooner,' he said thoughtfully. 'Then it would have seemed less important to me. It built up in my imagination over the years, but when I got there I found it very windy. Laxamýri is extremely beautiful, but I think it is too windy for me.'

There are harlequin ducks streaking overhead as Atli Vigfússon stops his pick-up truck at the waterfalls. Bobbing on the current, all dressed to party in their rakish red, white and black plumage, their effect is as salutary as that of the hens. You really can't mourn lost paradises in the middle of a riotous duck-ball.

And thank goodness for that. What Líney described as the power of this land's pull is not, after all, appealing to emotions I was fearful of discovering in myself. Laxamýri is evoking nothing covetous or proprietorial in my soul, but only this gleeful delight in the ordinary, this exhilaration at a loveliness which is strong and real rather than pretty and perfect: a landscape as big as the sky which I will remember for a long time, but too flat to be sublime, a little too exposed for comfort, certainly too full of vivid, humdrum life to be stuck in the mental museum our family has made of it.

For all that, I am distinctly awed when we walk to the edge of the cliff and look down, a long way down, into one of the pools into which the river plunges on its way to meet the sea a little way beyond. This stretch of the river is where Sigurjón twice fell in. It is terrifyingly fast. Snaking across the wide moor towards us, the Laxá suddenly starts spilling at ferocious speed into a series of black bowls of swirling foam, from which it then surges out to join the sea. I think about Sigurjón, caught under his boat in one of these whirling eddies in what he described in his memoir as a 'death-grip'. No wonder he took to drink afterwards.

'Yes, people have died there,' Atli says, pointing to the islet on the west bank from which Sigurjón had been swept away and over the waterfall. 'Your kinsman was very lucky.'

Like yesterday, a light wind is whipping straight across the moors. Zipped to the neck in the anorak I swore I wouldn't wear again, I am standing directly above the place where the salmon gather their strength for the first of their three giant leaps from sea to spawning grounds. They have been leaping here ever since Sigurjón was a young farmer setting stone-weighted traps to catch them. They have been leaping since Iceland was no more than a rumour of Snow Land and Laxamýri an undiscovered pocket of heaven.

How many times did my great-great-grandfather stand up here on this alarmingly crumbling cliff, with fulmars floating above and the surf crashing on to the black shore beyond, and gaze out at all this wild emptiness? Did Sigurjón's stomach drop to his boots, the way mine is now, as he peered down into the inky depths of tumultuous water? Did his breath catch at the desolate wail of the gulls? Did he stare across at the ridge of the Kinnarfjöll and wonder at its stern grandeur? Did he, by any chance, fall in love with the harlequins?

Oh, don't be silly. My father, jacket flapping open again in the breeze, shouts to me to watch my step on the cliff edge. He must wonder why I'm grinning. Catch Sigurjón wasting a moment reflecting on the majesty of the mountains or cooing over striped ducks. He would have paused just long enough to scan the shore for beached whales or prize driftwood and the cliffs for trouble. He would have had a gun at his shoulder and a murderous eye on those rapacious seagulls. And then he would have carried on running.

In fact, he would probably have trotted back up the river to the eider nesting grounds, where Atli drives us next. He wants to show these to us from the anglers' lodge, where it costs more *krónur* to live and fish for a week than to have bought the whole estate in 1928. The lodge is a haven of fish-worshipping masculinity, with brisk leather sofas and rows of fly-books. The dark walls are hung with stuffed salmon, yawning at us malevolently with jaws like shelves. All caught here on the Laxá, Atli tells us proudly.

I can tell that my father is thinking he might just sink into one of these shiny armchairs for a leisurely puff in front of the window, while engaging Atli in further fascinating conversation about salmon poundage. His hand is ferreting in his pocket with intent.

'Sadly,' says Atli, who must also, mercifully, have read the signs, 'this is a non-smoking room. Why don't we go outside?' My father droops behind us to the verandah.

From here, looking south-west towards the Laxá, we are close to the meadows where Sigurjón made his hay, the area which always became a flood-plain in spring when the snows were melting. Along the river we can see the bushes where the eider-ducks nest as they always have done, plucking the down from their breasts to line the nests with insulation for the eggs in the cold spring. Atli says that when the ducklings have left the nest, the men collect the eiderdown and spread it on the ground in the sun, just as they did in the old days.

The eider are all over the place, nesting in the shelter of the dwarf willow shrubs which Sigurjón encouraged to grow here long ago. My dad is puffing contemplatively now, saying he can understand why the old boy used to guard his eider so obsess-ively and why the sensitive Jóhannes cared for them so tenderly. They look vulnerable down there as they potter around the bushes, dun-coloured for camouflage on the nest but all too visible none the less. We spot one or two black and white eider drakes in the distance.

'They spend the winter in great rafts at sea,' says my father, who seems to know all about ducks. He and Atli exchange the names of species I don't recognise in English, never mind Icelandic. What on earth are scaup? Mallard I can just about identify, but the harlequin are the only non-eider I really recognise. My new friends are partying in the fast-flowing water upstream as garishly as they were at the falls. 'Nothing they like better than a good current,' says my father fondly.

Above our heads, two greylag geese croak past. The rift in the stillness makes me think of those waterfalls again. Funny, I never noticed the roar when I was near them; I suppose the noise of water crashing down sheer rock belongs too obviously to the scene to be remarkable. But Líney is right: further away is when you start to hear that sound, if you listen for it. And there it is now, a low, steady murmur on the breeze, the hint of delights not seen but always remembered.

How fitting that I should find myself feeling emotional about the waterfalls as soon as I can't see them any more. How very Laxamýri.

The last act of my family's Laxamýri saga played itself out with an inexorability worthy of *Eyvindur of the Mountains*. But there was to be no dramatic climax of the sort that art likes to impose on story, although some of the more imaginative of my kinsfolk had no trouble in constructing one for future audiences. Dark deeds of perfidy and betrayal are more satisfying to the Jóhann in all of us than division of inheritance and lack of capital investment.

In January 1924 Egill died at the age of fifty-seven, after a long and painful illness; Líney thought it might have been cancer. Inheritance problems, pre-empted in previous generations and eased in the short-term by Jóhannes's departure, immediately burst to the surface. Both Egill's father and grandfather had lived far enough into old age to pass Laxamýri on at a time and in a state of their choosing. But Egill, with four sons, two daughters, a depleted farm, no capital and a debilitating illness, was not in a position to organise the future so neatly.

His eldest son, Sigurður, found himself in charge of an estate which he could not possibly hope to purchase outright. To buy out his siblings was beyond his means. Such an extensive farm required a large workforce and, since his own children were all still too young to work themselves, he would have had to hire in all the labour. As Sigurður surveyed the balance sheets, already thick with debts, the sums didn't add up. Nevertheless he and his widowed mother Arnthrúður and younger brothers made a go of it together for a few years.

Sigurður renovated the old storehouse, where his grandfather's shadowy coffin had once hung from the ceiling, and moved his wife and children in. His brothers, all unmarried, continued to live with Arnthrúður in the farmhouse next door. When he was interviewed many years later, Sigurður maintained that this new venture in co-operative farming was going well enough and that it was a complete surprise when a farmer from another district in the north suddenly turned up on their doorstep one day to announce that he had a brother down south who wanted to buy Laxamýri.

Atli says it couldn't have been that much of a surprise since the farm had been placed on the market; or so he was always told. But Sigurður insisted in his newspaper interview as an old man that it was only when Hallgrímur Thorbergsson came knocking for a second time on behalf of his brother Jón Helgi that the family seriously considered selling Laxamýri. Right to the end, like everything in this saga, nothing was simple.

Sigurður Egilsson said he was in an agony of indecision as the family sat down to consider what everyone agrees was a good offer from the southern farmer known to all as Jón H. Thorbergsson. He totted up the advantages of selling: his mother was growing too old to run a large household; his brothers had skills which would enable them to flourish in other lines of work; there was no way he personally could afford to buy them out; the farm was heavily in debt and lenders were not merciful to farmers when the harvest was bad. Some of the reasons on his list seem weaker than others, and it may be that if the rest of the family had been for keeping Laxamýri, Sigurður would not have found the cumulative weight of argument so compelling. But others in the partnership wanted to sell and he was tortured by the thought that if this extremely good sale went down, it might lie for ever on his conscience, since who knew what the future would bring?

In fact, within only a couple of years the future was to bring the disastrous economic downturn of the Great Depression, which the business would have been ill-equipped to withstand. So Sigurður, who came to bear the brunt of opprobrium for the decision, was probably right to do what he did. But it was with heavy, unconvinced heart that he agreed to the sale of the Laxamýri estate in 1928, ninety years and four generations after his great-grandfather Jóhannes Kristjánsson had moved in.

'There is nothing I have done more unwillingly than this in my entire life,' he said.

It was one of Sigurður Egilsson's younger sons, by a second wife, who had met us last night under Húsavík's midnight sun. Björn Sigurðsson told us that his eldest brother Páll, who was eleven years old when the estate was sold, used to weep whenever he came near Laxamýri after that; like Líney, he never recovered from its loss. Björn himself was not born until 1946 and lives too close to Laxamýri for the luxury of romantic dreams. But he admitted to a stab of sadness for his father's dilemma: custodian of a place with such potential, but unable to develop it and frightened of the future. He hoped those who still believed it had been lightly thrown away would realise how difficult that decision had been.

Björn had stirred his coffee and lifted the cup towards his lips. But before drinking, he had stopped. 'You must understand that it is all in the past for me now,' he said, looking at us keenly. 'I would never say anything that might hurt the man who is living there now. Atli Vigfússon is my friend.'

Atli drives us back down the track towards the farmhouse, surprising a snipe which darts up from the roadside at speed, beak like a pencil. Moments later a golden plover flutters by, followed by a group of harlequins on their way to the party. The traffic in the skies is ceaseless. But Atli is pointing to the ground. Over there, he says, he has been planting lupins to help him reclaim the bare land near the river. They colonise and grow very quickly, he explains, and then move on, leaving dead foliage behind to fertilise the land they were on so that other plant life can move in and thrive.

It occurs to me that Sigurjón's clan were lupins, too: purple ones, yellow, blue and pink, flamboyant and gorgeous, though some were always too slender to survive. Their job was to colonise, enjoy and move on, to let others live more securely on the land they had prepared. Naturally I keep this insight to myself; ninety years of lupinhood is not something you want to rave about without a glass of wine in your hand.

But while my father and Atli are busy with the finer details of land reclamation, I raise a furtive imaginary glass to four generations of Laxamýri lupins: to Jóhannes the rich and Sigurjón the mighty; to Egill and Jóhannes, who loved this place but had to leave its soil for others; to Lúðvík and Snjólaug and Jóhann, who never forgot it as long as they lived; to Sigurður, who felt he had no choice but to abandon his roots to let the new life in; and to Líney, dear Líney, who found the whole process so very painful.

'But these are very special hens, Magnús.'

There is nothing like a blast of hen to bring a flight of fancy plummeting back to earth. Atli is earnestly outlining the pedigree of those black ones we had encountered on our way in. They are pure-bred Viking hens, he explains, and not only is this one of the few Icelandic farms to keep them, but their eggs taste better than any others we are likely to sample anywhere in the whole world.

Yes, this is the Laxamýri I know and love: purer, more aristocratic and higher quality than anywhere else on earth. And that is just the hens.

15

Back to Akureyri

Even in death, Sigurjón of Laxamýri could not stop running. His last journey on this earth was the same as the one my father and I are making now, away from Laxamýri, down through the valley and across the mountains to Akureyri. His was made in 1918, in the middle of the November snows and, typically, it was eventful.

Ponni, the retainer entrusted with the task of hauling Sigurjón's coffin over the snow on a horse-drawn sledge, was well tanked up for the ride. When he reached the churchyard at Ljósavatn, he decided to stop again to give the horse a rest and himself another liquid fortification. After unhitching the sledge at the top of a generously iced brae, he settled down comfortably with his bottle, only to be disturbed shortly afterwards by the alarming sight of the sledge taking off. He stumbled to his feet in time to see the black coffin skidding down the hillside at a most un-funereal pace.

Ponni had never moved so fast. He raced down the brae after it, yelling into the snowy emptiness, 'That old fellow! He can't wait to get on his way again.'

Still feeding his own legend even in death, Sigurjón eventually made it to the burial chamber high above Akureyri to join his wife. We are not far from the town ourselves now. Soon my father and I will be flying back to Reykjavík and then home.

We have driven most of the way in silence. There has been a

lot to absorb, not least the *hangikjöt* which had indeed been presented for lunch as we had been hoping. The dark-red smoked lamb, cooked to exquisite tenderness, was offered with boiled potatoes, peas, turnips and white sauce, and my father was in his seventh heaven. That the owner of Laxamýri should prove to be hospitable, artistic and thoughtfully appreciative of the past was boon enough; that he should serve *hangikjöt* at his table made him a god.

In the course of the meal we learned that even Atli's grand-father, Jón H. Thorbergsson, a farmer to his fingertips, had found Laxamýri a challenge which almost broke him. He had been born in the nearby Reykjadalur area in 1882, during the desperate decade of fierce winters which forced many of Iceland's emigrations. Today Jón H. would be called a miracle baby, born after one of the longest and coldest of these winters in the middle of a measles epidemic which was scything its way across the country. His mother caught the disease and gave birth pre-maturely to a grossly underweight baby who was already suffering from measles. Atli told us the baby lived to be nearly one hundred years old.

Jón Helgi's passion was sheep. He studied agriculture in Norway and Scotland and acted as an agricultural adviser all over Iceland, before buying, in 1917, the estate of Bessastaðir, on the Álftanes peninsula near Reykjavík, to put his knowledge into practice. But Bessastaðir, later to become the official residence of the Icelandic president, proved too close to the expanding capital for his liking, with barely enough grassland for his sheep. He began to look for somewhere else. Laxamýri, with its big, windswept moorlands so close to where he grew up, seemed ideal.

After clinching the deal in the capital in the spring of 1928, he rode back home to Bessastaðir to tell his wife Elín, meeting on the way a young boy by the name of Sigurjón Sigurðsson, my great-uncle, who was shocked to learn that the fabled family estate was gone.

Jón H. and Elín loaded their three children, their entire stock of five cows with calves, fifty sheep, a dog, some hens and three horses, as well as every stick of furniture they possessed, on to a boat, the *Dronning Alexandrine*, bound for Akureyri. From there they chartered it on to Húsavík, milking cows and frantically delivering lambs all the way.

Jón H. was a twentieth-century man in the Sigurjón mould, an entrepreneur steeped in the agricultural business who applied himself to farming with zealous determination. He was the sort of man who would get up at 4 a.m. to write pamphlets about farming, a man with a keen financial nose who, most importantly for Laxamýri, came to it as a single owner with a steady focus. Yet even he was almost overcome by the magnitude of the task.

He borrowed a great deal of money to invest in new farm buildings and was then hammered by the Depression, remaining heavily in debt for the next twenty years. In the 1940s, with workers in short supply as people poured south to booming Reykjavík, he was so near to despair that he thought seriously about selling Laxamýri. He often spoke with sympathy of the difficulties which Sigurður Egilsson and Arnthrúður had faced before him. He said there was no way they could have run that farm successfully, with so many children to divide it among and no money to run the place, never mind invest in it.

Elín struggled to cope in the dilapidated farmhouse. In one of the many ironies of the Laxamýri saga, Sigurjón's wonderful 1874 house felt cramped and old-fashioned to the new owners. It was cold and badly in need of renovation they could not afford. While the legend of the lost Laxamýri idyll was breeding in the minds of people who felt they had been cruelly dispossessed, Elín and Jón H. spent twenty years collecting their water from an outside well and living with damp and subsidence. While my grandmother and her sisters in their modern Reykjavík apartments were dreaming of blue mountains, Elín was stuck in a draughty house in the sticks, wistfully remembering the big shops in the capital.

If any of my family, busily telling their stories and dreaming their dreams as far away as Scotland, had realised how much of a strain it was proving to make a living in this nirvana, would it have made a difference? Would a dose of reality have suppressed the sighing rancour? Might they not have found it, metaphorically at least, as windy as Líney's son Jóhannes did when he swallowed his pride and visited at last? I wonder.

In 1948 Jón Helgi's finances finally improved enough to enable him to renovate the old house. The outer frame was left exactly as it was, but he ripped out all the timber from the ground floor, enlarged the cellar and rebuilt the floors with concrete. This brought the floor down a little, which raised the ceiling height. He then added two garrets on either side of the attic roof, giving the house the shape it has today. In 1953 he bought his first tractor and a jeep, and his son Vigfús, Atli's father, began farming with him, followed three years later by another son, Björn. Laxamýri was at last on its way to joining the rest of Iceland in the booming second half of the twentieth century.

Listening to Atli's story against the clatter of infant spoons around the table gave us a reassuring sense of continuity. Hard to believe, but his own Laxamýri saga was already into its fourth generation. At one point he reported, disarmingly, that his family always said our lot were too clever for farming.

'Your ancestors were artists, not farmers, you know. That was the problem.'

There, tossed lightly into the conversation, was the most simple explanation of all for the mystery which had brought us to Iceland. With sudden clarity I understood not only why Laxamýri had to go, but why we who followed could not let it alone. Artists cannot help making a song and dance and endless story about things, and that is exactly what this family of poets, playwrights, authors and journalists had been doing for generations. Doubtless the descendants of Sigurjón will continue to debate the finer details for years to come; for all I know, these will be remembered, like the last defence of Gunnar, for as long as this country is lived in. But I hope we will all remember, too, the quiet judgement of a man who knows this business and loves this land of Laxamýri as well as any who came before.

Atli himself is both farmer and word-artist, a modern businessman who can strike a hard bargain with the anglers and clocked early to the benefits of internet trading, but who also writes articles and children's books, someone whom I might once have been tempted to present as the synthesis of Sigurjón and his sons, in whom the tensions of the past are finally resolved. But not any longer. I am purged now of romantic simplifications. I hope Guðni is proud of me.

'Come here whenever you like,' Atli said as we took our leave. 'Your family is always welcome at Laxamýri.'

I started up the engine and eased the car away from the house my great-great-grandfather built the year the king visited Iceland, permitting myself only the tiniest sentimental reflection that the lupins had done their job well in this place. Laxamýri is not the kingdom of heaven, nor an earthly one, either, to be inherited by divine right. It is a fragment of tamed loveliness, profusely and raucously blessed with nature's riches, but always better served by tough heads than bleeding hearts.

We can see Akureyri ahead of us now, nestling close to its fjord in the first burst of sunshine we have seen all afternoon. My father, just for a change, is smoking his pipe.

I lean across to click on the tape-recorder for what he must be hoping is the last time and brace myself to ask something I really must know.

'Was it worth it then, this journey?'

He waits just long enough to unnerve me and then smiles. 'Oh, it was worth coming here, certainly.'

I could have done with something a little more effusive. 'Thank you, dear daughter, whose organisational skills I grossly underestimated, for dragging me here for the most rewarding three days of my life' would have done nicely. But my father is taking the question seriously.

'The most fascinating thing has been discovering the grain of sand of truth which produced those pearls of story-telling I've been inflicting on you over the years,' he says at last. 'It happened all over the place, didn't it?'

He pauses, puffs, considers, staring straight ahead. 'My mother was so intensely proud of belonging to the *Laxamýrarætt*. They all were. It's a fabulous place and it's clear from talking to people that it was considered an important dynasty which had produced an array of famous people. But I now realise that my mother, and perhaps her mother too, were beginning to see a Laxamýri that never was.'

He pauses again. 'But you know what I most enjoyed about this trip?'

I think I can guess. There is a mischievous flash in his eye as he turns towards me in his seat.

'It was seeing the house where my dad was born, and going through the book of the carter dynasty at my cousin Hallgrímur's house, and seeing what a wonderful job has been made of renovating Hótel Borg in Reykjavík. All that side of things was kept so quiet when I was growing up.'

My own head is still full of the place we have just come from. It was Laxamýri which drew me to Iceland, captivated by the romance of it like the rest of the female line; but I have sensed all along that my father's heart was really with the kinsfolk who were rarely talked about at home, the ones considered too lowly to stand comparison with the great line of Laxamýri. Of all the men called Jóhannes we have encountered lately, surely as numerous in Iceland as chefs called Siggi, there is one who claims my father's enduring allegiance.

'I'll tell you something I was thinking the other night,' he says. 'Jóhannes á Borg may have been a bit of a rough character, the son of a carter, a peasant in the eyes of the educated Laxamýri folk. But what he managed to do was unbelievable. To earn enough as a professional wrestler and strongman abroad to fulfil his stated ambition to build a decent hotel in Iceland – I think that's an astonishing feat. And he started building his hotel in 1928, the year Laxamýri was sold. I can't help noticing that his monument to posterity was rising when Laxamýri was in a mess.'

The schoolboy gleefully baiting his mother with Carter Dynasty Rules OK is not far below the surface here. I am glad we have had a chance to trouble some of the dust on the family line they never talked about in Edinburgh, as well as dampen a little of the polish on the other.

So expansive and genial is my father becoming that I take a chance on one last suggestion. Akureyri is upon us. How about a quick scout around for Sigurjón's grave on the way to the airport? We have aeons of time before the plane to Reykjavík takes off. Almost an hour at least.

He accedes with a less accommodating humph than I might have wished, but I am off up the hill before he thinks better of it. The car winds up a dizzying slope to the hill-top cemetery, set at an angle so acute that Ponni, astride his tired horse, must have been praying fervently that the coffin would stay on board until they made it to the top. With the fjord shimmering below us in the late afternoon sunshine, we round the summit at last.

Even I can see there is a problem here. This is nothing like the little field in Húsavík where Jóhannes the patriarch reposes among the shrill oystercatchers, but an ocean of graves stretching as far as the eye can see; quite possibly, my father reckons, from here to the next mountain-range. You don't come much closer to heaven than Akureyri's municipal cemetery, but it is far too big for casual grave-hunting, especially when one of the party is convinced that the circling dot on the blue horizon is the incoming flight from Reykjavík. Personally I had this down for a hawk, but I know when I'm beaten.

We head back down the hill for the airport. I wish my father wouldn't keep looking at his watch like this. There is something I'm trying to find the words to tell him.

I want to tell him that I, too, reckon what we have been doing is worth it. I want to find a way of saying that all his stories have been valuable, every one of them, because, like the sagas themselves, they are what have carried the old times and the old places, even when they were exaggerated and romanticised, even when there was only the smallest grain of truth in them. Now more than ever I know they have to be examined and repaired before they are handed on, if the past is not to fester. Maybe some of our stories would have benefited from inspection years ago.

So listen, Dad, I'm saying to him in my head as we speed towards the airport. I'll try to be faithful to what we have learned on this journey. I'll try to get the stories straight and tell them with all the affection for these newly discovered kinsfolk we have found welling up in us along the way. And perhaps in the writing of it, I will also find a way of saluting what you have been sharing with me since I was a few years old, this thing of great price we call our heritage.

What do you think of that, oh crusty one?

'I think we're going to miss that plane,' says my father.

Epilogue

Early in 2003 I was back in Iceland. I walked one afternoon towards Reykjavík city centre through swirling January snow to take a closer look at a statue I had been passing by for years without a second glance. It stands outside Government House in Lækjargata, a few metres away from a matching statue of Iceland's first Prime Minister, Hannes Hafstein.

King Christian IX, his hair curling generously above the ears at either side of a handsomely balding pate, is ramrod straight in his uniform, epaulettes bristling. A Napoleonic naval hat is tucked under his left arm; the other is outstretched towards the city. In his right hand is the rolled-up 1874 constitution, which he is offering to Icelanders.

It is a symbolism not always immediately obvious to foreigners. Looking at the statue from the side as you walk down Bankastræti (as a fan I felt I should observe his demeanour from all angles), it is hard to tell what Christian is actually brandishing in that right hand. 'Why', a foreign visitor once remarked to President Vigdís when she was pointing out the city landmarks, 'is that man pointing a gun?'

It makes you wonder what other invigorating impressions of Christian's role in Icelandic history have been carried away from Reykjavík to the ends of the earth. My father's little flurry of misinformation might seem quite tame by comparison.

It is pleasant to listen to the birds chirping, as Halldór Laxness

213

said. But it would be anything but pleasant if the birds were always chirping the truth.

Glossary of People

Aðalsteinn Magnússon (1892–1953) Ship's captain in Akureyri. Eldest son of Magnús Jónsson.

Anna Thorláksdóttir (1824–1901) Farmer's wife in Eyjafjörður. Wife of Jón Jónsson.

Arnthrúður Sigurðardóttir (1866–1963) Laxamýri housewife. Wife of Egill Sigurjónsson.

Árni Björnsson (1863–1932) Clergyman in Sauðárkrókur and then Hafnarfjörður. Husband of Líney Sigurjónsdóttir and brother of Sigurður Björnsson.

Árni Sigurjónsson (born 1955) Literary historian. Youngest son of Sigurjón Sigurðsson.

Atli Vigfússon (born 1956) Laxamýri farmer and writer. Son of Vigfús Jónsson and grandson of Jón H. Thorbergsson.

Björn Sigurðsson (born 1946) Coach franchise holder in Húsavík. Son of Sigurður Egilsson.

Egill Sigurjónsson (1867–1924) Laxamýri farmer. Third son of Sigurjón Jóhannesson.

Hallgrímur Aðalsteinsson (born 1918) Retired farmer and agriculturalist. Son of Aðalsteinn Magnússon.

Ingeborg Blom (1872–1934) Danish housewife. Wife of Jóhann Sigurjónsson.

Ingibjörg Sigurðardóttir (1905–83) Housewife in Edinburgh. Daughter of Sigurður Björnsson and Snjólaug Sigurjónsdóttir, and mother of Magnus Magnusson.

215

Jóhann Sigurjónsson (1880–1919) Poet and playwright. Youngest son of Sigurjón Jóhannesson.

Jóhannes Helgason (born 1946) Reykjavík banker. Son of Helgi Bergsson and Líney Jóhannesdóttir.

Jóhannes Jósefsson, known as **Jóhannes á Borg** (1883–1968) Wrestler and hotel builder. Son of Jósef Jónsson.

Jóhannes Kristjánsson (1795–1871) Laxamýri farmer, patriarch of the clan. Son of Kristján Jósepsson.

Jóhannes Sigurjónsson (1862–1933) Laxamýri farmer and school-teacher. Eldest son of Sigurjón Jóhannesson.

Jón Jónsson (1818–83) Farmer in Eyjafjörður. Father of Magnús Jónsson and Jósef Jónsson.

Jón Helgi Thorbergsson (1882–1979) Farmer at Bessastaðir and Laxamýri. Grandfather of Atli Vigfússon.

Jósef Jónsson (1859–1927) Carter in Akureyri. Brother of Magnús Jónsson and father of Jóhannes á Borg, the wrestler.

Kristján Jósepsson (1770–1840) Farmer at Halldórsstaðir. Father of Jóhannes Kristjánsson, Laxamýri patriarch.

Líney Jóhannesdóttir (1913–2002) Reykjavík housewife. Daughter of Jóhannes Sigurjónsson.

Líney Sigurjónsdóttir (1873–1953) Housewife in Sauðárkrókur and then Hafnarfjörður. Eldest daughter of Sigurjón of Laxamýri.

Lúðvík Sigurjónsson (1871–1938) Ship-owner and schoolteacher. Fourth son of Sigurjón of Laxamýri.

Magnús Jónsson (1871–1919) Student and carter in Akureyri. Father of Sigursteinn Magnússon.

Magnus Magnusson (born 1929) Writer and broadcaster. Younger son of Sigursteinn Magnússon and Ingibjörg Sigurðardóttir.

Mamie Magnusson (born 1925) Glasgow journalist and housewife. Wife of Magnus Magnusson.

Margrét (Didda) Bennett (1928–96) Edinburgh housewife. Elder daughter of Sigursteinn Magnússon and Ingibjörg Sigurðardóttir.

Margrét Sigurðardóttir (1873–1912) Wife of Magnús Jónsson in Akureyri.

Sesselja Bergsdóttir (1765–1818) Mother of Jóhannes Kristjánsson, Laxamýri patriarch.

Sigurður Björnsson (1867–1947) Teacher, shopkeeper and director of Reykjavík fire insurance. Husband of Snjólaug Sigurjónsdóttir.

Sigurður Egilsson (1892–1969) Laxamýri farmer and schoolteacher. Son of Egill Sigurjónsson.

Sigurjón Jóhannesson, known as **Sigurjón of Laxamýri** (1833–1918) Laxamýri farmer, son of Jóhannes Kristjánsson.

Sigurjón Sigurðsson (born 1915) Former Reykjavík police chief. Youngest son of Sigurður Björnsson and Snjólaug Sigurjónsdóttir.

Sigurlaug Elísabet Björnsdóttir (1868–1928) Sister of Sigurður Björnsson and Árni Björnsson.

Sigurlaug Kristjánsdóttir (1800–59) Farmer's wife at Laxamýri. Daughter of Kristján Andrésson and wife of Jóhannes Kristjánsson.

Sigursteinn Magnússon (1899–1982) European export manager of SÍS and Icelandic consul-general for Scotland. Son of Magnús Jónsson and father of Magnus Magnusson.

Sigurveig Jóhannesdóttir (1832–99) Servant in her brother Sigurjón Jóhannesson's home at Laxamýri and then dressmaker in Argyle, Manitoba. Daughter of Jóhannes the patriarch.

Snjólaug Sigurjónsdóttir (1878–1930) Reykjavík housewife. Youngest daughter of Sigurjón Jóhannesson of Laxamýri.

Snjólaug Thorvaldsdóttir (1839–1912) Laxamýri housewife. Wife of Sigurjón Jóhannesson of Laxamýri.

Soffía Sigurjónsdóttir (1875–1940) Masseuse in Akureyri. Middle daughter of Sigurjón Jóhannesson of Laxamýri.

Thórdís Thorsteinsdóttir (1875–1921) Laxamýri housewife. Wife of Jóhannes Sigurjónsson.

Thorvaldur Sigurjónsson (1865–96) Second son of Sigurjón Jóhannesson of Laxamýri.

Bibliography

Books

A Guide to Icelandic Architecture, Association of Icelandic Architects, Reykjavík, 2000.

Auden, W. H., and MacNeice, Louis, *Letters from Iceland*, Faber, 1937.

Boucher, Alan, *The Iceland Traveller: A Hundred Years of Adventure*, Iceland Review, 1989.

Cornwallis, Graeme, and Swaney, Deanna, *Iceland, Greenland and the Faroe Islands*, Lonely Planet Publications, 2001.

Dufferin, Lord, *Letters from High Altitudes*, John Murray, 1903.

Einarsson, Stefán, *History of Icelandic Prose Writers 1800–1940*, Cornell University Press, 1948.

Eyrbyggja Saga (trans. Hermann Pálsson and Paul Edwards), Penguin Classics, 1989.

Guðmundsson, Gils (ed.), *Öldin sem leið: Minnisverð tíðindi 1861–1900*, Iðunn, Reykjavík, 1956.

Gylfi Þ. Gíslason, *The Problem of Being an Icelander: Past, Present and Future* (trans. Pétur Kidson Karlsson), Almenna bókafélagið, Reykjavík, 1973.

Hjálmarsson, Jón R., *History of Iceland: From the Settlement to the Present Day*, Iceland Review, 1993.

Jóhannesdóttir, Líney, *Það er eitthvað sem enginn veit:*

Endurminningar Líneyjar Jóhannesdóttur frá Laxamýri (with Þorgeir Þorgeirsson), Iðunn, 1975.

Jónsson, Hallgrímur, *Á slóðum manna og laxa*, Akureyri, 1985.

Jósefsson, Jóhannes, *Icelandic Wrestling*, 1908, hosted on the internet by American Heritage Fighting Arts Association, http://ahfaa.org/glimabook.htm, Pete Kautz, 2000.

Jósepsson, Þorsteinn and Steindórsson, Steindór, *Landið þitt Ísland*, Örn og Örlygur, 1980.

Karlsson, Gunnar, *Iceland's 1100 Years: The History of a Marginal Society*, Hurst and Co., London, 2000.

Krossaætt I–II, edited by Björn Pétursson, Mál og mynd, 1998.

Lacy, Terry G., *Ring of Seasons: Iceland – Its Culture and History*, University of Michigan Press, 1998.

Laxamýrarættin, compiled and published by Skúli Skúlason, Reykjavík, 1958.

Laxdæla Saga, trans. Magnus Magnusson and Hermann Pálsson, Penguin Books, 1969.

Laxness, Halldór, 'Jarðarför Jóhanns Sigurjónssonar', in *Ungur eg var*, Helgafell, Reykjavík, 1976.

Leffman, David, and Proctor, James, *The Rough Guide to Iceland*, Rough Guides, 2001.

Magnusson, Magnus, *Iceland Saga*, Bodley Head, 1987.

Magnusson, Magnus (trans. and introduced), *The Icelandic Sagas, Vols 1 and 2*, Folio Society, London, 1999 and 2002.

Magnússon, Sigurður A., *The Icelanders*, Forskot, Reykjavík, 1990.

Magnússon, Sigurður A., *Northern Sphinx*, Snæbjörn Jónsson, Reykjavík, 1984.

Marion, Stefan J., *Travel Guide to Iceland*, Mál og menning, Reykjavík, 1995.

Moore, Tim, *Frost on my Moustache: The Arctic Exploits of a Lord and a Loafer*, Abacus, 1999.

Morris, William, *Icelandic Journals*, Mare's Nest Publishing, 1996.

Njal's Saga, trans. Magnus Magnusson and Hermann Pálsson, Penguin Books, 1960.

Philpott, Don, *The Visitor's Guide to Iceland*, Moorland Publishing, 1989.

Sale, Richard, *Xenophobe's Guide to the Icelanders*, Oval Books, 2000.

Sigurjónsson, Jóhann, *Eyvindur of the Mountains*, Helgafell, 1961.

Sigurjónsson, Jóhann, *Ljóðabók*, Almenna bókafélagið, 1994.

Sigurjónsson, Jóhann, *Ritsafn I–III*, Mál og menning, Reykjavík, 1980, including essay by Gunnar Gunnarsson, 'Einn sit ég yfir drykkju', reprinted from *Skriðuklaustur*, 1940.

Sveinsson, Hallgrímur (ed.), *The National Hero of Iceland Jón Sigurðsson: A Concise Biography*, Vestfirska forlagið, Hrafnseyri, 1996.

Þorsteinsson, Björn, *Thingvellir: Iceland's National Shrine* (trans. Peter Foote), Örn og Örlygur, 1986.

Vigfússon, Atli, *Ponni og Fuglarnir*, Bókaútgáfan Skjaldborg, Reykjavík, 1992.

Articles

Benedictsson, Margrét J., 'Icelanders on the Pacific Coast' (trans. Árni Magnússon), Almanak Ólafs Þorgeirssonar, 1925.

Gill, A. A., and Clarkson, Jeremy, 'Dripping Yarns', in *The Sunday Times Magazine*, 2 April 2000.

Haraldsson, Jón, in *Tíminn*, 23 December 1951, recalling a meeting with Sigurjón Jóhannesson in the winter of 1918.

Jónsson, Björn, 'Jóhann Sigurjónsson og hugmyndin um hafnargerð við Höfðavatn', in *Lesbók Morgunblaðsins*, 15 February 1970.

Kristjánsson, Karl, interview entitled 'Sigurður Egilsson frá Laxamýri', in *Heima er bezt*, November 1967.

Magnússon, Árni, 'An overview of Vestur-Íslendingar of the Laxamýri Family', unpublished paper, Reykjavík, 1998.

Magoun Jr, Francis P., 'Jóhann Sigurjónsson's Fjalla-Eyvindur: Source, Chronology and Geography', in *Publications of the Modern Language Association of America LXI*, 1946.

Morgunblaðið, 14 March 1947, article on Sigurður Björnsson.

Nordal, Sigurður, 'Johann Sigurjónsson', in *Mál og menning* magazine, 19 June 1940.

Schonberg, Sylvia, 'The Thorðarson Family History', unpublished paper, 1995.

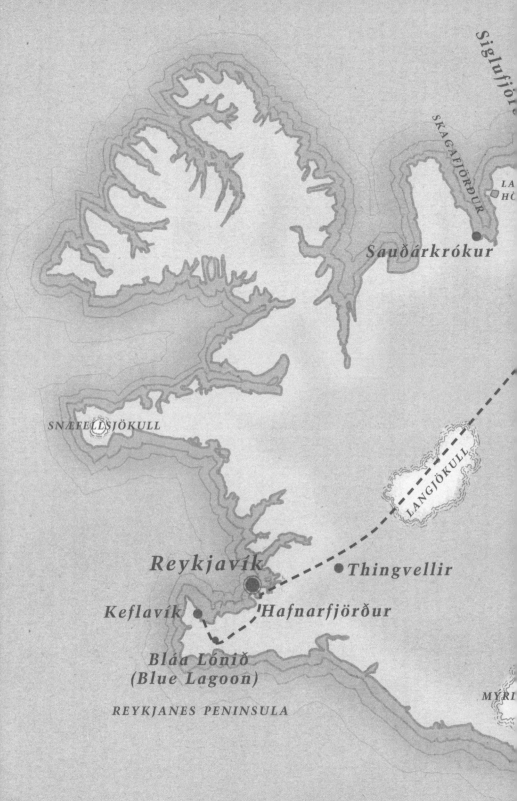

Siglufjör

SKAGAFJÖRÐUR

SKAGAFJÖRÐUR

LA
HÖ

Sauðárkrókur

SNÆFELLSJÖKULL

LANGJÖKULL

Reykjavík   ● **Thingvellir**

Keflavík ●   ●'**Hafnarfjörður**

**Bláa Lónið
(Blue Lagoon)**

REYKJANES PENINSULA

MÝRI

ICELAND JOURNEY